READER'S BLOCK

READER'S BLOCK

A History of Reading Differences

Matthew Rubery

Stanford University Press

Stanford, California

Stanford University Press
Stanford, California

Printed in the United States of America on acid-free, archival-quality paper

Library of Congress Cataloging-in-Publication Data
Names: Rubery, Matthew, author.
Title: Reader's block : a history of reading differences / Matthew Rubery.
Description: Stanford, California : Stanford University Press, 2022. |
    Includes bibliographical references and index.
Identifiers: LCCN 2022003997 (print) | LCCN 2022003998 (ebook) |
    ISBN 9781503632493 (cloth) | ISBN 9781503633421 (ebook)
Subjects: LCSH: Reading—Physiological aspects. | Reading disability. |
    Neurodiversity.
Classification: LCC QP399 .R83 2022 (print) | LCC QP399 (ebook) |
    DDC 612.8—dc23/eng/20220211
LC record available at https://lccn.loc.gov/2022003997
LC ebook record available at https://lccn.loc.gov/2022003998

Cover design: Notch Design
Cover image: Stocksy
Typeset by Newgen North America in 10.2/14.4 Minion Pro

This one's for The Razor.

Contents

READER'S BLOCK

Introduction: The Unideal Reader

THIS BOOK TELLS the stories of atypical readers and the impact had on their lives by a spectrum of neurological conditions affecting their ability to make sense of the printed word. The first history of neurodivergent reading, it relies on personal testimonies that have been left out of conventional histories of reading to express how cognitive differences shape people's experiences both on and off the page. A key premise of the book is that there is no single activity known as reading. Instead, there are multiple ways of reading (and, for that matter, *not* reading) despite the ease with which people use the term in conversation and act as if everyone does it in essentially the same fashion. Take a moment to consider what the term "reading" means to you. Whatever your conception of reading may be, and no matter how well you think you understand it, the examples presented here will push you to rethink the term's scope. My aim is to defamiliarize reading, to make you sit up, like Dickens's Joe Gargery, and say, "How interesting reading is!"[1]

The savant Kim Peek offers one of the most compelling examples of reading outside the box. Peek could read two pages at the same time: one with his left eye, the other with his right. It made no difference whether those pages were sideways, upside down, or reflected in a mirror. He was among the world's fastest readers, too, finishing Tom Clancy's doorstopper of a novel, *The Hunt for Red October*, in under ninety minutes.[2] You might think of Peek as a scanner as much as a reader since it took him approximately fifteen seconds to store away two pages of a paperback novel with near total recall. Hence his nickname: the "Kim-puter."[3] Peek's behavior was the inspiration for *Rain Man*, an award-winning film about an autistic savant with an extraordinary ability to calculate numbers. That film drew attention to not only savant abilities but also savant disabilities, for the real-life Rain Man needed help showering, dressing, and brushing his teeth. In short, Peek exemplified the variability of human minds both through his talent for memorizing entire books and through the challenges he faced in navigating a world that was not designed for minds like his. Today he would be understood more sympathetically through the lens of "neurodiversity" as someone who thinks, behaves, and interacts with the world differently than most other people.

The concept of neurodiversity emerged in the 1990s in recognition of the tremendous amount of variation found in our brains.[4] Disability rights activists introduced the term to replace the notion of a so-called normal brain with a continuum of neurological differences among people: the brain versus brains. All brains are different, and dissimilar brains lead to different ways of thinking, even among people thought to be neurotypical or to have similar cognitive architecture. As neuroscientist-turned-novelist Laura Otis observes, "People's mental worlds vary astonishingly."[5] The campaign for neurodiversity seeks recognition for neurological variations as differences rather than as defects or pathological symptoms to be marked off a checklist in accordance with the *Diagnostic and Statistical Manual of Mental Disorders (DSM-5)*. What began as a movement to appreciate cognitive differences among individuals diagnosed with autism has since expanded to embrace numerous other conditions, including many that affect the ability to read. (I'll be using the phrase "reading differences" instead of "reading disabilities" to move away from a framework that emphasizes deficits and difficulties over potential strengths.)

This book's focus on neurodiversity aims to transform our understanding of the very concept of reading. Neuroscientists have long insisted that we learn most about the brain when something goes awry.[6] *Reader's Block* makes a similar proposal concerning reading—that much can be learned about its complexity, versatility, and seemingly inexhaustible richness by attending to those edge cases that defy expectations. My book thereby directs attention to exceptional instances—say, a stroke survivor who reads with his tongue—compelling us to rethink the term's contours. This is merely one example of how disrupting the customary reading pathways may lead individuals to seek out alternative ways of doing it—not so much reading against the grain as reading against the brain.

Reader's Block ventures beyond the typical reader (if there is such a thing) in order to recover the testimonies of neurodivergent readers whose encounters with print have been affected by various neurological conditions: from dyslexia, hyperlexia, and alexia to synesthesia, hallucinations, and dementia. Before going any further, then, a few diagnostic explanations may be in order, starting with the three lexias. While it is well known that dyslexia disrupts the process of learning to read during childhood, not everyone is aware that alexia, historically known as acquired illiteracy or word blindness, can deprive literate adults of the ability to read, usually as the result of a stroke, an illness, or brain trauma. A third variant, known as hyperlexia, applies to children's precocious ability to decode words (usually before they have learned to talk) and even to memorize entire books without seeming to understand them, one of the symptoms associated with the autism spectrum.

Cognition influences reading in other ways, too. Synesthetes might see the letters of the alphabet in different colors, even when they are printed in black ink. Vladimir Nabokov's *Speak, Memory: An Autobiography Revisited* memorably describes seeing a polychromatic alphabet in which the letter "a" holds the tint of weathered wood. Others experience sensations of touch, sound, smell, or even taste while reading (for one person, the word "jail" has the flavor of bacon).[7] Atypical perception blurs the line between reality and imagination in ways that go beyond the power of ordinary books. In some cases, a hyperactive visual word form area (VWFA) in the brain can induce lexical hallucinations that are difficult to distinguish from real print. These phantasms range from religious visions (the writing on the wall at Belshazzar's feast in the Book of Daniel) to the psychotic breaks with reality associated with schizophrenia. Finally, people with dementia may struggle to read as a result of memory loss, evoking the Struldbruggs in *Gulliver's Travels* who abandon books "because their Memory will not serve to carry them from the beginning of a Sentence to the end."[8]

Advances in brain imaging technology and psychological assessments now make it easy to diagnose a wide range of reading differences. What has yet to be fully considered is, on one level, the influence these differences may have on specific textual encounters and, on another level, their impact on people's lives, well-being, and sense of identity in societies that historically have stigmatized the inability to read. *Reader's Block* proposes that, despite formidable obstacles, we can begin to formulate the neurodivergent reader's phenomenological experience through personal testimonies recovered from literature, film, life writing, social media, scientific journals, medical case studies, and other sources expressing what it feels like to read in unconventional ways. Hence, the ensuing chapters set out to recover atypical responses to books that have been passed over by nearly all accounts of reading and yet warrant inspection if we want to comprehend the term's full meaning.

THE READING SPECTRUM

The idea for this book came while I was finishing another one looking into debates over what counts as "real" reading. Time and again I encountered people who insisted on drawing a sharp line between reading and closely related activities they judged to be impostors (in that case, listening to audiobooks). It was not their verdicts that held my attention so much as the confidence that there was a single, coherent entity known as reading that could be neatly set apart from everything else people did with books. Is reading really that simple?

As this book contends, the most productive way to think about reading is as a loosely related set of behaviors that belong together owing to family resemblances, in Ludwig Wittgenstein's understanding of the phrase, without having in common a single defining trait.[9] Consequently, efforts to cordon off reading from nonreading are doomed to fail because there is no agreement on what qualifies as reading in the first place. The more one tries to figure out where the border lies between reading and not-reading, the more edge cases will be found to stretch the term's elastic boundaries. My book attempts to marshal together these exceptional forms of reading into a single forum, one highlighting the challenges faced by anyone wishing to patrol the boundaries over where reading begins and ends.[10] *Reader's Block* moves toward an understanding of reading as a spectrum that is capacious enough to accommodate the disparate activities documented in the following chapters along with any new ones that will inevitably surface beyond its pages.

It is a curious feature of the humanities that there is no agreed meaning for one of its fundamental terms. "Mysteriously, we continue to read without a satisfactory definition of what it is we are doing," observes Alberto Manguel in *A History of Reading*.[11] The term is taken to be so obvious that there is no need to specify exactly what is meant by it. After all, most people read just fine without knowing what is happening in their minds. Reading is an example of what the philosopher Daniel Dennett calls "competence without comprehension."[12] Cognitive neuroscientists share the view that our enjoyment of reading in no way depends on grasping the neural operations underpinning it. To cite one example, Mark Seidenberg recently observed that "people tend to be good at reading without knowing much about how they do it."[13] In my experience, literary critics tend to be *very* good at reading without knowing much about how they do it. This is a group consisting of what cognitive neuroscientist Stanislas Dehaene calls "overtrained readers" who have lost sight of the act's complexity.[14]

Historians have all but thrown up their hands at the prospect of trying to define what happens when someone picks up a book. Steven Roger Fischer begins *A History of Reading* by observing that there is no simple answer because reading is a variable term, not an absolute one.[15] What reading means to us today is not the same as what reading meant in past cultures or will mean in future ones. The definition continues to evolve along with humanity. "For, like thought itself," Fischer concludes, "reading can really be anything we choose."[16] Let us avoid choosing too narrow a conception, then, lest we risk excluding the endless forms of reading (to use a Darwinian figure of speech) visible all around us.

If one aim of this book is to defamiliarize reading, another is to denaturalize it. To put it bluntly: There's nothing natural about reading. The view of literacy as something that will just happen if kids grow up surrounded by books is a utopian one—literally, according to the future imagined in William Morris's *News from Nowhere*.[17] Philip Gough and Michael Hillinger's less idealistic study "Learning to Read: An Unnatural Act," by contrast, cautions that the average child learns to read slowly, with difficulty, and with lots of instruction.[18] From an evolutionary perspective, reading's gradual emergence over several millennia partly explains why there is so much variation in how people do it. Reading is an acquired skill, a gift of exaptation and neuroplasticity. "We were never born to read," cognitive neuroscientist Maryanne Wolf reminds us.[19] Because our brains are not hardwired or genetically programmed for reading (as they are for speech), there is no universal design for doing it. Instead, there are multiple pathways to literacy, which may vary confoundingly from one person to the next. One motive for writing this book was the sense that my own peculiar reading habits set me apart from other people in ways that I wanted to better understand. Years of speaking to people about their reading habits, covertly observing those of others, and accumulating unorthodox examples of it for this book have confirmed for me, at least, that there is no standard way of reading: There are *ways* of reading.

Surprisingly, one of the earliest exponents of this viewpoint was Sigmund Freud, a figure associated in literary circles less with reading than with overreading. Freud began his career as a neurologist, though, and his first book, *On Aphasia*, probably his least-read book among humanists, distinguishes between different types of reading in the most literal sense:

> Everybody knows from self observation that there are several kinds of reading some of which proceed without understanding. When I read proofs with the intention of paying special attention to the letters and other symbols, the meaning of what I am reading escapes me to such a degree that I require a second perusal for the purpose of correcting the style. If, on the other hand, I read a novel, which holds my interest, I overlook all misprints and it may happen that I retain nothing of the names of the persons figuring in the book except for some meaningless feature, or perhaps the recollection that they were long or short, and that they contained an unusual letter such as x or z. Again, when I have to recite, whereby I have to pay special attention to the sound impressions of my words and to the intervals between them, I am in danger of caring too little about the meaning, and as soon as fatigue sets in I am reading in such a way that the listener can still understand, but I myself no longer know what I have been reading.[20]

Freud captures three variants that most people would agree count as reading without necessarily agreeing that they are the same kind of reading. (The auditor of Freud's recitation might even represent a fourth type—of comprehension without, strictly speaking, decoding.) If we break down the reading process into two key components, word recognition and comprehension, then it becomes apparent that the emphasis can be placed on either one. The equation discerned by Freud is now orthodoxy among educationalists: the more cognitive resources spent on decoding, the fewer available for comprehension. This explains why a person may be said to have read a book even if that person confesses afterward to not having understood a word of it. Freud was ahead of his time in acknowledging that there is no single way to read but rather an assortment of techniques that we use depending on our circumstances, situations, and purposes. Proof reading, deep reading, reading aloud: All three are strategies that people deploy and switch between throughout the day. If the term can comfortably accommodate these three conflicting methods of reading, then why not more?

Educational psychologists have long recognized the need to expand the term's definition to accommodate different ways of doing it. The psycholinguist Frank Smith once declared that searching for a single definition would be pointless; for him, disputes over what we mean by reading are really disputes over language.[21] Even generic formulations along the lines of "being able to understand text" or "getting meaning from print" capture only one aspect of the process while saying nothing about what readers do, either physically or mentally, to achieve that goal.[22] Such imprecision may be strategically necessary, of course, since not everyone reads in the same way. To insist otherwise would be to endorse what cognitive psychologist Sally Andrews calls the "uniformity assumption," the supposition that all readers share identical cognitive architecture enabling them to read in a similar fashion.[23] The varied forms of reading identified by my book will thus be unrecognizable to anyone accustomed to doing it in a particular way.

Literary critics themselves have taken notice of how many ways there are to read. Although this group tends to be preoccupied with different methods of interpretation (close, distant, slow, hyper, and so forth) over other aspects of the process, a resurgence of interest in reading has moved the conversation away from hermeneutics and toward the various ways people do it.[24] Scholars have drawn on fields as different as education, history, neuroscience, psychology, sociology, and computational science to gain a better understanding of reading practices—not "doing a reading" but reading, actually. This renewed attention to the term's heterogeneous meanings encompasses everything from the mechanics of reading to the affective, cognitive, and physiological dimensions of it that vary from one person to the next. Perhaps the one thing everyone agrees on is that the meaning of the term "reading" is anything but self-evident.

The humanities' reluctance to pin down the concept may even turn out to be a virtue. Whereas quantitatively minded disciplines such as neuroscience, cognitive psychology, and computer science have sought to define the term with algorithmic precision, many humanists remain comfortable with a fuzzy, unconstrained usage pointing in several directions at once. In fact, much recent scholarship advocates expanding the term further to make room for emerging, marginal, or misunderstood forms of it (think of outliers like audiobooks, braille, and sign language). Media theorist Katherine Hayles has called for a reconceptualization of reading in response to the multimedia ecologies of the twenty-first century, for example, and media historian Mara Mills advocates an expansive understanding of the term to include accessible formats designed for people with physical disabilities.[25] *Reader's Block* pushes this evolution one step further by asking us to consider neurodiversity, too.

Bringing attention to emerging genres of life writing, from dyslexia to dementia memoirs, alongside alternative perspectives on more familiar titles (from *The Adventures of Sherlock Holmes* and *Little Women* to *The Bell Jar* and *Still Alice*), *Reader's Block* contributes to longstanding interest among literary critics in analyzing the methods, ethics, and representations of reading by evaluating atypical styles of doing it. Drawing on the latest research on reading from multiple disciplinary perspectives, it seeks to expand our understanding of a fundamental term in literary studies, sharpen the figurative terms ("close," "paranoid," "surface," and so forth) used to describe various methods of doing it, and assess the potential influence alternative modes of reading have over textual encounters. Specifically, *Reader's Block* pushes literary studies to recognize how neglected aspects of the reading process—from decoding and comprehension to affect, attention, memory, perception, sensations, and mental imagery—precede or feed into interpretation to shape people's understanding of texts.

Before going any further, it is worth restating that there is no hard border between neurodivergent and neurotypical readers. We are talking about a spectrum of reading abilities here. Many individuals classified as neurodiverse read in conventional ways, just as those presumed to be neurotypical can interact with books in ways that might raise an eyebrow. To take a famous example, the iconic media theorist Marshall McLuhan insisted on reading only the righthand pages of books while relying on his brain to supply the missing info.[26] (Neurological patients who are genuinely oblivious to one side of the page are sometimes encouraged to tie a brightly colored ribbon onto their left wrist.[27]) Can McLuhan be said to have "read" those books? This would be a hard question to answer satisfactorily using our existing vocabulary and classifications, both of which this book seeks to expand.

No sooner do we define reading than we run into exceptions. Bearing that lesson in mind, this book resists the temptation to replace one definition of reading with another. Whereas the prevailing approaches begin with a definition of reading before adjudicating whether subsequent examples fit, my approach starts with examples and then asks how our conception of reading can accommodate them. This method of exemplification, again influenced by Wittgenstein, seeks to reach an understanding of the term via concrete instances instead of a common element.[28] Presenting atypical styles should help clarify the concept of reading as an ensemble of disparate activities that sometimes fall outside of general formulations describing what happens when somebody picks up a book. Proceeding by way of example stretches the catchall term "reading" to accommodate the sorts of behavior that do not fit comfortably within existing definitions of the term. But enough talk about reading. Let me show you what I have in mind.

ON THE VARIETIES OF READING EXPERIENCE

Few absolutes exist when it comes to reading. Nearly every convention associated with the activity of reading (that it involves visually decoding graphic symbols, moving from left to right across the page, proceeding horizontally instead of vertically) turns out to apply only to particular ways of doing it. People can decode words using senses besides vision (namely, touch, hearing, even smell). Sentences can be written from left to right (as in English and modern European languages), right to left (as in Arabic, Farsi, and Hebrew), or alternate between the two (as in the Greek system known as boustrophedon). With practice, it is possible to read in any direction, even if you are accustomed to a particular orientation. When it comes to reading, there are so many exceptions to the rule because there is no rule. Choose any aspect of reading you think essential, and I will show you someone who does it in a different way.

This book's chapters focus on those neurological conditions most relevant to reading: dyslexia, hyperlexia, alexia, synesthesia, hallucinations, and dementia. But neurodiversity encompasses other conditions, too (ranging from depression and bipolar disorder to epilepsy and Tourette syndrome), that influence reading less pervasively but no less profoundly. The following illustrations offer a sense of how neurological and psychiatric conditions not covered elsewhere in this book may shape people's textual encounters. For clarity, these readers will be placed into two categories: those who have experienced the onset of symptoms gradually over time and those who find their lives suddenly disrupted by illness, injury, or other traumatic events.

Let's start with the conditions that emerge over the course of one's life. Bibliotherapy has drawn considerable attention to reading's impact on mental health.[29] My book turns that equation on its head by looking at how mental health influences reading—or, it bears repeating, *not* reading. Bibliotherapists may advocate the therapeutic benefits of literature, but such regimens only work if someone is able to read in the first place. People may struggle to read when they are anxious, depressed, manic, stressed, traumatized, sleep-deprived, or otherwise psychologically maladjusted. The right state of mind is a prerequisite to immersing oneself in a book.

For anyone in a troubled state of mind, books represent both cause and cure. John Stuart Mill famously turned to poetry for consolation at his lowest ebb.[30] Robert Burton's *The Anatomy of Melancholy*, by contrast, warns the impressionable reader to skip over the tract's list of symptoms lest "he trouble or hurt himself."[31] The very act of reading has a therapeutic effect for some people. Samuel Johnson kept a book next to his bed to ward off the "black dog" that kept him awake at night; books played a crucial role in what he referred to as "the management of the mind."[32] But unmanageable minds stop others from seeking refuge there in the first place. Merely opening a book, never mind reading one, might be too exhausting when in the black dog's company. As Andrew Solomon recalls in *The Noonday Demon*, leafing through a magazine felt like a Herculean task even though he was usually a voracious reader. Libraries offered no consolation: "My house is full of books I can't read."[33]

The correlation between depression and a distaste for books is a venerable one. A key symptom of the medieval notion of *acedia*, a spiritual torpor related to depression, was that it prevented monks from deriving solace from sacred texts. Thus the *Regula Benedicti* appointed two elder monks to look out for any member "not intent upon his reading" who might be in need of the brethren's intervention.[34] Historically, reading has been diagnosed as both a source and a symptom of melancholy—too much and too little reading were considered equally risky to one's health. If overexerting the mind led to melancholic thoughts, as physicians of antiquity believed, reading remains on the modern psychiatric list of clinical symptoms of depression, too, albeit in the inverted form of patients who find it difficult to follow what they are reading.[35]

Knowing what you are missing out on makes reading's absence feel even worse. The psychologist Stuart Sutherland spent most days reading and writing before a mental breakdown in his mid-forties. As he explains in his memoir, "so unremitting and painful were my thoughts that I was virtually unable to read."[36] The inability to read even the newspaper was "a singularly refined torture" for that inveterate reader.[37] If some people seek comfort in books at their lowest moments, mental illness blocks other people from reading when it is most needed. Those who have gone long spells without reading may therefore experience its restoration as a step toward recovery. After coming out of a prolonged depression, the writer Matt Haig found himself reading with an intensity he'd never known before, turning from someone who "liked" books into someone who "*needed*" them.[38]

Mental health can influence not only whether you read but also what you read. According to *Monkey Mind: A Memoir of Anxiety*, Daniel Smith's bibliotherapy consisted of randomly choosing library books whose opening lines soothed his feelings of unease. Anything that succeeded in thawing the icicle in his chest (Smith's equivalent to the "tingling spine" used by Nabokov to gauge a book's worth) went home with him: Saul Bellow, E. L. Doctorow, Ernest Hemingway, William Styron, and John Updike all made the cut.[39] Triggering sentences stayed on the shelf (with apologies to John Cheever, Don DeLillo, William Faulkner, William Gaddis, Henry James, Flannery O'Connor, and Thomas Pynchon). Self-medicating in this way helped him to find not just a double but a diagnosis in the likes of Philip Roth's Nathan Zuckerman.

The title of clinical psychologist Kay Redfield Jamison's memoir, *An Unquiet Mind*, points toward the potential downsides to bipolar disorder. If manic highs made Jamison feel like she could do anything, the inevitable lows blocked her from doing something as simple as reading a book. Her lapses in concentration match those found in other accounts of depression. "I would read the same passage over and over again only to realize that I had no memory at all for what I just had read," she tells us. "Each book or poem I picked up was the same way. Incomprehensible."[40] The medication keeping her moods level simultaneously keeps her away from books. Jamison rightly worried less about lithium's physical side effects (nausea, vomiting, occasional toxicity) than its psychological ones (impaired concentration, attention span, and memory) since she ends up going from reading three to four books per week to not reading a single one in over a decade. Sometimes rereading lines while taking copious notes was enough to counteract the medication. "Even so," she admits, "what I read often disappeared from my mind like snow on a hot pavement."[41] The following advice appears on her list of "Rules for the Gracious Acceptance of Lithium into Your Life": "Try not to let the fact that you can't read without effort annoy you. Be philosophical. Even if you could read, you probably wouldn't remember most of it anyway."[42] A key stage of recovery for Jamison, as for so many others affected by depression, comes when she is able to resume reading.

The poet Susanne Antonetta likewise blamed bipolar disorder for a case of reader's block that stopped her from finishing books despite her desire to do so. "I wanted to read, and my books had charm for me," she recalls in *A Mind Apart*, "but the words slid off the page or stuck, gnarls in a river."[43] Antonetta found her reading derailed by arbitrary word aversions that repelled her like the wrong pole of a magnet. Such is the force of these trigger words that she felt unable to repeat them even in her own book. Word infatuations could be equally debilitating. When Antonetta's eyes paused to linger over captivating words like "smooth" and "lush," she found it difficult to resume reading.

Anyone who has experienced seizures triggered by print will have good cause to remain wary of books. For them, continuing to read after the appearance of symptoms like facial muscle spasms and jaw clicking may lead to convulsions and loss of consciousness.[44] What is called "reading epilepsy" might have been responsible for the travails of the Victorian polymath Herbert Spencer, who experienced unpleasant "head-sensations" while finishing *The Principles of Psychology* (1855). As Spencer recalls in his *Autobiography*, "One morning soon after beginning work, there commenced a sensation in my head—not pain, nor heat, nor fullness, nor tension, but simply a sensation, bearable enough but abnormal."[45] Over the coming months Spencer found himself unable to read novels without suffering from what he called "hot head."[46]

People may not even know that they have reading epilepsy until waking up in an ambulance after losing consciousness midway through a sentence.[47] These readers usually recall feeling a sense of confusion while viewing the page, followed by a blackout. A teenager described himself "sticking to a word" immediately before a fit.[48] For this group, more than aesthetic preferences are at stake when choosing a font. One woman found that certain fonts (say, Times New Roman) provoked seizures, whereas reading the identical passage set in other typefaces had no effect. Minutes after starting to read a hazardous font, she felt a "strange sensation in her throat," followed by an unresponsive staring spell lasting for several minutes.[49] An electroencephalogram (EEG) confirmed the disparity by measuring the electrical activity in the woman's brain while she read the opening pages of Dickens's *A Tale of Two Cities* in multiple fonts. Researchers attributed the difference to serifs, the extra strokes used by typefaces to finish off letters.

Many of the preceding examples illustrate how mental health affects literacy: mind over manuscript. Our brains influence every aspect of literacy, from the deciphering of graphic symbols down to the way we feel about those symbols and even about books themselves. But the brain plays an equally prominent role in conditions like Tourette syndrome and obsessive-compulsive disorder that are not usually associated with reading disabilities. The tics or convulsive movements and sounds made by people with Tourette's may have an impact on their intellectual lives as much as their social lives. Carl Bennett's obsessive tendencies, a common trait among those with Tourette's, made it difficult to complete homework while attending medical school. "I'd have to read each line many times," he recalled.[50] The need to align paragraphs symmetrically in his visual field; to balance syllables; to make punctuation proportionate; to check a letter's frequency; and to repeat words, phrases, or lines all made fluent reading difficult. His symptoms interfered with his capacity to read until he stumbled upon a breakthrough:

The ritual of riding an exercise bike while smoking a pipe at the same time calmed him enough to read without tics (except for the occasional hoot).

Bennett's regime calls to mind one of history's best-known, and most idiosyncratic, readers: Samuel Johnson (who it has been speculated also had Tourette's).[51] Johnson was renowned for his ferocious appetite for books, as we know from vivid eyewitness accounts. One spectator recalled watching Johnson reading a book "over which he seesawed at such a violent rate as to excite the curiosity of some people at a distance to come and see what was the matter with him."[52] Perusing pages seems to have been therapeutic for Johnson, who rocked back and forth while holding books in a contorted posture that soothed his nerves. This was bibliotherapy in the most literal sense of the word.

Others found books impossible to put down—and not because they were page-turners. The completionist drive to finish everything could be exhausting for readers. According to a biographer, Nikola Tesla started the works of Voltaire before realizing that, in order to find peace of mind, he would have to finish close to a hundred volumes written by "that monster."[53] Compulsive reading drove others to read the same text multiple times. (Clinical tests used to screen for obsessive-compulsive behavior sometimes ask whether a patient feels the need to read passages more than once.[54]) The television host Marc Summers found himself reading the same paragraph thirty times. "I couldn't stop myself. I had no idea why," he explains in *Everything in Its Place: My Trials and Triumphs with Obsessive Compulsive Disorder*. "We have to do whatever it is that we do over and over until it's perfect."[55] Perversely, *repetitive* reading—not to be confused with the more benign practice of *repeat* reading—interfered with efforts to remember what has been read. One woman affected by reading compulsions recalled being too fixated on reading every sixth word six times to recall anything from the text.[56] Yet the elaborate rules governing this group's reading habits were not without compensatory benefits, including holding at bay distressing thoughts. Summers used to worry that reading a paragraph in the wrong way would kill his parents.[57]

"NORMAL" READING

Now on to those who come to see the world differently as a result of head injuries, illnesses, strokes, or other calamities—a group of survivors philosopher Catherine Malabou calls "the new wounded."[58] One misconception about literacy is that it lasts a lifetime. Tell that to the stroke survivors for whom words on the page have turned to gibberish. Patients in the neurology ward are quick to recognize the appropriateness of the clinical use of the word "insult" to describe brain damage. Literacy offers no protection against cerebrovascular accidents, which, in the blink of an eye, can take away your decoding abilities, along with speech, mobility, and cognition. Joe Torchio was among those who gave up reading for this reason. He would barely finish a sentence before "the words seemed to scatter in front of him like pigeons in a park."[59]

Even the most accomplished readers remain vulnerable to brain trauma. Robert McCrum's storied career at Faber, for instance, could not shield him from a stroke at the age of forty-two. While recovering, one of Britain's most influential editors found himself having to depend on other people to read to him—what Alberto Manguel once referred to as "vicarious reading."[60] Childhood favorites such as *Alice's Adventures in Wonderland*, *Charlotte's Web*, and *The Lion, the Witch and the Wardrobe* were not only consoling but also calibrated just right to a mind relearning how to read. McCrum was typical of stroke survivors in viewing his altered standing as a regression to childhood instead of a new phase of adulthood. "I feel like a child, and helpless like a child too," he admitted after being read to by his parents.[61] Midway through occupational therapy, he wondered what Kazuo Ishiguro, Milan Kundera, Mario Vargas Llosa, and other clients would think about seeing their editor playing with colored plastic letters.

The links between literacy and trauma became difficult to ignore after the First World War. Shell-shocked soldiers listed the inability to concentrate on books among the symptoms brought back from the trenches.[62] Yet reader's block was only half the story. Neurologists also noticed how resourceful trauma survivors could be after losing the ability to read. One of Kurt Goldstein's patients, for example, stopped recognizing letter shapes after having iron shrapnel extracted from his skull. He saw only spots on the page after the surgery. But the soldier learned to read again by following letter contours with the macula of his eyes, moving his head along the page without moving the eyeballs themselves, while simultaneously tracing those patterns with his hand. According to Goldstein's account, "he 'wrote' with his hand what his eyes saw."[63] The patient's presumption that everyone else read in this laborious way too offers proof that even the most unorthodox style of reading will come to feel natural to the person doing it.

As should be clear by now, this book is as much about reader's block as it is about the ingenious stratagems devised to unblock reading. Survivors of traumatic brain injuries have shown a knack for finding workarounds to continue reading after losing their decoding skills (a topic explored in Chapter 3). For example, if someone with hemianopia, which restricts the field of vision and eliminates any preview of upcoming text, might be unable to read horizontally, then why not read vertically instead? An art professor who could no longer read Hebrew after experiencing a stroke did exactly that by rotating the page ninety degrees and proceeding to decipher the row of letters as a column.[64] Studies have confirmed that anyone can read upside down with enough commitment.[65] When it comes to reading, practice makes proficient.

Jim Carollo is one of many people in this book for whom reading consists less of decoding (the mental process of translating printed words back into speech) than of recoding (converting print into other types of graphic symbols). No one expected Carollo to live after a car accident left him in a coma. When he woke up, a skull fracture had endowed him with exceptional mathematical abilities while at the same time stripping him of the ability to read fluently. Although he had been an avid reader before the accident, Carollo could no longer remember a sentence from start to finish. Today he largely avoids reading, and, even when he does pick up a book, he is really doing arithmetic since he has developed an intricate system for assigning numerical values to letters. "I was constantly adding and subtracting letters and words in my head," he explained—essentially reading by numbers.[66]

For some survivors, though, reading never gets any easier. In *I'll Carry the Fork! Recovering a Life After Brain Injury*, Kara Swanson describes how it felt to read a book after being hit by a van. What stands out in her account is the loss of control over a process that used to be automatic. Instead of proceeding sequentially through the narrative, Swanson bounces from one line to the next, randomly snatching words from the beginnings, middles, and endings of sentences. The smooth process of gliding across the page now felt as if she "were reading in the back of a truck while driving over the potholes of a Michigan springtime."[67] Swanson's memoir includes the unusual disclaimer that it hasn't been read by the author.

Brain injury survivors who once led successful, high-functioning lives may find it especially difficult to accept their new status as nonreaders or what this book will be calling "postliterate." Barbara Lipska spent her life studying other people's mental illnesses at the National Institute of Mental Health before a brain tumor triggered one of her own. Words no longer made sense: "When I try to read, I go faster and faster over the words but have little idea what I've read."[68] Knowing how the brain works offers surprisingly little consolation when it stops working.

Reading tends to be thought of in cerebral rather than corporeal terms. But, just like your organs, reading can fail. The art critic Tom Lubbock gradually lost the ability to read as glioblastoma spread through his brain. Whereas his pre-cancer self would have easily detected mistakes like substituting "walterkly" for "weightlessly," his eye could no longer tell the difference between sense and nonsense.[69] Lubbock continued reading despite widening delays between decipherment and comprehension, a kind of letter lag. The damage left him stranded in a literacy limbo that will be familiar to many neurodivergent readers: "My understanding of phrases was neither with, nor without sense, but in a kind of blur, in between."[70] Brain tumors and literacy sometimes find themselves locked into an antagonistic relationship in which one's growth corresponds to the other's decline. "Reading seems to have given up entirely," Lubbock reports as if he were a spectator to his own literacy's demise.[71]

The artist Marion Coutts stopped reading about the same time as Lubbock, her husband, a reminder that the sources of reader's block can be psychological as well as physiological—sympathetic reader's block, perhaps. Coutts found herself too preoccupied with events in the real world to heed imagined ones any longer. As she explains in her memoir,

> My eyes can't focus, they skit across, landing on words and skimming them for meaning as if they were simply a platform for something else more important. Fiction is impossible. Why would you want to make anything up?[72]

Neither spouse is reading independently by that point: Lubbock holds onto words but can no longer decipher them, whereas Coutts can decipher words but no longer takes an interest in them. Yet the couple find a way to continue reading, or at least co-reading, by working together symbiotically, a true marriage of minds.

Mastering the art of reading is an ambition that may wane with age, especially when the brain refuses to cooperate once someone's health begins to deteriorate. To take a dramatic example, Oliver Sacks's *Awakenings* sketches the lives of patients emerging from prolonged catatonic states caused by an epidemic of *encephalitis lethargica* or "sleeping sickness." The psychoactive drug responsible for restoring these patients to life also restores their ability to read—though not always in the way they had been accustomed to doing it. Sacks's patients show how easy it is for readers to devolve into nonreaders. Prior to taking medication, Mr O. could no longer concentrate enough to sustain his love of books, for intrusive thoughts "dart" into his mind while reading or, alternatively, "thoughts suddenly vanish, smack in the middle of a sentence sometimes . . . They drop out, leaving a *space* like a frame minus a picture."[73] Mr P. either read too fast to take anything in or became transfixed by a single word.[74] And a counting compulsion stopped Miss H. from losing herself in Dickens the way she used to; it is difficult to follow the plot when you are counting every "e" on the page.[75]

The newly awoken readers under Sacks's care, by contrast, undergo equally dramatic reversals. Although Leonard L. had never gotten beyond Dante's *Purgatorio* before drug therapy, he went on to read straight through the *Paradiso* with tears streaming down his face. Unfortunately, this drug-induced zeal soon tipped his behavior into mania: talking too fast, harassing nurses, masturbating for hours. Leonard's reading turned into just another compulsion as surges of energy drove him to read faster and faster, without concern for sense or syntax—what Sacks diagnosed as "festinant reading."[76] Snapping the book shut after every passage was the only way for Leonard to make sense of what he read.

A premise of this book is that brains and bodies cannot be separated when it comes to discussions of reading. But, strictly speaking, you do not need a brain to read—or at least not a whole one. Patients have been known to maintain the ability to read after undergoing hemispherectomies, a surgical operation to remove one of the brain's two halves. In the case of a patient named Kate, her language abilities remained intact after surgery since the right side of her brain took over the malfunctioning side's cognitive tasks (including essential language functions such as speech, comprehension, and reading). Three decades later, cognitive assessments confirmed that Kate's verbal ability remained in the average range. Ironically, removing part of her brain had the unexpected outcome of turning Kate into a reader. Although she had never read for pleasure before the operation, the encouraging results of cognitive tests completed after the surgery motivated her to take up fiction.[77] This was a serendipitous instance of what has come to be called "disability gain": Kate has read more novels with half a brain than most people do with a whole one.[78]

Brain injuries need not be the end of reading. Still, not everyone is comfortable reading to the beat of a different drum. Blocks may arise not only from neurophysiological sources but also from a person's conviction that there are right and wrong ways to read. Take the cautionary tale of Ted, a former courier for the Royal Air Force whose stroke made it difficult to identify the initial letters of words. Tracing the missing letters on his hand and other workarounds enabled him to continue reading accurately. But Ted refused to use these techniques because he felt that, in his words, "It's not normal reading."[79] Alt-literacy may be worse than illiteracy in some people's eyes. And that is where this book seeks to make a difference: by changing perceptions about what counts as "normal" reading.

TOWARD A HISTORY OF NEURODIVERGENT READING

Neurodiversity poses a challenge to book historians and historians of reading. Those fields have long sought to record the varied, distinctive, and marginal ways of reading, and even the "strangeness" of those ways of reading, found throughout the world from ancient times to the present day.[80] Documentary work has shifted attention away from abstract theoretical constructs of an idealized reader—what Karin Littau calls "a disembodied mind" reflecting contemporary literary theory's mentalist bias—toward the heterogeneity of actual readers coming from different social backgrounds and shaped by sociological factors such as age, class, education, ethnicity, gender, nationality, race, religion, and sexual orientation.[81] Such efforts have been remarkably successful in unearthing the wealth of reading practices exhibited in different time periods, locations, and communities.[82] Yet these studies focus on cultural, not cognitive, differences among readers. Despite their attention to demographic diversity, historians of reading have worked almost exclusively with neurotypical reading communities, that is, those for whom the act of reading operates according to identical cognitive or psychological processes—the uniformity assumption, again. The field may have stopped treating reading as an "anthropological invariant" (a charge levied by Roger Chartier and Guglielmo Cavallo) but not as a neurological one that would enable historians to account for differences in cognition.[83] What, then, should a historian of reading do with people whose responses to books reflect brains over backgrounds?

Brains have been on the minds of book historians since the field's inception. In "First Steps Toward a History of Reading," Robert Darnton observed the need to obtain neurological evidence in order to understand how readers decipher words.[84] Although we may be a long way from recovering what Darnton called the "inner dimensions" of the reader's experience, this book proposes that we can still make use of textual evidence preserving insider perspectives on unorthodox ways of reading in past cultures.[85] Let's follow Darnton's lead in thinking of my project as "First Steps Toward a History of Neurodivergent Reading," one that sets out to recover atypical responses to literature that have largely been passed over by cognitive literary studies and related narratological approaches invested in the mental processes shared by all readers.[86]

In place of "the ideal reader" envisioned by reader-response criticism and other theoretical schools, room should be made for "the unideal reader" whose disabilities make reading difficult or even intolerable.[87] Testimonies from across the spectrum of cognitive abilities point toward the need for a model of reading capacious enough to accommodate differences in the way minds work. Recent scholarship bringing together histories of reading with the insights of disability studies suggests one pathway toward documenting the cognitive dimensions of reading alluded to by Darnton while at the same time not losing sight of neurodiversity.[88] As we will see, neurodivergent ways of reading warrant attention both for what distinguishes them from neurotypical reading as well as for what they have in common.

Oliver Sacks's name has come up more than once in this introduction. The approach taken by *Reader's Block* differs markedly from those of the medical professionals who have written the bulk of scholarship on neurological disorders. Their case studies tend to focus on clinical symptoms relevant to medical diagnosis, discarding merely personal details. But my approach is indebted to Sacks's humane treatment of individual cases. The British neurologist was renowned for his bestselling books describing patients with unusual neurological conditions. More important, he is remembered for taking an interest in people as much as pathologies. When describing his methods, Sacks criticized the Hippocratic tradition of case histories for focusing too much on disease. To remedy this neglect, Sacks proposed making the patient—"the suffering, afflicted, fighting, human subject"—central to these histories.[89]

Sacks's case histories or "clinical biographies," as he called them, shift the balance from pathology's physiological dimensions toward its psychological ones: biography meets pathography.[90] His handling of cases was influenced by the detailed profiles found in nineteenth-century medical journals and, later, the book-length narratives of the Russian neuropsychologist Alexander Luria (not to mention Sacks's own experience listening to patients tell their stories). My approach builds on this rich tradition of clinical observation by singling out personal, emotional, and psychological—let's call them paramedical—details offering insight into patients' lives. As it turns out, Sacks wrote about many of the conditions featured in this book. This is hardly surprising considering his devotion to reading ("I need to read; much of my life is reading"); he contemplated suicide for the first time in his life when sciatic pain stopped him from being able to read.[91]

My method differs from Sacks's in one crucial respect: His case studies were built on consultations with patients. By contrast, my evidence consists primarily of testimonies gleaned from historical sources—an archive comparable to what Walter Benjamin referred to as his "Library of Pathology."[92] As a historian of reading working with print instead of people (and mindful of critiques put forward by the field of disability studies), I read the existing body of textual evidence with an eye toward those revealing personal details that have been downplayed, if not discarded altogether, by impersonal, heavily mediated clinical accounts of a patient's symptoms. Yet my goal remains in part the same as that of the clinicians: to gain a better understanding of the impact reading differences have on people at a time when reading is figured as a crucial aspect of our identities; a signifier of status, privilege, and power; and possibly even a prerequisite to leading a meaningful life.

This book remains wary of presenting a neurological freak show in which one brain dysfunction after another is paraded onstage for us to marvel at: someone reading upside down, then someone tracing letters with their toes, then someone seeing the alphabet in colors, and so forth. The charge of being a latter-day P. T. Barnum has been made against Sacks.[93] But plenty of people come away from Sacks's portraits with an enriched understanding of the individual lives about which he is writing. In my estimation, his sympathetic handling of cognitive differences goes beyond the medical gaze to probe questions about identity relevant to us all. Many readers gain from Sacks's books a renewed sense of our shared humanity despite any differences setting apart our minds.

My project likewise presumes there to be no conflict between reading in an unorthodox manner (or not at all) and leading a dignified, meaningful life. Several steps have been taken to communicate the stories of neurodivergent readers in a responsible manner. First, I have attempted to recover the experiences of readers who have been marginalized, stigmatized, or left out of the historical record. Second, my approach gives people of varying cognitive abilities the opportunity to speak for themselves—the historian's equivalent to listening to patients (a responsibility that clinicians have not always upheld).[94] This is hardly a straightforward task, of course, when working with clinical case reports that historically have privileged medical perspectives over the patient's voice.[95] Third, I erase any sharp lines between ability and disability that would reinforce the perception of some people being second-class readers. Fourth, *Reader's Block* foregrounds a shared cognitive ability—literacy in all its guises—in order to advance our understanding of how literate minds work. And finally, I emphatically reject the idea that there is a "normal" way of reading in the first place. Through its attention to the diversity of reading styles and methods, *Reader's Block* seeks to promote an understanding of reading as an inclusive activity in which people find all sorts of ways to participate.

As I mentioned earlier, the most effective way to demonstrate reading's breadth is simply to lay out the various ways people do it. Consequently, this book relies heavily on miscellaneous accounts of individual behavior ("everyone loves anecdotes," Sacks once wrote).[96] Anecdotes have a poor reputation among a medical profession that has become increasingly beholden to statistics and other forms of quantitative evidence.[97] Many historians share this dim view.[98] Saying that a book relies on anecdotal evidence is a surefire way to condemn it. Despite the limitations of qualitative evidence, however, historians of reading have long turned to anecdotes to learn about obscure forms of reading that would be difficult to investigate in any other way.[99] Unconventional readers who fall outside the statistical average are precisely those whose stories tend to be preserved informally. As literary scholar Kathryn Montgomery Hunter observed of the medical profession, "almost all anecdotes are about the variant or anomalous."[100] Variant and anomalous forms of reading are precisely what this book seeks to bring to our attention. It therefore exhibits unusually high levels of tolerance toward unconventional sources (fictional ones included) that invite new ways of thinking about what might otherwise feel like a familiar concept.

In fact, fictional examples can be among the most revealing, especially when it comes to opening up medicalized frameworks to alternative points of view. Aldous Huxley's *Point Counter Point*, for example, illustrates what happens when a novelist encounters the neurologist Henry Charlton Bastian's *The Brain as an Organ of Mind*, an 1880 study in which an aphasic patient asked to read aloud the College of Physicians' bylaws pronounces the line "It shall be in the power of the College" as "An the bee-what in the tee-mother of the trothodoodoo."[101] What the medical profession views as a textbook example of a neurological disorder—reading gone wrong—makes a very different impression on Huxley's protagonist, who finds himself mesmerized by the enchanting sounds of the phonemic distortions. "Marvellous!" he says to himself. "What style! what majestic beauty!"[102] The episode invites us at least to consider the positive aspects of cognitive differences before reflexively dismissing the patient's speech as gibberish. But it is not necessary to share Huxley's *jouissance* here to appreciate the larger point: that fiction provides space in which to represent acts of reading as well as a vantage point from which to reflect on their meaningfulness.

My reliance on sources ranging from memoirs to medical case studies points toward another challenge: bridging the gap between the separate and, according to some, antithetical fields of the medical humanities and disability studies.[103] The core dispute: A medical model tends to locate disability in individual bodies, whereas a social model locates it in an unaccommodating environment. The conflicting orientations are evident in perspective (diagnostic versus activist), vocabulary (disorder versus difference), and emphasis (deficits versus strengths).[104] Nevertheless, I have found elements of both approaches useful to understanding the complex history of reading differences. The following chapters draw from each side's toolkit, and occasionally the friction between them, to delve into the evolving medical histories of neurological impairments before then reframing these histories by bringing in the firsthand perspectives of individuals directly affected by cognitive differences.[105] These accounts give patients a chance to speak back to medical frameworks that reductively treat their cognitive differences in pathological terms without recognizing the value that alternative forms of reading may hold for them.

My allegiances lie with disability studies' emphasis on wresting away from medical authorities the power to determine what counts as "normal." The entire thrust of this book is away from an idea of "normal" reading that would leave out many textual encounters. In fact, writing this book would not have been possible without the vital work of disability studies scholars such as Michael Bérubé, G. Thomas Couser, Eva Feder Kittay, Ralph Savarese, and Tobin Siebers, among others, combined with evolving attitudes toward cognitive disability over the past century.[106] Take the example of children with Down syndrome, who were once considered ineducable. Outdated works like *Mongolism: A Study of the Physical and Mental Characteristics of Mongolian Imbeciles* (1928) cautioned against teaching these children to read since they were thought to be incapable of recognizing even the simplest words.[107] Being told by teachers that "Mongoloids cannot read" did not stop Nigel Hunt, though, from publishing his own book subtitled *The Diary of a Mongoloid Youth*.[108] Substantial progress has been made in terms of expanding educational opportunities and expectations for children with cognitive differences thanks to campaigning by parents, advocacy groups, and the disability rights movement. Today, these children are no longer written off. We have reached the point where Bérubé can talk about reading the Harry Potter series with his son, who has Down syndrome and whom no one expected to progress beyond *Chicken Little*.[109]

But the insistence by some in the field of disability studies on focusing exclusively on strengths over deficits conflicts with a core goal of this book: to document the consequences of reading's loss. In order to prevent characterizing disability in terms of lack, some disability rights activists frown on (to put it politely) unfavorable comparisons between old lives and the new when it comes to discussing changing abilities. It is certainly true that people can live fulfilling lives without being able to read visually, especially now that audiobooks, text-to-speech software, and other assistive technologies offer alternative ways to access print—"reading by other means," as Georgina Kleege calls it.[110] Still, following the lead of writers like Tobin Siebers, Susan Wendell, Tom Shakespeare, Christina Crosby, and Michael Davidson, this book pushes back against a prevailing ethos of disability studies by refusing to reduce literacy to just another skill.[111] We can still recognize how acquired print disabilities may be experienced as a loss without devaluing the lives of other people who can't read. Those who were once invested in literacy as a cultural ideal may wish to spend time mourning its absence, exploring its residual influence, and reflecting on how identities evolve alongside changes to one's status as a reader. After all, people's impassioned relationship to reading is what makes testimonies about reader's block so compelling.

My book provides space for people to express complicated responses to the many forms taken by reader's block: struggling to learn to read, struggling to stop reading, losing the ability to read, favoring unorthodox styles of reading, figuring out workarounds to resume reading, adjusting to life after reading. What all this book's cases have in common is a sense that reading matters at a profound level that may be difficult to put into words. I have been influenced by testimonies from people like Claudia Osborn, a physician who sustained a traumatic brain injury and chafed afterward at being told to appreciate what she had instead of dwelling on what she had lost. As she wrote in her notebook,

> I am keenly aware of how much I have to be grateful for in my life, including being alive. However, when my impaired reading skills leave me too confused to sort my mail, it doesn't soothe my pain to record here that I am glad I am not in a coma. Nor do I, who crave my former relationship to the printed word, want to be told there are a multitude of impoverished folks who cannot read.[112]

Osborn's stance will be a common refrain throughout this book—the sense that being a reader is fundamental to many people's identities and that testimonies about their changing relationship to reading deserve to be heard.

HOW TO READ THIS BOOK

I'm sometimes asked about this project: Why should ordinary readers care? Bizarre ways of reading may pique our curiosity without necessarily being valuable to anyone else interested in literature. William Empson, for example, dismissed the sensory disturbances produced by migraines, epilepsy, and psychedelic drugs as unimportant to poetry readers.[113] My response: Understanding other people's ways of reading is a necessary step to understanding your own (which may not be as ordinary as you think). Being exposed to multiple styles of doing it offers a chance for people to reflect on the nature of reading in ways that can be difficult to do without provocation. It is worth thinking about reading from an outsider's point of view, as William James did by asking what his fondness for books must look like to his dog.[114] My book takes the dog's eye view on reading. The following six chapters—each focused on a particular reading difference—set out to examine the nature of the relationship between neurotypical and neurodivergent reading and ultimately to call into question whether there is such a thing as a typical reader.

The first half of *Reader's Block* covers the three lexias. Chapter 1 starts with the best-known set of reading differences: dyslexia, how the medical profession describes difficulties with word recognition and decoding skills that interfere with an individual's ability to read fluently. The experiences of dyslexic readers upend one of the most fundamental assumptions about how humans apprehend books: "typographical fixity," the expectation that a page of text will remain identical from one viewer to the next. This assumption of typographical fixity was a key benefit delivered by Johannes Gutenberg's invention of the printing press, and it has grounded how books have been conceived for hundreds of years. Dyslexic readers, however, confront what might be called "typographical fluidity": a page whose appearance changes from one reader to the next or even from one *reading* to the next. Of course, two people reading the same book can and often will interpret its contents differently. Dyslexia, by contrast, introduces a similar divide at the level of decoding, where brains play a decisive role in determining whether two readers will see the same printed words in the first place. Holding identical copies of a book is not itself a guarantee that readers will perceive identical contents.

On one level, Chapter 1 shows how the experience of typographical fluidity influences dyslexic readers' encounters with books. It does so by directing attention to the little-studied genre of the dyslexia memoir, whose authors give first-person accounts of the impact of reading differences on everything from their personal lives to the perception of print. I contend that these testimonies restore to view elements of the interpretive process taken for granted by audiences for whom reading has become an automatic, streamlined procedure. Specifically, these accounts single out misrecognized letters, moving words, mixed-up sentences, and other perceptual distortions that disrupt the word processing stage preceding interpretation. Memoirs with titles like *The World Through My Dyslexic Eyes* articulate the precise ways in which atypical perception sets people with dyslexia apart from other readers by confronting them with incompatible versions of the same page. Drawing on encounters with classic novels such as *Little Women*, dyslexia memoirs thus invite fluent readers to witness how dyslexia—and reading differences more broadly—influences a book's reception by generating competing versions of it before interpretation has even begun.

On another level, the chapter enables us—once these elements of the interpretive process are restored to view—to recognize the underappreciated role played by decoding (and misdecoding) in all acts of reading. Whereas neurotypical readers tend to assume that everyone decodes in more or less the same fashion before then proceeding to interpret texts differently, dyslexic readers complicate this scenario by decoding texts in disparate ways that hold implications for interpretation down the line. The average reader will have a sense of how this works from occasionally misreading a word—as even an exemplary reader like Marcel Proust acknowledged doing—and then having to double back on the passage to confirm its meaning.[115] In other words, the discrepancies assumed by most people to take place only at the level of interpretation (say, a group of students close reading a passage in which everyone agrees on the words before proceeding to disagree on their meaning) can also be seen at work in earlier stages of the reading process.

Chapter 2 turns from children who start reading late to those who start reading early. Perhaps too early. It is not unusual for children on the autism spectrum to exhibit a precocious ability to read and even to remember entire books without seeming to understand a word of them—a condition known as hyperlexia. The experiences of autistic readers challenge the conventional understanding of reading as an interpretive activity. Instead of reading to understand a text's meaning, as people usually do, many readers on the spectrum prefer what this chapter calls "surface reading," a preoccupation with a book's surfaces, from the shapes of its words to the textures of its cover, binding, ink, paper, typefaces, and so forth. If theories of reading generally focus on hermeneutics, or methods of interpreting texts, then this style of reading stands out for its refusal to delve beneath the surface. Surface readers prioritize the senses over making sense.

My chapter on the neglected history of autistic reading practices captures how variations in the ways brains process information affect people's interactions with books. It argues that autistic readers' distinctive cognitive profiles predispose many of them to appreciate aspects of textuality that tend to go unnoticed or unacknowledged by other readers. Drawing on the insider perspectives of autistic people—who, since the publication of trailblazing books like Temple Grandin's *Emergence: Labeled Autistic* (1986), have written profusely about their experiences of neurodiversity in memoirs (sometimes called "autiebiographies") and on social media—this chapter singles out uncommon forms of textual engagement: stimulating the senses by touching, tasting, or smelling books; decoding as an end in itself; manipulating word shapes; memorizing entire manuscripts; and fixating on extraneous typographical details such as hyphens and serifs. These ways of interacting with texts contribute to the reading experience, even if they may be perplexing to neurotypical audiences or, worse, dismissed as "nonreading." Whereas clinical accounts of the so-called idiot savants of the late nineteenth century and the savant skill of hyperlexia in the twentieth century once focused on deficits or deviations from a supposed norm, as this chapter documents, a growing corpus of life writing by individuals from across the spectrum now offers a counter-perspective, articulating the potential benefits (from blocking out unwanted stimuli to immersing oneself in print's unique sensory gratifications) of using unconventional methods to engage with books.

Testimonies about autistic ways of reading therefore invite neurotypical audiences to reflect on the boundaries marking what qualifies as reading and, more important, the full extent of their own bookish pleasures—some of which may even fall outside those boundaries. For despite the presumed link between reading and interpretation, all reading to some extent involves the forms of surface reading prized by autistic readers before the customary processes of interpretation have even begun. Viewing these methods of surface reading as different versions of the behavior exhibited by everyone who interacts with books, and not as alien forms of gratification experienced by autistic readers alone, makes it possible for book historians and cognitively oriented humanists alike to recognize how highly specific, idiosyncratic features (maybe the feel of a well-thumbed paperback edition or an excerpt from its pages preserved eidetically in the mind's eye) contribute to textual encounters that are often recollected in generalized terms applicable to all readers.

Chapter 3 takes as its starting point the dystopian scenario imagined by Nabokov's *Pale Fire*: "What if we awake one day, all of us, and find ourselves utterly unable to read?"[116] While the risk of an illiteracy epidemic may be remote, individuals occasionally do wake up as nonreaders. Alexia, or what is sometimes referred to as acquired illiteracy, can happen to anyone as the result of a stroke, an illness, or a head injury. Such accidents confound a deeply entrenched belief that literacy is a permanent condition by showing how easily it can be lost. This chapter proposes that formerly literate adults should be thought of as "postliterate" to distinguish their situations from those of people who have never read. The most revealing way to assess the value of reading in people's lives may be to scrutinize instances in which it has been taken away. Hence, this chapter draws on over a century's worth of medical case studies, memoirs, and even detective fiction featuring alexic sleuths to gauge the impact of postliteracy on people's sense of identity in societies that increasingly take literacy for granted and stigmatize those who lack it.

Paradoxically, incidents of reader's block can sharpen our understanding of how reading works in the first place. Chapter 3 argues that accounts of postliteracy—that is, of what it feels like to go from being a reader to a nonreader—bring into view the mechanics of a process to which people pay little attention after learning to do it as children. Postliteracy narratives expose how what may feel like a smooth, automatic process instead consists of multiple neurological operations that can go awry at any given moment: from attention and visual recognition to decipherment and meaning-making. Accounts of seeing letters without being able to make sense of them underscore the extent to which reading depends on the reciprocity between bodies and brains. This is a point vividly borne out by the resourceful ways devised by individuals with alexia to continue reading, whether by proceeding on a letter-by-letter basis or by tracing the shapes of letters on the back of one's hand or even (using the tongue) the roof of one's mouth, all labor-intensive techniques—slow reading by necessity— that bring the procedures of reading into potential conflict with the enjoyment of texts at an imaginative level. Or to put it another way, how we read affects how we respond to reading. Exposure to such workarounds encourages fluent readers, in turn, to reflect on the nature of the reading process in two opposing directions: first, as a neurophysiological set of procedures executable in more ways than one, as opposed to a single, "correct" way of reading; and second, as an activity whose worth to individuals far exceeds its mechanics, thereby highlighting the extent to which reading is as much an identity as it is an action or activity. As this chapter will show, the specter of literacy's loss forces a reckoning not only with what it means to read but also with what it means to be a reader.

The second half of *Reader's Block* turns from the lexias to three other neurological conditions affecting readers: synesthesia, hallucinations, and dementia. The first of these stands out less as a disability than a superability: sensing phenomena imperceptible to everyone else. One of the most common types of synesthesia involves the perception of color in response to print. Where most people see plain black letters, a synesthete like Nabokov saw them in the blue shades of huckleberries and thunderclouds. Synesthetic readers experience what I call a bibliographic double consciousness consisting of both the original page and an array of colors overlaying that page. This dual perspective complicates the prevailing view holding that audiences mutually apprehend a book's graphic design before proceeding to interpret it in different ways, for the synesthete may perceive an entirely different page than other readers do. Hence, this chapter considers synesthesia's relevance to literary criticism by asking: How might seeing the alphabet in a spectrum of colors influence the experience of reading?

Chapter 4 elucidates how synesthetic readers' bibliographic double consciousness—a mental image shared by the entire audience supplemented by a private one existing in the synesthete's mind alone—influences their responses to books. Drawing on personal testimonies, scientific case studies, journalistic profiles, social media, and other textual evidence of what it feels like to read in color, it argues that the perception of sensory effects generated less by the manuscript than by the reader's mind have played an unacknowledged role in the textual reception of neurodivergent readers.

Namely, a word's hue may trigger intense feelings of attraction or repulsion that can potentially shape responses to classic titles such as, say, *The Scarlet Letter*. The perception of color can also enhance or disrupt the reading process itself, either by supporting the synesthete's ability to concentrate on words displayed in alluring hues or by disrupting that attentiveness when the sensations generated by the page overwhelm the reader's ability to make sense of it.

At the same time, this chapter points toward the relevance of synesthesia to understanding the mental imagery perceived by the average person. As remote as synesthetic imagery (oatmeal-tinged letters, orange-tinted words, novels in a green shade) may seem, synesthesia represents an extreme version of the mental imagery perceived by all readers, for, as each of this book's chapters demonstrates, the page is as much a product of the brain as the eye. Since readers tend to think of perception as neutral or at least unbiased, understanding what takes place in the minds of synesthetic readers can guide literary critics toward a more refined understanding of how perception itself is capable of acting as a form of interpretation. The confessions of the synesthetic reader—to adapt a phrase from Nabokov—encourage audiences to become aware of idiosyncratic preferences (say, a fondness for a particular font) that may play a role in aesthetic taste and ultimately even textual interpretation.

Chapter 5 takes up another formidable type of mental imagery: hallucinations. Such misperceptions exemplify the mind's capacity to come between a person and the page. It is widely believed that books supply a shared framework enabling audiences to judge the validity of various interpretations of their contents. But the hallucinations documented here undermine this pretense of consensual understanding by introducing phenomena imperceptible to anyone other than the hallucinator. Such readers visualize letters, words, sentences, books, and even other readers that no one else can perceive—what this chapter calls seeing "things." Just as dyslexic readers encounter a fluid page whose appearance changes from one reader to the next, those prone to hallucinating can never know for certain whether they are viewing the same page as other people—or even a page at all.

Hallucinatory imagery affects all readers, to some extent. As William James's *The Principles of Psychology* once noted of novel readers: "More than half of the words come out of their mind, and hardly half from the printed page."[117] This ratio is out of balance in the case of readers affected by mental illness, however, who may not be able to distinguish between the two. Testimonies gathered from various sources, ranging from the Bible to memoirs written by patients with firsthand experience of psychosis, illustrate the many ways hallucinations can disrupt efforts to read. My view is that these testimonies call attention to how competing imagery generated by the mind and the page can make it difficult to tell the difference between them. In some cases, readers have trouble distinguishing between fact and fiction. The figure of the paranoid reader epitomizes this tension between mind and manuscript. In others, a hyperactive visual cortex causes people to see lexical hallucinations consisting of letters, words, or entire sentences emblazoned across the walls. The testimonies presented by this chapter convey the full extent to which the reader's mind can transform narrative imagery in the very process of receiving it.

Reader's Block concludes with the challenges awaiting readers late in life. Whereas the opening chapters focus on children learning how to read, the final one leaps forward in time to adults forgetting how to do it. Dementia and neurogenerative diseases make it difficult to concentrate on books or even to remember what's in them. As the author of a book subtitled *My Life Turned Upside-Down by Alzheimer's* asks, "Did you ever . . . Read for hours and hours, having enjoyed it while you were reading it, but then it's all gone?"[118] Testimonies like this one undercut the widespread supposition that memory is a necessary component of reading. Contrary to expectations, many people with dementia continue to derive pleasure from books long after they have ceased being able to read them in the familiar sense of the term.

Chapter 6 examines how memory loss affects people's ability to engage with texts ranging from classics such as Dickens's *A Christmas Carol* and Arthur Conan Doyle's *The Adventures of Sherlock Holmes* to contemporary novels like Lisa Genova's *Still Alice*. It does so through the help of an expanding genre known as the dementia memoir, whose authors (or caregivers) seek to communicate their experiences of cognitive decline, including a changing relationship to print. Drawing on firsthand accounts as well as my own analyses of classic narratives adapted for audiences experiencing memory loss, I demonstrate how testimonies about living with dementia single out aspects of the reading process that have been undervalued by a literary discourse invested in plot and the retrospective comprehension of narrative—or what is popularly referred to as closure. These accounts celebrate aspects of reading associated with what might be called "continuance" instead, a way of engaging with narratives whose value does not depend on completing them. People who read in "the eternal present tense" (a phrase applicable to anyone affected by amnesia, dementia, or other memory disorders) seek pleasure in ruminating on small chunks of text, reading aloud captions, looking at pictures to trigger reminiscences, tracing letter shapes with their fingers, or merely holding a book in their hands. They may also devise resourceful strategies to continue reading books by jotting down plot summaries in the margins, skimming for the gist, co-reading them with caregivers, or privileging the page over the plot—a newfound appreciation of form expressing interest less in the matter of whodunnit than in howsitdun. Such testimonies shift attention from the pleasures of rereading books—familiar territory among memoirs about aging—toward the counterintuitive pleasures of being unable to reread them. The dementia memoir's attention to "de-reading" thereby invites narratologists with even the most spotless memories to appreciate seemingly peripheral components of the reading process as meaningful in themselves rather than as mere steps toward retrospective understanding of a text.

A brief disclaimer: these six chapters treat reading differences as distinct phenomena for the sake of clarity. Outside of this book, of course, neurological conditions lack sharp boundaries and inevitably overlap in messy ways—as is made clear by titles like *Neurodiversity: A Humorous and Practical Guide to Living with ADHD, Anxiety, Autism, Dyslexia, the Gays, and Everyone Else*.[119] The diagnostic categories discussed by this book will inevitably evolve, merge, or even disappear altogether in a few years' time. The approach taken here recognizes the fluidity of these diagnostic categories, which vary across time and culture, while still finding the testimonies of the individuals who have been personally affected by them useful resources with which to rethink the concept of reading—itself a fluid and provisional category.

In closing, it is a convention of scholarly publishing to advise audiences on the best way to read your book. This introduction makes no such presumption. Since everyone reads differently, as I have been insisting, tackle this book in whatever way you feel comfortable. Read it from cover to cover, out of sequence, or piecemeal. Read it upside down, sideways, or in a mirror. Feel free to read two pages at the same time or only every other page. You're welcome to memorize the pages for later consultation, too. For just as there is no right way to read, there is no right way to read this book. What matters is that you are doing something with it—something that I'm proposing should be called "reading."

1 Dyslexia

"I love everything about books, except actually reading them."
—Philip Schultz, *My Dyslexia*

THE VOICES OF PEOPLE WITH dyslexia are conspicuously absent from most histories of dyslexia. Until recently, that history was seldom told by them; it was told for them. In 1970, for example, the neurologist Macdonald Critchley recounted the story of an unnamed Trinidadian woman of color who found being dyslexic so distressing that she decided to move to a foreign country to learn how to read. It took the woman four years to save enough money for a ship's passage to London, a city where she had never been and everyone was a stranger. Once there, the woman sorted rags in a factory before finding a cleaning job at a hospital, whose chaplain gave her reading lessons.[1] Her plight reflects the powerful stigma associated with reading differences. But what exactly made life so intolerable? How did she feel about leaving behind her home, family, and friends? And was reading ultimately worth the sacrifice? There is no way of knowing, since the woman never speaks for herself.

Public understanding of reading differences has improved markedly since that woman's journey across the Atlantic. Derived from the Greek roots "dys" (difficulty) and "lexis" (language), "dyslexia" is the term used by the medical profession to describe difficulties with word recognition and decoding skills that interfere with an individual's ability to read fluently.[2] Since there are variations in how dyslexic brains process information, dyslexia should be thought of less as a fixed category than as a continuum of developmental differences related to the numerous components of reading (as well as writing and spelling).[3] No two dyslexics will describe their experiences in the same way.

It is now customary to speak of dyslexia in terms of cognitive differences instead of deficits. In fact, there are many instances of what might be designated "dyslexia gain": pattern recognition, spatial reasoning, intuitive problem-solving, a knack for design, and so forth. Numerous studies have confirmed the potential benefits of dyslexia, especially when it comes to creativity.[4] Celebrated figures like Leonardo da Vinci, Alexander Graham Bell, and Thomas Edison are no longer thought to have succeeded despite their dyslexia but because of it. This overdue shift in perspective, though, should not erase how much people have suffered over the past century because of reading differences. As the physician Sally Shaywitz once noted, "Dyslexia inflicts pain."[5] And, as this chapter will show, that pain carries over into people's responses to books.

The difficulties faced by some people in learning to read reflect the fact that there is nothing natural about doing it. "Literacy is a cultural invention," as the cognitive neuroscientist Maryanne Wolf put it.[6] Unlike speech, reading is not hardwired into our brains. Instead, reading is an acquired skill that depends heavily on the brain's plasticity or ability to repurpose older circuits designed for other cognitive tasks. Given the complexity of the act—one that depends on synchronizing a staggering number of affective, cognitive, linguistic, perceptual, and physiological processes—it should hardly be surprising that some people can't read. What's surprising is that anyone can do it at all.

Not everyone finds learning to read difficult, of course. Gifted children may start reading without any help. Rudolf Flesch's classic study of literacy, *Why Johnny Can't Read*, holds up the exceptional case of President Andrew Johnson, a tailor's apprentice who taught himself to read using the speeches of distinguished statesmen.[7] Or to take a more recent example, the science-fiction writer Isaac Asimov learned to read before starting school. When asked how he did it, Asimov replied, "I don't know. I just figured it out."[8] But most children find learning to read challenging, at least at first. They resemble Dickens's Pip, who "struggled through the alphabet as if it had been a bramble-bush; getting considerably worried and scratched by every letter."[9]

Years of instruction may be necessary to turn that bramble-bush into a rose garden—if it ever blooms at all. And then there are the children who find learning to read excessively difficult, even painful. Gustave Flaubert, who did not learn to read until age nine, found deciphering letters so taxing as a child that he frequently burst into tears. Jean-Paul Sartre's biography refers to him as "the slave of the alphabet."[10] These are the readers—Flaubert's fellow slaves of the alphabet—who, in this chapter, get to express in their own words how reading differences have influenced not only their disposition toward books but also their understanding of them.

It was not until late into the twentieth century that researchers began to take an interest in the impact reading differences can have on people's lives. Dyslexia research initially focused on the neurological mechanisms underpinning reading deficits, along with the optimal remediation techniques for improving children's literacy. Critchley's *The Dyslexic Child* was among the first studies to recognize the psychological toll of living with reading differences: "The dyslexic is apt to find himself an alien in a critical, if not hostile, *milieu*; mocked, misunderstood, or penalized; cut off from opportunities for advancement."[11] Subsequent scholarship drew on interviews, ethnographies, case studies, and other qualitative methods to explore the condition's fallout. *The Scars of Dyslexia*, *The Reality of Dyslexia*, and *The Human Side of Dyslexia* are representative titles seeking to convey "the dyslexic experience" that would otherwise remain invisible to other people.[12] It was only a matter of time before dyslexics found ways to speak for themselves.

Today, stories written (or dictated) by people with dyslexia are easy to find. Personal accounts of dyslexia are now widely available as a result of advances in literacy instruction, expanded publishing opportunities, and evolving attitudes toward disability.[13] The situation has changed since the 1960s and 1970s, when a shortage of firsthand accounts held back research. As Eileen Simpson explained at the start of her pioneering memoir, *Reversals: A Personal Account of Victory over Dyslexia*, "Experts in the field have been hampered in their research because they have not been able to find out what it is like, from the inside, to live in a literate society and be unable to read and write."[14] Simpson was among the first to supply one of these insider perspectives. Since then, numerous accounts of dyslexia "from the inside" have appeared in print and online, constituting what this chapter recognizes to be a genre in its own right: the dyslexia memoir.

After being shushed for much of their childhoods, dyslexics are finally getting the chance to tell their side of the story. Whereas the initial accounts of dyslexia were written from a medical standpoint seeking to figure out what had gone wrong with people's brains, the life writing produced by dyslexics introduces a distinctly personal slant on how cognitive differences may shape perception of everything from one's place in society to the pages of an ordinary book.[15] As children's author Patricia Polacco once put it, "What you perceive is different than what other people see."[16] This difference in perspective is made vividly apparent through the genre's personal testimonies about reading. Memoirs with titles like *The World Through My Dyslexic Eyes* take on the formidable task of formulating the precise ways atypical perception sets people with dyslexia apart from other readers by confronting them with competing or even conflicting versions of the same page. In doing so, the dyslexia memoir restores to view elements of the interpretive process that usually go unnoticed by audiences for whom reading has become an automatic, streamlined procedure. By directing attention to the crucial role played by decoding in the act of reading, dyslexia narratives seek to make audiences recognize how reading differences can shape encounters with books before the process of interpretation has even begun.

SOMETHING FUNNY ABOUT ME

The historical record offers an occasional glimpse into the impact dyslexia had on past lives. Since at least the seventeenth century, cases have been reported of literate people suddenly becoming "illiterate" after a brain injury. In 1652, for example, the Swiss physician Johann Jakob Wepfer reported the case of a stroke survivor who forgot how to read even though he was still able to recite the Lord's Prayer (a condition now known as alexia, the subject of Chapter 3).[17] The German physician Adolf Kussmaul introduced the term "word blindness" (*wortblindheit*) in 1877 to describe a perplexing condition in which patients saw words on the page but were unable to make sense of them, and, a decade later, Rudolf Berlin referred to these instances of acquired illiteracy using the term "dyslexia."[18] The medical literature initially adopted Kussmaul's phrase, though, to describe the various difficulties people had with reading. Although word blindness misleadingly linked the condition to the eye rather than the brain, Kussmaul and those influenced by him nevertheless recognized there to be a neurological dimension to word processing.[19] This insight marked the beginning of the medical profession's investigations into the nature of reader's block.

Clinicians soon began to treat reading differences present since birth. Before the advent of mass literacy, the dramatic reversals in fortune associated with acquired reading difficulties made them easier to detect than congenital ones. Less conspicuous difficulties only became noticeable once increasing numbers of children began attending school in the late nineteenth century. In 1896, James Kerr, a medical superintendent in England, added a boy with word blindness to his list of students affected by what he called the "most *bizarre* defects."[20] That same year, the physician W. Pringle Morgan identified similar behavior in a fourteen-year-old student "Percy F.," noting, "Words written or printed seem to convey no impression to his mind."[21]

The catalyst for Morgan's report was a case study of word blindness published by James Hinshelwood in the *Lancet*, a prominent medical journal.[22] The Glaswegian ophthalmologist encountered parents who, understandably, attributed their child's reading woes to eye problems. Over the next decade, Hinshelwood's detailed clinical reports identified the key traits of what would come to be known as dyslexia. These cases ranged from a twelve-year-old boy who recognized only five words ("it," "is," "to," "can," and "not") to a girl who was unable to remember the alphabet after nine months of practice. The children found reading exhausting; one child's father observed that "reading seemed to take a good deal out of him."[23] They evoke modern instances of dyslexia not only through their decoding deficits but also through their subsequent experiences of social exclusion. It is no wonder so many of these students masked their dyslexia at school by memorizing the instruction booklets before being asked to read aloud. One mother confided to Hinshelwood that classmates' derision exacerbated her son's problems with print—an ordeal memorably anticipated by Dickens's David Copperfield, who felt the words in his head "all sliding away" at the very sight of his tyrannical stepfather, Mr. Murdstone.[24]

Hinshelwood supposed dyslexia to be more common than was suggested by the number of recorded cases. In his estimation, most cases simply had not been diagnosed.[25] "It is a matter of the highest importance to recognise the cause and the true nature of this difficulty in learning to read which is experienced by these children," concluded Hinshelwood, "otherwise they may be harshly treated as imbeciles or incorrigibles and either neglected or flogged for a defect for which they are in no wise responsible."[26]

Hinshelwood's suspicions proved correct. Cases of dyslexia were soon being reported all over the world; one study estimated that there were sixty-four cases of word blindness documented between 1896 and 1916.[27] Unfortunately, Hinshelwood also turned out to be right about the harsh treatment awaiting these supposedly "defective" children.

Although the medical profession handled the initial cases of dyslexia, it would not be long before educationalists and clinical psychologists turned their attention to reading differences, too. Learning difficulties came to be understood primarily as educational problems. One outcome of this reorientation was to overturn the prevailing view of reading as an automatic process. According to an article titled "Learning to Read" published in the *Elementary School Teacher* in 1911,

> The adult gives no more thought to his reading than he gives to his walking. The process has become automatic; when he sees the printed symbols he reads in spite of himself. He can no more tell how he reads than he can tell how he walks; he simply reads. He has so far forgotten the time and energy he spent mastering the process that he is not even aware of its complexity. Reading sometimes tires his brain and sometimes tires his eyes; further in the analysis he does not go.[28]

No one with dyslexia had the luxury of forgetting about reading's complexity, of course. Dyslexia's prevalence among schoolchildren upended any notion of reading as an "automatic" process by showing just how many things could go wrong.

Much of the ensuing research into dyslexia moved toward theories of cognitive development. In 1925, Samuel Orton presented a paper to the American Neurological Association that galvanized interest in reading disabilities in the United States. Based on clinical observation, Orton's essay disputed the longstanding association between reading disabilities and low intelligence.[29] As the psychologist Marion Monroe observed, teachers at that time assumed any student who could not learn to read "must be either lazy or stupid."[30] Although researchers worked to dispel the link between reading deficits and intelligence (Orton recommended swapping the terms "defective" and "disability"), it would take decades to devise effective teaching methods to help children with dyslexia.[31]

Motivated by his findings, Orton sought to rescue students with reading differences from the pool of students sent to the Iowa State Psychopathic

Hospital clinic for being "dull, subnormal, or failing or retarded in school work."[32] He was interested in students like "Clarke C.," who showed average intelligence in every category except for literacy: "Mother says there is something funny about me because you could read anything to me and I'd git it right away, but if I read it myself I couldn't git it."[33] The remedial methods developed by Orton to help children like Clarke C. have been enormously influential over the past century. He was among the first to advocate for phonics instruction and would later collaborate with Anna Gillingham and Bessie Stillman on multisensory learning methods that have contributed to today's phonological understanding of reading.

Support for dyslexia grew following the Second World War, as literacy skills among the professional classes became crucial to prosperity. The Word Blind Centre for Dyslexic Children opened in London in 1963, for example, followed by other institutions established specifically to teach dyslexic children, provide support for their families, and carry out research. Organizations including the Orton Dyslexia Society (a title that would eventually be changed to the International Dyslexia Association) in the United States and the British Dyslexia Association raised the condition's profile, too.[34] In fact, people agreed on the condition's existence long before they could agree on what to call it.

Dyslexia is a recognized condition today largely because of decades of campaigning by people with dyslexia (and their families), disability rights advocates, and educators.[35] Use of the term "dyslexia" did not become widespread until late in the twentieth century, when it supplanted the label "word blindness" and other terms including "script blindness," "mind blindness," "developmental alexia," "symbolic confusion," "legasthenia," "typholexia," "word amblyopia," "analphabetia partialis," "amnesia visualis verbalis," and "verbal deafness."[36] (In 1918, a German doctor had even proposed the phrase "partial idiocy in connection with reading of words alone."[37]) The term "dyslexia" continues to elude precise definition, though, and has developed over time in line with changes in medical understanding, educational imperatives, and social values.[38]

Modern dyslexia research emerged in the 1970s with a wave of psychological studies into the relations among speech, language, and reading development. The growing consensus that dyslexia was a language-based disorder overturned previous theories attributing it to problems with vision and perception. Studies showed that the visual reversals associated with dyslexia (mixing up the letters "b" and "d" or "p" and "q") arose from the child's difficulties attaching the correct verbal labels to these sounds, not perceptual deficits. As one study demonstrated, children could draw letters accurately even when giving them the wrong names.[39] Other tests have since confirmed that children with dyslexia do not perceive the constituent parts of words in the same way as other readers.

Scientific understanding of dyslexia continues to evolve in line with advances in neurological research. Neuroimaging technology has improved our understanding of the anatomy, activity, and functioning of dyslexic brains in ways that could only have been dreamed of by the previous century's neurologists.[40] Research teams have used functional imaging to locate the precise neural networks involved in reading and to observe the differences between dyslexic and non-dyslexic brains when it comes to deciphering print. These findings have played a crucial role not only in improving the medical understanding of dyslexia but also in rebutting the skeptics who blame reading difficulties on poor teaching, inhospitable family environments, or, most damaging of all, a child's laziness.

Whatever disagreements there may be over the precise nature of dyslexia, everyone agrees that reading differences can have a detrimental impact on people's lives. What remains to be charted is the felt experience of dyslexia during eras in which the condition was poorly understood. To that end, the following sections will focus on "neuroimaging" in a metaphorical rather than a literal sense: narrative representations of how dyslexic brains affect people's sense of identity. This approach radiates outward from neurological challenges to the social ones faced by people with dyslexia within societies that factor literacy into estimations of social status. The testimonies to follow express what it feels like to live with reading differences as well as the specific mechanisms through which society makes life intolerable for people suspected of harboring them. As one of these "nonreaders" protested, "I can live perfectly well with the dyslexia. I accept it. It's not so much the dyslexia I'm fighting as society."[41]

THE HIDDEN INJURIES OF CLASSROOMS

The dyslexia memoir is an improbable genre. Why would anyone who has seemingly suffered so much from the printed word choose to communicate using the very medium responsible for those woes? Grievance provides one motivation since many dyslexics—the name says it all—grow up being defined by what they cannot do. As Girard Sagmiller announces at the beginning of *Dyslexia, My Life*, "I was told it was impossible for me to write a book."[42] Authorship represents a defiant rebuttal—not least when authors insert mischievous disclaimers about being unable to read their own books. The very fact of authorship can be seen to redefine the dyslexic's relationship to words in affirmative rather than antagonistic terms. As Naomi Folb observes in her introduction to *Forgotten Letters: An Anthology of Literature by Dyslexic Writers*, "It asks: who gets to be an author? Who authorises it? And how [do] they get to have that authority?"[43] The prevalence of self-publishing confirms that publication may be viewed as an end in itself by many of these aspiring men and women of letters. But writing a book does more than simply refute charges of illiteracy. It also enables dyslexics to trace the roots of an antipathy toward reading that has colored their encounters with books ever since childhood.

A genre produced for readers by so-called nonreaders, the dyslexia memoir comes in as many guises as the condition itself. The most prominent branch describes individuals triumphing over adversity (an all-too-familiar storyline for anyone acquainted with disability). The following ungainly title reflects this trajectory: *Former NFL Veteran Robert Tate Reveals How He Made It from Little League to the NFL: Overcoming His Secret Battle with Dyslexia*.[44] But if adversity narratives imply that individuals achieve success despite their disability, there is now a countertradition emphasizing dyslexia's advantages. John Rodrigues's equally inspiring *High School Dropout to Harvard* credits much of his success to undiagnosed dyslexia.[45]

The very titles of dyslexia memoirs make visible the effects of an invisible disability—what might be called the hidden injuries of classrooms. The spelling mistakes preserved in *Trainwreck: My Life as an Idoit* and *Look Mom, I'm the Dumest One in My Clas!: One Boy's Dyslexic Journey* convey the linguistic challenges faced by their authors.[46] *Please Don't Call Me Dumb!* launches a preemptive strike against the insults aimed at learning differences, by contrast, while *Brilliant Idiot* subverts that name-calling by reclaiming one of the most stinging phrases to its advantage.[47] Since the expectations for dyslexic children were once anything but great, the title *Most Unlikely to Succeed* should be taken as a tongue-in-cheek way to introduce an author whose success is meant to inspire.[48] The most recent titles reflect a sea change in attitudes toward reading differences. It would have once been unthinkable to emphasize the condition's advantages through titles like *Dyslexia Is My Superpower*.[49]

Authorship offers people with dyslexia a chance to tell their side of the story after lifetimes spent being excluded from storytelling—what might be thought of as the dyslexic writer's attempt to dismantle the master's house using the master's tools. Some authors feel compelled to write about dyslexia after failing to escape from it. Dick Kraemer's rationale for writing about his childhood echoes the accounts of trauma survivors. "I never wanted to go back there before, because I didn't want to remember those days," he tells us. "When I started writing, I couldn't stop."[50] Other memoirs trace how a seemingly minor reading disability could spread like a cancer. Jo Rees wrote her memoir to portray dyslexia's reverberations beyond the page: "I wanted to show you how it leaks into everything we do, how it spills into every hour of every day, and how we can never get away from it."[51] Numerous memoirs confirm this insight: Dyslexia's grasp exceeds its reach.

Most dyslexia memoirs share a similar arc. Think of it as a tale of two childhoods: a state of blissful contentment disrupted at school by reading difficulties that drive a wedge between the child and their classmates. Reading lessons are usually the turning point. Frustrations with letters then radiate outward, interfering with the child's relationships with peers, teachers, and family, especially once the "F" grades start appearing on report cards—one more letter to worry about. Much of the child's energy will be spent navigating the school system to avoid potentially embarrassing situations involving reading. Dyslexia narratives map survival tactics (say, how to make up a book report) to avoid attention and maintain a low profile. But, ultimately, the combustible moments stand out: name-calling by students; punishments from teachers who mistake learning difficulties for defiance; and clashes with parents who misinterpret poor grades as evidence of laziness. The threat of violence lies just beneath the surface in these narratives. Despite reputations to the contrary, no one takes reading more seriously than dyslexics do since something as trivial as mispronouncing a word can escalate into delinquency, depression, or even suicide attempts.[52]

The genre features traumatic scenes involving homework, exams, discipline, bullying, even going to school itself (one boy used to vomit beforehand).[53] But the flashpoint inevitably comes when the narrator is ordered to read aloud. "What kid wants to get up in front of his class and feel humiliated and think of himself as stupid?" asks Louise Baker.[54] As we saw with David Copperfield, the pressure has less to do with reader's block than with the spectacle of it. Abraham Schmitt compared reading aloud to "a death experience" in which his self-worth was repeatedly annihilated in front of the entire classroom.[55] Classrooms were akin to courtrooms at such moments since the punishment came from being judged by a jury of one's peers. "I was faced with a classroom full of kids watching me fail," the author of *Faking It* recalled, "and realized that I could no longer hide the fact that I was stupid."[56] Reading aloud terrified him so much that he once blacked out when called on by the teacher.

You do not need to be a psychologist to detect the dyslexic narrator's discomfort. The symptoms are hidden in plain sight. "When I have to read out loud," Steven Bonfield explains, "my nose will run, my eyes water and occasionally I'll even start to wheeze."[57] Other dyslexics share this allergic reaction to reading aloud. As Jeff Nichols puts it, "Show me a man who breaks out in a rash when he is asked to read aloud, and I will show you a dyslexic person."[58] Nichols (who has said he would prefer a public enema over reading aloud) stopped going to Alcoholics Anonymous meetings to avoid reading the organization's five-line preamble in front of the other members.[59] Even a support group might not be supportive enough to counteract the humiliation of reading out loud.

Fear of reading aloud is not something everyone grows out of, either. For many dyslexics, this discomfort perversely increases with age since the discrepancy between a child's age and reading level can turn the performance into a spectacle. Classmates inevitably taunted a ten-year-old boy who was asked to read aloud from *Thomas the Tank Engine* by making "choo choo" sounds.[60] Silent reading offered scarcely more cover. A Kentucky coal miner held excruciating memories of being forced to read with the first-graders when he was in the ninth grade—shortly before he dropped out of school.[61]

Dyslexic students may go to extreme lengths to avoid reading aloud, way beyond excuses like "I forgot my glasses." Physical trauma might be preferable to psychological trauma. While some resorted to self-harm—one girl would scratch her nasal cavity to be excused with a nosebleed—others favored corporal punishment; Victor Villaseñor preferred being hit with the teacher's ruler over public humiliation.[62] He was the archetypal dyslexic who would rather be the delinquent than the dunce. After being smacked for refusing to read, Villaseñor retaliated by biting the teacher's hand: "She screamed out in pain! I loved it!"[63] Biting the hand that reads to you might have offered distraction from painful situations, but it did little to prevent them from happening again. According to *Brilliant Idiot*, Schmitt grew up worrying about what he thought of as the "secret idiot" hidden behind the defiant pose: "No matter how defiant I became, something deep inside told me that I was a defective human being."[64] The dyslexia memoir captures how students internalized criticism through the very act of rebelling against it.

You will inevitably encounter the word "stupid" in dyslexia memoirs. In *Making the Grade*, for example, Dayle Upham describes feeling as if she wore a flashing neon sign announcing, "This kid is stupid, stupid . . ."[65] The dyslexic ego will be shaped by that word, or some variation on it ("dummy," "imbecile," "thicko"), from the moment a student's difficulties deciphering verbal codes become apparent to classmates. This revelation sets students apart from the rest of the class by marking them with what Erving Goffman's *Stigma* characterizes as "an undesired differentness."[66] Dyslexia memoirs emphasize the child's vulnerability to a stigma against which even celebrities insist no one is immune. As Formula One champion Jackie Stewart eventually revealed, "I was told I was dumb and so I believed it—and so would you if you were told you were dumb at a young age."[67] Stewart's memoir turns the tables on audiences by implicating them in the group dynamics before they have a chance to distance themselves from someone who could otherwise be thought of as an outsider.

Dyslexia memoirs maintain that reading differs from most other learned skills in constituting an essential part of people's identities. Fictional characters might be able to downplay the negative effects of dyslexic shame on one's self-esteem and prospects, as Somerset Maugham's illiterate verger did by getting along just fine without reading since he "didn't seem to 'ave the knack for it."[68] But, more commonly, literacy is thought of in modern societies as a defining element of selfhood and even as a proxy for intelligence.[69] The author of *Reading David* sensed this difference long before he encountered the term "dyslexia": "What does it mean when you can't read like other kids do? It means you're a mutant, a freak."[70] You do not need to know how to read to know that you are being turned into an outcast.

The presiding emotion in dyslexia narratives is inevitably shame. Reading is a fraught subject not because of its difficulty (lots of children find reading difficult, after all) but because it is bound up with anxiety, awkwardness, embarrassment, humiliation, and other ugly feelings. Literacy was inextricably linked to feelings of inadequacy for the fifty-three-year-old woman who exclaimed, "Oh, if only I could read and not be haunted by the excruciating fear of being humiliated!"[71] The passage of time makes little difference to a struggling reader's self-esteem, either. "Do you suffer daily embarrassment or humiliation? I do!" confessed a woman diagnosed with dyslexia at the age of forty-one. The slightest misstep compounded what she called "My Huemillyashon," a deliberate misspelling used to communicate her sense of how words will be weaponized against her.[72] Dyslexics often use emotive terms, instead of impersonal ones like "difficult" or "challenging," to describe what should ostensibly be a mechanical skill. "Reading is one of the most frightening things I ever had to learn in school," observed Chris Lee.[73] As dyslexia memoirs show, negative emotions toward reading arise less from the task itself than from the disabling environment. The dyslexic person's hell is other readers.

Studies have confirmed that dyslexic children are subjected to disproportionate amounts of physical abuse.[74] The mistreatment comes from peers, parents, teachers, and even from the dyslexic individuals themselves. Masculinity offers scant protection: The rugby player Kenny Logan used to punch himself in the head while standing in front of a bathroom mirror.[75] And children who have not yet internalized this aggression will still face it from other people. Dyslexia strains family relationships in particular if a child is perceived to be lazy or unruly. As one adolescent recalled, "When I was younger, my dad would sit me down beside him and tell me I was going to read or else, and it was usually else."[76] Tough love does not help promote a love of reading.

Teacher–student relationships could be especially fraught since reading difficulties were easy to misinterpret as defiance. According to *The Scars of Dyslexia*, one teacher whacked a student on the head with a broom handle for refusing to read.[77] Students returned the favor by holding authority figures responsible for their classroom humiliations. When one student was asked how he felt about being perceived as "thick" by teachers, he replied, "I felt like punching them."[78] Unsurprisingly, the narratives embraced by

children with dyslexia prominently feature the theme of injustice experienced by disempowered groups. At least one dyslexic reader identified with
Booker T. Washington's *Up from Slavery* in undergoing his own struggles
to obtain an education—a sincere (if disproportionate) attempt to equate
Sartre's "slaves of the alphabet" with actual enslaved people.

The violence that brought reading lessons to a halt should be understood
literally as well as metaphorically. Books could be weaponized by either
side—in this sense, the scenes of book-throwing in *Wuthering Heights* (no
matter whether authors have read that novel) provide the template for the
entire genre of dyslexia life writing. From the dyslexic child's perspective,
the book embodies literate society's power over anyone deemed unable to
read. As if to illustrate the point, W. B. Yeats's father found teaching his son
to read so infuriating that he once threw a book at the budding poet's head.[79]
Yet dyslexics turn their oppressors' tools against them, too, by recognizing how many uses there are for books besides reading—including hurling
them back at the teacher.[80] The book itself is an easy target for the dyslexic
reader's wrath since books that refuse to cooperate—unlike words—can
at least be forced into submission. As the cardiothoracic surgeon Graeme
Hammond recalled of his childhood frustration, "I would take it out on
the book. I'd take my pencil and grind it into the words that didn't make
any sense to me. I'd start beating on the books because I couldn't read the
words."[81] This is the dyslexic equivalent to hitting a broken machine to make
it start working.

As memoir titles like *Faking It* suggest, "passing" as a literate adult represented one of the easiest ways to evade violence. According to Tobin
Siebers, posing as able-bodied temporarily liberates people with disabilities
from prejudice while at the same time taking a toll on their mental health.[82]
Hence dyslexia memoirs about passing as neurotypical frequently emphasize the strain caused by painstakingly organizing one's life around con-
cealing reading differences from acquaintances and loved ones alike. "For
years now I have 'passed,'" explains Simpson. "Were it not for the periodic
threats of exposure—anyone who passes learns to live with them—I would
almost have forgotten what it was like to live in the limbo of illiteracy."[83] Not
everyone learned to live with the constant risk of being exposed, though,
especially in less tolerant eras. "I carry this dreadful secret always," a woman
who wished to conceal her identity confessed in 1936. "I live in fear of having to read out something."[84] The cost of passing was perpetual anxiety.

Impostor syndrome disproportionately affects dyslexics since their condition might be revealed at any moment. As the psychiatrist Howard Rome argues,

> Because of the great rewards in being considered normal, almost all persons who are in the position to pass as being fluent readers, even though they really are not, will do so. This puts the one who "passes" in jeopardy, for he is constantly liable to the threat of exposure.[85]

Dyslexia memoirs recount feelings of perpetual unease even among close friends. "I knew they had finally seen through my cover," Chris Lee explained after making a slip. "They called me stupid, and I knew I couldn't hide anymore."[86] The danger persisted long after graduation. According to *Last Reader Standing*, life still felt precarious for Archie Willard at the age of fifty-four since the slightest trigger could transport him to "that back-of-the-room desk in first grade, feeling the shame and pain I could not seem to erase."[87] There were no safe spaces for nonreaders. One fifty-three-year-old woman described living in fear that she would be asked to read the Bible during Sunday school.[88]

Since passing as a reader was an essential survival skill for dyslexic students who wished to avoid embarrassment, they mastered the performance of reading, if not reading itself. "I got exceptionally good at pretending to read," writes Rees. "None of the teachers ever noticed."[89] So much for the laziness myth: Pretending to read was usually more time-consuming than doing the reading. Every week Jennifer Smith memorized an entire book to make it look like she was reading from the page. As she would later explain, "In order to avoid embarrassment, I did what any other kid would do; I faked it."[90] Simulating literacy was a tactic to avoid scrutiny, one that led the author of *Backwords Forword* to refer to her school's independent reading time as "Look at the Pictures in a Book and Pretend to be Reading Time."[91] Even adults long past their schooldays felt pressured into reading fraud. The author of *Life with No Words* confessed to making up stories while pretending to read books to his daughter.[92]

People who found it hard to read words sometimes found it easy to read people. Rethinking the role of passing from the perspective of disability studies can help us to appreciate the degree of skill involved in mimicking the behavior of other readers. "Actresslike, I studied to improve my performance," Simpson explained of her attempts to pass as a reader at school.

"Over big words I pretended to stumble. From time to time, mimicking the other children, I appealed to the teacher for help on a word that was 'too hard.'"[93] Simpson's theatrical performance extended to moving her index finger across the page, hesitating between words, and covertly watching where other students turned the page since one false move would blow her cover. Similarly, memorizing the script in advance got Louise Green through school unscathed until the time when a teacher accidently turned two pages instead of one.[94]

The impostor syndrome felt by anyone passing as neurotypical partly explains why dyslexia memoirs often take the form of a public confession—hence the "My name is X and I have a reading problem" structure of many of these narratives. While there should be nothing shameful about finding it difficult to read, historically people with dyslexia have gone to extreme lengths to hide cognitive differences. Coming out as a "nonreader" therefore liberates many of these individuals from the pressure of pretending to engage with books in the same ways as other people. Instead, the genre enables dyslexics to present themselves as a distinctive kind of reader, one whose reading differences predispose them to react in ways that may not be typical and might even be hostile to books adored by everyone else. No reception history of children's literature would be complete without taking into account the responses of these unabashed book haters.

Bibliomemoirs—books about how much people love books—are a genre beloved by audiences who find reading effortless.[95] Writing about dyslexia, by contrast, might be thought of as the anti-bibliomemoir. You won't find any reminiscences about favorite books or the joys of reading there. Dyslexics are more likely to single out the golden age of children's literature as an ordeal; as one of the first women to write about dyslexia confessed, "*Black Beauty* is a nightmare to me"[96] (not that she finished it anyway). The genres present a stark choice between bibliophilia and bibliophobia: Dyslexia memoirs offered a platform to anyone who dislikes reading books—or reading itself. Fantasy writer Terry Goodkind spoke for this constituency when grumbling, "To me reading was torture."[97] If bibliomemoirs track how books change lives for the better, anti-bibliomemoirs offer a counterperspective emphasizing the worse. The dyslexic reader's reaction to a beloved novel like Louisa May Alcott's *Little Women* may be incomprehensible to other readers. Anna Quindlen channeled the feelings of countless bookworms when declaring, "*Little Women* changed my life."[98] The dyslexia memoir's countercharge would be: "*Little Women* ruined mine." Both sides find the book unforgettable—only for opposite reasons.

No one has expressed the dyslexic reader's antipathy toward classic books more eloquently than Eileen Simpson: A novel that has spoken to readers for more than 150 years did not speak to her. As Simpson recounts in *Reversals*, she found the narrator of *Little Women* patronizing, the dialogue prattling, and the characters indistinguishable. Seldom did she know who was speaking—"Was it Meg or Jo?"—or care: "And was it worth the effort to find out when the story was so *dreary*?"[99] This is a novel, after all, whose heroine describes her "greatest affliction" as not being allowed to read as much as she would like.[100] As someone for whom there was no such thing as a page-turner, by contrast, Simpson knew exactly how many pages (536!) there were in Alcott's novel. For dyslexic readers, size matters. While Alcott's fans might hang on every word, Simpson skipped over "unnecessary filler" including authorial interjections, dialects, diary entries, difficult words, dreams, letters, nature descriptions, poetic effusions, proper names, theatrical performances, syntactically complex sentences, and even Amy March's own difficulties with words, spelling, and "punchtuation"—in other words, most of the novel.[101] About the only thing spared was dialogue. Naturally, this ruthless self-abridging left Simpson with a very different understanding of the plot than other readers. It is hardly surprising that Simpson was one of the few readers to remain dry-eyed after finishing *Little Women* since she had skipped over Beth's death scene (meh). Her contrarian stance reveals less about taste, though, than it does about the influence cognitive differences can have over a book's reception.

ALPHABET SOUP

Testimonies from dyslexic readers vividly illustrate how the same page can be perceived differently by two separate readers. The usual way of thinking about the page of a book is as a stable entity that appears identical from one reader to the next. "Typographical fixity" was among the key benefits delivered by Johannes Gutenberg's invention of the printing press in the fifteenth century.[102] Dyslexic readers, by contrast, think of the page in terms of what might be called "typographical fluidity"—a state of flux typically associated with pixelated screens instead of paper. As Simpson's memoir puts it, atypical perception "can make of an orderly page of words a dish of alphabet soup."[103] Dyslexic readers decipher words just like other readers do. Their travails arise because they are not necessarily deciphering the *same* words as other readers.

What do dyslexics see when they open a book? The most common response is backwards letters. Titles such as *Reversals*, *Reversed*, and *My Backward Life with Dyslexia* all foreground difficulties with letter sequencing as central to the experience of reading differences.[104] Employing a tactic widely used by dyslexia memoirs, the cover of *Something's Not Right* even flips one of its letters ("R") to face in the wrong direction.[105] Visions of jumbled letters can be traced back to the first reported cases of reading difficulties, when eye problems, not brains, were suspected of being the source.[106] Samuel Orton referred to these distortions as "strephosymbolia" or "twisted symbols."[107] But the notion that dyslexic children see letters backwards turns out to be a misconception. The issue lies not with faulty vision but with mislabeling visual information—namely, converting graphic symbols into sound. Numerous tests have confirmed that children can copy letters just fine even when they have trouble naming them. In other words, the issue is linguistic, not visual. Cognitive neuroscientist Stanislas Dehaene called this shift in understanding a "revolutionary" idea: reading difficulties are in fact difficulties with processing speech.[108]

Eye issues are no longer thought to be the primary cause of dyslexia since children with learning differences usually possess the same levels of vision as other children.[109] Although vision remains fundamental to print reading, and faulty vision can certainly interfere with it, what matters most is how the brain interprets information. "Not the eyes but the brain learns to read," as a group of ophthalmologists once put it.[110] The challenge faced by dyslexia memoirists lies in persuading neurotypical audiences how much more there is to reading than meets the eye. Long before digital apps made it possible to simulate dyslexia, people wishing to experience the condition for themselves were advised: Try reading the page upside down.[111]

Dyslexic narrators have experimented with various ways of portraying the obstacles thrown up by the fluid page. Susan Hampshire, once known as "the actress who doesn't like to read," begins *Susan's Story: An Autobiographical Account of My Struggle with Dyslexia* by warning audiences not to mistakenly assume their view of the page to be universal:

If you have read what I have written so far without any difficulty, your eyes
gliding easily along the lines, seeing sentences as a whole, not flicking back,
checking and rechecking the last few words; if you have not misread words,
or read them in the wrong order, then it would happily appear that you and
I do not have the same problem.[112]

Flicking, checking, rechecking, misordering, misreading: The passage de-
naturalizes the act of reading by restoring friction to prose skated across
by fluent readers. Similar passages emphasize the degree to which dyslexics
struggle with aspects of word processing taken for granted by other people.
The dyslexia memoir faces the challenge of communicating exactly what
its author sees on the page, where letters may appear to dance or duplicate, flash or flicker, glow or grow, pulsate or rotate, shimmer or shrink. For
people with dyslexia, the page is a moving target.

Dyslexic narrators may resort to idiosyncratic metaphors to convey
what it feels like to have reader's block. Something in Hampshire's head
made it difficult to respond when asked the seemingly simple question:
What does "C-A-T" spell? "The string inside my head stopped me from an-
swering," Hampshire explained. "It actually felt as though my skull housed
a whole ball of string, with an end sticking out of my crown. I thought that
if I pulled at this, I could get the string out, empty my head of it, unravel the
tangle in my brain."[113] What's happening in the narrator's skull competes for
attention with what's happening on the page, the image suggests, while at
the same time giving the illusory impression of clarity being within reach.

For much of the twentieth century, investigations into dyslexia used
the phenomenon known as mirror reading to understand the distortions
perceived by some readers. Troubles with letter orientation initially led researchers to suspect links between dyslexia and other "backwards" forms of
decoding. In 1900, a Minnesota neurologist recorded the case of a twelve-
year-old boy who could easily read reversed writing, not to mention books
held sideways or upside down.[114] Subsequent studies confirmed that a text's
orientation made no difference to some readers, and Critchley proposed
that reading a book upside down might even help dyslexics.[115] The alleged
link between dyslexia and mirror reading, however, turned out to be based
on another misconception. Although both involve unconventional ways
of reading, letter reversals can be seen in the early stages of development

among all children; dyslexics are no more prone to mirror reading than anyone else.

Nor is the complementary technique of mirror writing—sentences written in the opposite direction from the usual and with letters reversed, as if reflected in a mirror—still taken to be evidence of dyslexia. Consider the famed example of Leonardo da Vinci, who filled thousands of pages of his notebooks with reversed writing (Figure 1). As the Florentine artist Giorgio Vasari observed,

> [H]e wrote in letters of an ill-shaped character, which he made with the left hand, backwards; and whoever is not practiced in reading them cannot understand them, since they are not to be read save with a mirror.[116]

Although da Vinci may indeed have been dyslexic, or at the very least a neurodivergent reader, his mirror writing is hardly conclusive proof since most people can write backwards with a bit of practice.[117] (As one study of mirror writing points out, you can try it for yourself by writing on a sheet of paper pressed against your forehead.[118]) Lewis Carroll memorably entertained acquaintances with "looking-glass" letters designed to be read in a mirror, for instance, and one of Alice's first discoveries in *Through the Looking-Glass* is a book printed in mirror-script.[119]

The association between dyslexia and mirror imagery nevertheless persists in the popular imagination for good reason: It remains useful at a figurative if not a literal level. For mirror imagery graphically expresses the contrasting viewpoints of neurodivergent and neurotypical readers, who may be reading the same page while at the same time seeing two different manifestations of it. This is one reason why the covers of *Dyslexic Dick* and numerous other dyslexia memoirs print their titles both forwards and backwards.[120] Reversed letters serve the purpose of distilling a complex array of cognitive differences and word processing difficulties into legible form.

In reality, dyslexics may have trouble reading no matter which direction the letters are facing. Whereas most readers eventually learn to decode words, others might never crack the code. For them, letters will remain opaque inkblots instead. In *Making the Grade*, Upham recalls how confusing she found the alphabet as a first-grader: "The squiggles on the page, the sounds they made, and the words read when several squiggles were put together made no sense at all."[121] It would take years for her to realize that

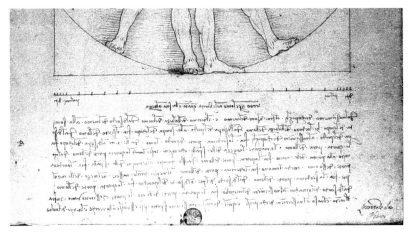

FIGURE 1. Leonardo da Vinci's mirror writing, from *Vitruvian Man* (c. 1490).

different combinations of squiggles formed words. *Why Johnny Can't Read* and other books about dyslexia offered no help to aspiring readers who were confused by the very concept of decoding words.

For some readers, words seldom looked the same from one appearance to the next. Whereas most children accumulate a mental bank of individual words, a dyslexic first-grader described himself as "a fast forgetteror."[122] Words might still appear alien even after repeat viewings. According to *Living with Dyslexia*, it took one child three years of practice to recognize the word "said," and Upham could no longer make sense of the words "was," "want," "what," "which," "went," "where," "why," and "who" if someone changed their original sequence.[123] A dyslexic military veteran recalled being told as a child that he would have to "over learn" words by writing each of them a hundred times.[124] Similar-looking words could be especially tricky to tell apart. A dyslexic reader of the *Aeneid*, for instance, might mistake Achates, Anchises, and Ascanius for the same character.[125] Two different words ("genetically" and "generally") might be misread as the same one, or, conversely, the same word ("Ascomycota" versus "ascomycota") might be mistaken for two different ones.[126] Dictionaries were useless to anyone who lacked the spelling and letter recognition skills to locate words in the first place. Hampshire failed to find "indifferent" in the dictionary after searching for "endefarint," "endifarent," and "endeferent," for example, and still couldn't find the "i" section even after being told the correct spelling.[127]

The handwritten passages reproduced in some memoirs graphically portray how differently language comes across to dyslexics than to other people. *Dyslexia: I Live with It* begins by placing images of the author's original and edited scripts side by side for comparison.[128]

What people with dyslexia mean by "reading" and what other people mean by that term may be two different things. In fact, the phenomenological accounts of reading presented in dyslexia memoirs call into question the usefulness of applying that same term to different minds. As Simpson recounts, "I understood that whatever I had been doing it could not be called reading."[129] Her mind transposed letters ("nad" for "and"), added or subtracted them ("bfore" instead of "before"), or inserted extra syllables ("examimine"). An even more striking difference in perception can be seen between a static page and one that appears to be in perpetual motion. Sophie Conran's account of words "dripping down the pages like wet paint" could have been taken straight out of a literacy horror film, whereas the lines in books "seemed to melt before they made sense" to John Corcoran, author of *The Teacher Who Couldn't Read*.[130] Other people found words jumbling together or merging into a "confusing muddle of non-sensible mess" that defied understanding.[131] Chameleon-like words changed not only their shapes but also their colors, at least from the perspective of Phyllis Snyder, who gave up reading because of what she described as rainbows flashing on the page.[132]

Reading would be easier for these people if the words would just stand still. Various accounts fret about words jumping and dancing, flashing and swirling around the page in a way that can make reading feel like an impossible task. According to *The Reality of Dyslexia*, a spelling list reduced a ten-year-old student to tears because the words moved around so much; roving words similarly thwarted a high school student's efforts to finish Jane Austen's *Emma*, a novel whose opening line introduces a heroine "with very little to distress or vex her."[133] Worse, words not only moved but seemed to float off the page altogether when Stephen Sutton tried reading aloud to his elementary school students.[134] Dyslexics might as well be reading on an Etch A Sketch. The clarity of digital screens could help, by contrast; as one computer user reported, it "made the words stand still."[135]

Dyslexic narrators frequently turned to screens when seeking analogies to describe the page's fluctuations. Abraham Schmitt's harrowing account of the fluid page compares books to TV, a medium more commonly taken to be the book's antithesis:

> My eyes seem to pulsate as the words go in and out of focus. The page looks like a television picture during a storm when the antenna sways back and forth in the wind. I read in spurts as the page clears and then blurs again. I feel as if I should put my hands at the edge of every line to keep the print from floating away. I must grab every word and hold it in place until I finish reading it; otherwise the letters scramble or the word simply vanishes altogether. Some words do just disappear and I read on as if they never existed.[136]

No wonder some people find reading exhausting. The emphasis here is disproportionately on decoding—or not decoding—over other aspects of the reading process since the words appear legible only for short windows. As Schmitt's unorthodox method of "reading in spurts" suggests, dyslexia influences not just what people read but also how they read, driving aspiring close readers to settle for being close enough ones.

The concept of the fluid page helps to explain why this group consists of slow and speed readers alike. For some people, moving letters slow the pace of reading to a crawl. It might take someone with dyslexia hours to read a five-page book.[137] (One dyslexic author's tip: Enlarging the text on a Kindle makes it feel as if you're reading quickly.) But fluctuating pages can have the opposite effect, too, of spurring readers to keep up with the receding alphabet. Jennie Peel read as quickly as possible to beat the "jumping" of the print.[138] Similarly, Christopher Lee raced through passages to keep pace with the class. "Glancing has become my major reading compensation strategy," he explains in his memoir.[139] Since comprehension often exceeds decoding skills, a person who stumbles through a script may still grasp its meaning, or at least a loose approximation of it. One dyslexic who relied heavily on guesswork referred to reading as "free translation."[140]

Still, slow reading beats no reading. In many cases, textual cues have to compete with non-textual ones for the reader's attention. Anyone's mind can wander. (Your thoughts have probably strayed more than once before reaching this paragraph.) But minds will be especially susceptible to distractions when dyslexia overlaps with closely related conditions such as attention deficit disorder (ADD) or attention deficit hyperactivity disorder (ADHD)—a number estimated to be as high as 45 percent.[141] Whereas dyslexia covers difficulties processing language, ADHD pertains to focus. For anyone falling into the latter category, even minor distractions can be fatal to reading. Schmitt's mind was especially susceptible to ambient noises ignored by other people: "I am reading in the quiet of my living room and a car drives past. My mind leaves the page and follows the sound."[142] Schmitt's mind wandered no matter how desperate the measures used to force himself to concentrate on the increasingly fluid page:

> I remember gripping my cheeks with my fingers in order to hold my head in place. I dug my fingernails into space. The printed page seemed to float away, the letters became fluid and only with extreme effort could I keep them in place long enough to read.
>
> At times my eyes would follow the lines carefully but I read nothing. My brain had departed. I envisioned myself literally grabbing my brain to keep it functioning and my eyes focusing on each word. I refused to let my mind drift again and with great determination was able to read several paragraphs before I slipped off again.[143]

In the Mennonite village where Schmitt grew up, students were expected to read books silently until achieving fluency, a pedagogical method that brings to mind Frank Smith's wrongheaded advice: "The cure for dyslexia is to read."[144] This is the literacy equivalent to throwing a child who cannot swim into the pool.

Hyperactive minds may find it difficult to concentrate long enough to read a book. One ADD guide welcomes its audience with the announcement: "We know that many of you, our readers, are not actually readers at all."[145] This is less an insult than acknowledgment that wavering concentration drives people away from books or at least makes those books feel less like entertainment than endurance tests. As the psychiatrist Gail Saltz observes, "Reading can be particularly agonizing for the child with ADD."[146] Students who have little trouble focusing on material in which they are interested may find their minds straying when disengaged, severing any connection between the eyes and the brain. Tom Nardone failed eight-grade English because he found it difficult to focus on books. "It was not because I was lazy," explains Nardone, "I just couldn't figure out how to silence my brain long enough to read a story."[147] He inevitably lost track of the plot after two or three pages.

The earliest portraits of hyperactive readers could be found in books aimed at audiences who found it easy to pay attention. Reading difficulties featured prominently among the symptoms exhibited by archetypal hyperactive children like Fidgety Philip and Window-Watchin' Wendy.[148] The press would go on to resurrect these caricatures with modern incarnations like Billy the Wall Climber for the restless child who could not sit still long enough to read.[149] In an attempt to target anxious parents, marketing campaigns by the manufacturers of Ritalin and other psychoactive drugs portrayed the hyperactive child's metamorphosis into a compliant student. In one news story, six-year-old "Jackie D." fought with classmates, tore up his homework, and struggled to read until Ritalin transformed him into a model student—the seductive prospect of better reading through chemistry.[150]

For readers affected by ADD or ADHD, medication could indeed have a noticeable impact on concentration. Those who struggled to finish a short story might find themselves reading voraciously under the influence of stimulants. Nichols read the entire *New York Times*. "That is what I would do on Ritalin: read," he explains. "Reading was so much more interesting on Ritalin. I inhaled newspapers and books as my scalp tingled with euphoria and hope."[151] The high did not last, however. To avoid addiction, Nichols flushed the pills down the toilet—along with any chances he had of finishing a novel.

Cases of reader's block suggest how difficult it can be to find the right balance between the attention and inattention necessary for reading. Concentrating too little interfered with reading, of course, but concentrating too much proved equally counterproductive. One boy concentrated so hard while reading that he forgot to blink.[152] Others devoted so much energy to decoding individual words that they missed the gist—cautionary tales of *too* close reading. "I would open my eyes wide, get close to the piece of paper and stare at the word," recalls Hirschman in *Backwords Forword*:

> I figured that if I concentrated hard enough, I would get it. I focused so much on that grouping of letters that I would forget what I had been reading. All my attention was on that one menacing word.[153]

Hyperawareness of the page became its own distraction since a degree of inattention is required for the medium of communication to disappear from view. "The difficulty seems to me to be that I am distracted when read-ing by the act of reading itself," explains one lawyer.[154] Mistakes, misprints, or even a missing dot from the letter "i" all diverted his attention from the passage's meaning.

Too much focus on decoding also interfered with people's ability to combine various parts of a text into a coherent whole, since those compo-nents swiftly disappeared from working memory. "I tried to read books but the information didn't stay in my brain," recalls Paul Nixon. "I would read one page, turn to the next page and then not remember what was on the page before. I just couldn't hold on to that information."[155] The clock started ticking the moment a book shut. One student could not remember a poem for more than fifteen minutes before it vanished from memory, since, as she put it, "Nothing stays in my brain."[156] Other people forgot not only *what* they read but even *while* they read. Simpson was among the first to voice how dyslexia affected textual recall—or the lack of it. For her, reading was akin to amnesia since everything would be forgotten by the time she looked up from the page. Simpson's mind seemed to switch off during these lapses in concentration or what she humorously called "fugues": "While my eyes had been going through the motions of reading, my mind had been else-where. But where?"[157] Mind-wandering is an ever-present hazard for people affected by dyslexia, who seem particularly susceptible to daydreaming while reading—escaping from escapism itself.[158]

Mind-wanderers may have to read a passage more than once—or twice, for that matter. Argie Hoskins inevitably had to ask herself, "Now, what was that I just read?"[159] It took readers like her four or five traversals for passages to stick since the initial pass was reserved solely for decoding. As one of the teenagers interviewed by Orton explained, "It takes me so long to spell out some words that by the time I read them I forget what was ahead of them."[160] Comprehension was only manageable after subsequent passes. Hence, Rees could not understand anything without reading it at least five times.[161] This was not exactly rereading; it was more like rereading some-thing for the first time.

For people whose dyslexia makes them feel anxious about books, the easiest way to read may be to ignore the fact that you are doing it. The poet Philip Schultz only made progress with books when his inter-est level surpassed the anxiety generated by reading them. Otherwise, self-consciousness would bring the entire process to a halt. "And when I make the mistake of becoming aware that I am reading," he explains in *My Dyslexia*, "and behaving in a way that enables this mysterious, electrically charged process to take place, my mind balks and goes blank and I become anxious and stop."[162] The obvious resemblance between this account of reader's block and the more familiar concept of writer's block suggests that blank and black pages alike can lead to debilitating self-consciousness. Schultz only finished Walker Percy's *The Moviegoer* because, in his telling, "I read without realizing I was reading."[163]

READING BY THE COLORS

Back in the dyslexia dark ages, when there was little understanding of reading differences, people would try just about anything to attain literacy. Gail scribbled "HELP ME" in the corner of school assignments (though no one could read her handwriting).[164] Natalie Nielson prayed every night before bed.[165] And Nelson Lauver secretly watched *Sesame Street* in his twenties.[166] Desperation drives other people affected by reading differences to look at the world through rose-colored glasses. If mirrors offer one metaphor through which to understand the dyslexic viewpoint, as we saw earlier, then the tinted lenses prescribed for people with reading difficulties represent another way to grasp these differences in perspective. Colored eyeglasses epitomize the dyslexic reader's tendency to see the same page through a different lens, so to speak, than other readers. This chapter's final section traces how the use of tinted lenses to help struggling readers may have failed to resolve their reading difficulties but succeeded at raising awareness of the perceptual distortions interfering with some people's ability to decipher texts.

Throughout the twentieth century, educators developed teaching methods to improve the reading skills of students once thought to be uneducable. As mentioned, the Orton-Gillingham-Stillman method—which teaches students how to say, write, hear, and make clay models of words—is still used by schools today. Yet other methods have been more controversial: Eye exercises, play therapy, vitamin mega-doses, and even hypnosis have all been promoted as remedies for learning differences. One of the most popular treatments for reading differences involves the therapeutic use of color. According to some authorities, colored filters can help students suffering from "visual stress," a condition whose symptoms include light sensitivity, textual misrecognition, and perceptual distortions.[167] Some eye care practitioners screen customers for the condition by asking, "When you read, do the letters do anything they should not do?"[168] Letters appearing to blur, double, flicker, grow, move, shrink, or reverse direction could all be diagnosed as symptoms of visual stress. Consequently, parents and teachers are encouraged to be on the alert for the following behaviors while reading: rubbing one's eyes; covering one eye; blinking excessively; wearing sunglasses; moving unusually close to or far away from the script; yawning, fidgeting, or looking away from the page; or tracking the text with a finger.

Color's impact on reading became apparent as early as 1958, when pediatricians encountered a nine-year-old boy who could recognize a word printed on yellow cards but not white ones.[169] The potential benefits only became apparent, however, once educators tried placing translucent plastic sheets in varying tints over the page. In 1980, a New Zealand schoolteacher named Olive Meares proposed that laying sheets of colored plastic over print could alleviate the perceptual distortion—blurring, moving, jumping, flickering, and so forth—reported by some students when learning to read. Colored overlays seemed to reduce the contrast of black-and-white print, for instance, that bothered some children. "'It's not fair!'" one student complained of book publishers:

> They make the covers so you can read them, and then you want to read the book and you can't because it's all black and white and glaring. They know it gives you a headache but they don't care.[170]

Filters made the background appear less dazzling to many of these readers with aching heads.

Three years after Meares's breakthrough, the American psychologist Helen Irlen extended the treatment to the colored plastic lenses used in eyeglasses. The commercial success of tinted eyeglasses led to the opening of Irlen Institute testing centers along with the uptake of colored overlays among schools, both in the United States and abroad.[171] Irlen's presentation at the American Psychological Association's annual conference attributed reading problems to the way the brain processes visual information. Students diagnosed with what she called *scotopic sensitivity syndrome* or *Irlen syndrome* reported experiencing high levels of discomfort while viewing the page. *Reading by the Colors: Overcoming Dyslexia and Other Reading*

Disabilities Through the Irlen Method targeted anyone who avoided books for one simple reason: "Reading hurt!"[172]

The most provocative finding of Irlen's guide (for historians of reading, at least) may be the personal testimonies confirming that not everyone is on the same page when it comes to reading. Struggling readers seemed to see an altogether different page than proficient ones. As Gertrude Stein might have put it: A rose is not a rose is not a rose. Many of these struggling readers grew up assuming that everyone else saw distorted letters too. As the writer Ayofemi Folayan explained to Irlen, "I didn't know that other kids could look at a page of print and the lines would stay neatly [instead of moving] at a crazy angle like worms trying to squeeze out the neck of a bottle."[173] As testimonies like this one suggest, efforts to correct dyslexic readers' distorted perception confirmed how differently those readers saw the page in the first place.

The perceptual distortions cataloged by Irlen's study corroborated the notion that some students apprehended an entirely different page than others did. Anyone influenced by what she labeled the *halo effect* perceived a white glow around letters, whereas the *whiteout effect* inverted foreground and background. "Each word has a bright, white corona," reported a student. "If I concentrate on one area, the white spreads out between the letters and makes them disappear."[174] The *washout effect* made letters appear virtually interchangeable as the white background eroded their borders, leaving behind circles ambiguously resembling the letters "b," "d," or "o." What Irlen called the *rivers effect* made words appear to run together. "I see a bunch of letters, but I cannot see where one word stops and the next starts," observed a student.[175] And the *overlap effect* made it seem as if a sentence's words all sat on top of another "like one jumbled mess instead of a sentence."[176]

Other resolution issues noted by Irlen made letters appear to be in perpetual motion. Letters moving from side to side, up and down, or randomly were associated with the *swirl effect*. One student referred to the letters as a "dancing group of dots."[177] What Irlen called the *shaky effect* made words appear to pulsate, changing in intensity from black to gray and then back to black, whereas words and backgrounds blended together in the eyes of anyone witnessing the *blurry effect*. As one student protested, "The print disappears, and assorted colored shapes drift over the page."[178] Finally, the *seesaw effect* made it seem as if letters tilted, stretched, or overlapped with the other lines. In sum, Irlen's readers saw entirely different pages than other readers did. Where most people beheld a static page, unchanging from one reader to the next, Irlen's group perceived a fluid one that influenced the decoding process along with the potential range of interpretations that could be derived from it. The combination of visual stress and dyslexia proved especially difficult to overcome since it made the page almost totally illegible. (Irlen estimated that visual stress was present in 65 percent of people with dyslexia.[179]) As a student affected by both conditions unambiguously put it, "Reading is harrowing."[180]

It is hardly surprising, then, that children would be receptive to the idea of using tinted lenses in hopes of converting the fluid page into a static one. Testimonials confirm the difference tinted lenses made for some people. According to Lauver's dramatic before-and-after story, he initially saw a confusing mess on the page—"The best way I can describe it is like somebody placing a piece of window screen over the text and then moving it around while I try to read through it"—before colored overlays instantly improved his reading ability.[181] "It worked!," he writes. "Yellow cellophane filters helped calm the chaos and anxiety in my brain."[182]

Similarly, educational psychologist David Grant watched students improve their reading speeds by as much as 30 percent using lime-green overlays; one remarked that the plastic sheet made "the words look like words."[183] The testimony of Alison Hale, a scientist who found reading physically distressing before she began using colored lenses, is especially compelling. "I do not understand how my friends can possibly enjoy reading," Hale remarks in *My World Is Not Your World*:

> After all, it is clearly so painful. Reading obviously results in a headache as well as sore, achy eyes. In an effort not to lose my place, even my hands become sore because I use a bookmark to prevent myself from skipping lines and follow the letters with my finger so that they are not missed. How do people cope with the pain?[184]

Using colored lenses widened her focal vision, reduced glare and shadows, decreased movement, and diminished the amount of minute white bits or visual snow, improvements that enabled her to read for up to fifteen minutes before tiring—a marked improvement over her previous stamina (Figure 2). Hale credits tinted eyeglasses with helping her to understand how "normal" readers saw the page.[185]

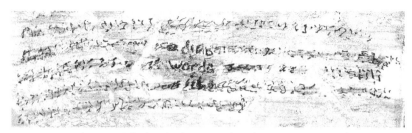

FIGURE 2. Alison Hale's sketch showing what she sees on a typical page.
Courtesy of Alison Hale.

Colored filters have clearly helped some readers. And yet, despite abundant testimonials, scientific trials have failed to confirm any benefits to using them. Although trials have found that colored overlays might improve a reader's comfort level, and possibly offer gains attributable to a placebo effect, the outsize claims for improved reading performance have not stood up under rigorous testing.[186] The term "Irlen syndrome" is thus less useful as a clinical diagnosis than as shorthand to describe various perceptual differences experienced by readers—what this chapter has been calling the fluid page.

No matter how appealing specially designed lenses might be, the most effective treatment for the cognitive language processing difficulties associated with the dyslexia spectrum remains proven remedial interventions. In other words, it probably won't be enough for dyslexic readers to view the world through rose-colored glasses. The main way tinted lenses have helped people affected by reading differences is by making everyone else aware of the very perceptual differences leading readers to see different pages in the first place.

The dyslexia memoir challenges widely held preconceptions about reading—that it is pleasurable, natural, automatic, consistent, necessary for success, or a proxy for intelligence. Testimonies given by these misreaders, nonreaders, and antireaders disrupt the familiar arc of literacy narratives moving from ignorance to enlightenment, all thanks to the newly acquired power of unlocking the written word. "Reading is not pleasurable," insists one of literacy's discontents, "it is work, and for me it is frustrating."[187] Firsthand accounts of textual encounters with a poor signal-to-noise ratio give voice to the personal, social, and mental health challenges left out of celebratory accounts of literacy. Yet these narratives simultaneously advocate for a more expansive understanding of reading itself by restoring to view elements of a process that for most people comes to feel routine. Specifically, these narratives highlight the crucial role played by decoding in the dyslexic reader's textual encounters, and perhaps those of anyone else for whom misreadings, however slight, factor into their understanding of books. The testimonies of dyslexic readers thereby push audiences to recognize how variant impressions emerge from the decoding process itself. Such accounts work toward supplanting the dyslexic's inner voice whispering "You can't read" with the more uplifting mantra "You can read—just differently than other people."[188]

The memoirs covered by this chapter insist that people affected by dyslexia deserve a place in conversations about reading, too. Dyslexia memoirs accomplish many things: recording the anguish felt by struggling readers; defamiliarizing the act of reading by describing it in corporeal as well as cognitive terms; showing how cognitive differences influence perception of the page; tracing how these differences affect people's identities; and giving dyslexics a platform from which to speak for themselves, since the history of dyslexia is also the history of people with dyslexia. Their testimonies offer a reminder that reading does not necessarily change lives—or at least not for the better. Compared to most literacy narratives, the dyslexia memoir's goal is a modest one: to record how reading becomes part of the nonreader's life at all. The last word goes to one of these authors: "I didn't read well, but I read. That was something, wasn't it?"[189]

2 Hyperlexia

"I couldn't get anything but words out of what I was reading."
—Donna Williams, *Nobody Nowhere*

KIM PEEK'S LIFELONG INTEREST in books shows the potential advantages offered by neurodivergent ways of reading. As we saw in the introduction, Peek could read two pages of a book at the same time—one with each eye—no matter whether those pages were sideways, upside down, or reflected in a mirror. He retained practically everything he read, too. Near total recall of over 12,000 books earned him the nickname the "Kim-Puter."[1] Today, Peek is remembered not just as a savant but as a megasavant.

Peek's accomplishments as a reader were especially impressive since it once looked as if he would not be able to read at all. Following brain injuries sustained during a difficult birth in Salt Lake City in 1951, a doctor pronounced Peek "mentally retarded" at the age of nine months.[2] According to his father, he nevertheless showed an early interest in books and began looking up words in the dictionary at age three. Soon he was reciting entire paragraphs at the mention of a book's page number, and by age six, when most children were reading Dr. Seuss, Peek had memorized the index to a set of encyclopedias. As an adult, he continued to read for at least three hours a day, immersing himself in practically anything in print: almanacs, atlases, catalogues, encyclopedias, magazines, telephone books. Occasionally, he would read two or three books at the same time, moving between them every few minutes. It was easy to tell when Peek was absorbed in a book since he squinted and held the tip of his nose about six inches from

FIGURE 3. Kim Peek reading a book.
Ethan Hill/Contour RA via Getty Images.

the page while making a low, guttural noise that sounded like a revving engine (Figure 3). Sometimes he would mumble names and dates, accompanied by whistles, whines, groans, grunts, or even giggles. This mnemonic "stimming" (self-stimulating behavior) helped him concentrate: the savant equivalent to white noise.[3]

Traumatic brain injuries that might be expected to endanger Peek's memory enhanced it instead. As his father observed, "He just seems not to be able to forget anything he reads or hears."[4] Peek's areas of expertise ranged from the Bible, the Book of Mormon, and Shakespeare to every story published in *Reader's Digest* over a three-decade span. When he was once asked about "The Nun's Story," for instance, Peek identified it as a tale written by Kathryn Hulme that was reprinted in volume four of the 1956 edition.[5] Throughout his life, he turned books upside down on the shelf to signal that he had finished them (and thus incorporated them into his mind's virtual library).

Peek came to public attention through *Rain Man*, a 1988 film about an autistic savant with exceptional calculating abilities. That film drew heavily on Peek's behavior, portraying the cognitive advantages as well as disadvantages associated with what would come to be called *savant syndrome*, for even though Peek could memorize an entire page in eight seconds, he needed help when it came to dressing, showering, and brushing his teeth. Peek represented what it meant to be an autistic savant both through his aptitude for storing information and for the obstacles he faced daily because of cognitive differences. (Like many people from his generation, Peek was not officially diagnosed as autistic, but he was understood to have autistic characteristics and would probably be diagnosed as such now that the neurotype is better understood.)

Savants challenge conventional ideas of what it means to be a genius by bringing together exceptional abilities and cognitive disabilities—what the psychiatrist Darold Treffert calls "islands of genius."[6] Savant talents usually fall into the categories of art, mathematics, music, calendar calculation, and mechanical or spatial skills. Many of these talents would be considered remarkable in anyone. A few examples of modern-day savants: Daniel Tammet recited from memory the number pi to 22,514 digits. Stephen Wiltshire sketched entire city skylines after a single helicopter ride. Ellen Bourdeaux could tell the exact time without looking at a clock. Twin brothers George and Charles Finn were able to name the day of any date on the calendar. And Leslie Lemke played Tchaikovsky's Piano Concerto no. 1 after hearing it once on television.

Prodigies, geniuses, and savants all exhibit exceptional abilities, and exceptional memories, too, though only savants' talents are inextricably connected to cognitive deficits. In fact, the first reported cases of savants were discovered at asylums and hospitals for people who were written off as incapable. Formerly known as idiot savants, these patients in some cases had memorized entire books without seeming to understand a word of them. As William James (using the medical terminology of his era) observed in *The Principles of Psychology*: "Imbeciles sometimes have extraordinary desultory memory."[7] "Savant syndrome" is now the preferred term for this combination of ability and disability, one that was misunderstood in previous centuries since it frequently overlaps with autism (a condition unknown in James's time).[8]

Autism itself was poorly understood until recently, and the criteria used to diagnose it have often failed to accurately characterize the subjective experiences of autistic individuals. As we now know, autism spectrum condition (ASC), a complex group of neurodevelopmental differences affecting how the brain processes information, can impact every aspect of behavior, including the way people read.[9] Diagnostic manuals tend to emphasize the autistic person's difficulties with communication and social interaction (ranging from awkwardness in conversations to the avoidance of eye contact), along with restricted interests and repetitive behavior (from hand-flapping to inflexible daily routines and intense fixations).[10] As a spectrum condition, autism can take a range of forms and behaviors, resulting in an elastic diagnostic category in which no two autistic people are exactly alike. The spectrum covers everyone from Aspergians with successful careers, to nonspeaking autistics who write poetry, to those supported in residential care.[11]

In contrast to that medical framework, disability rights advocates rightly insist that autism should be viewed not in terms of deficits but as a form of neurodiversity.[12] It is possible to recognize variations among brains without pathologizing those differences, attending instead to the distinctive capabilities and resourcefulness of autistic people when it comes to activities such as reading.[13] Douglas Biklen's "presuming competence" model points toward an alternative way of treating autistic people—as just as complex, if not more so, than other people in terms of their behavior.[14] This chapter on the neglected history of autistic reading practices thus reframes the evidence found in medical, psychological, and neuroscientific case studies by placing it alongside the testimonies of autistic people themselves.[15] The restoration of their voices is meant to highlight the risks of misconstruing the behavior of a group who have already been painfully misinterpreted by neurotypical audiences (exhibit A: the "mind-blindness" theory that autistic people are incapable of understanding that other people have minds of their own) and, until recently, have had few opportunities to speak for themselves.[16]

This chapter is not proposing that there's an autistic way of reading— autistic *ways* of reading, maybe. Autistic reading can itself be considered a spectrum covering everything from photographic memories to tracing letter shapes or fanning a book's pages. To adapt a common slogan, "If you've met one reader with autism, you've met one reader with autism." In fact, many autistic people read in the same way as neurotypical readers. Kamran Nazeer recalled his teacher's disappointment when he didn't do anything extraordinary like recite chapters from memory.[17] A video made by Mel Baggs similarly undercuts expectations by juxtaposing scenes of their face smothered in a book's pages alongside scenes of them reading in the conventional way, flaunting their status as what Gillian Silverman calls "multiliterate."[18] Recent scholarship on autistic reading, especially that of Silverman and Ralph Savarese, has documented how singular forms of sensory engagement with books, bewildering as they may be to other people, can contribute to the reading experience in meaningful ways.[19]

This chapter expands that scope further by documenting autistic reading across three different eras: the so-called idiot savants of the late nineteenth century; those diagnosed with a savant skill termed "hyperlexia" in the twentieth century; and contemporary accounts written by individuals from across the spectrum. Whereas autistic ways of reading may appear strange or even "alien," to use a word frequently—and misguidedly—brought up in conversations about autism, these ways of reading should be thought of as different versions of the behavior exhibited by all people who interact with books—what this chapter calls *surface reading*.[20] Its mission, then, will be to expand our understanding of reading to include ways of interacting with books that have been excluded from the prevailing understanding of the term or even stigmatized as nonreading.

READING WITHOUT CONSCIOUSNESS

Wouldn't it be useful to remember everything you read? Some people do— people like Antonio Magliabechi, one of Italy's most renowned librarians.

Born in Florence in 1633, Magliabechi rose from humble origins to become the Medici Grand Duke of Tuscany's librarian, famed throughout Europe for his comprehensive knowledge of books. "The universal library," as he was called, allegedly knew every one of the collection's volumes down to the very page on which information could be located.[21] He once informed a patron that the book he sought was the seventh one on the second shelf to the right as you entered the Grand Signore's library at Constantinople.

Print fascinated Magliabechi from an early age. Before he could read, he pored over the leaves of old books used as wastepaper in his master's shop, growing up to become a compulsive reader of whatever he could find, whatever the topic.[22] Magliabechi possessed what today would be called a photographic memory. According to anecdotes, he once reconstructed from memory an entire manuscript after the original one had reportedly been lost; when it was found, a comparison between the two manuscripts confirmed the duplicate's accuracy down to its misspellings. Magliabechi went on to devise his own version of speed reading, or at least speed scanning, to expedite his way through the vast libraries at his disposal. The Magliabechi method entailed scrutinizing a book's title page; dipping into the preface, dedication, and advertisements; then examining all division, section, or chapter breaks. A contemporary described him as "An universal Index both of titles and matter."[23]

The Florentine librarian represents a now familiar type: someone more at home with books than people. For Magliabechi's unworldly devotion to books was matched by an indifference toward mundane considerations involving self-presentation and personal hygiene. A reputedly eccentric bachelor surrounded at all times by stacks of books, he was said to dress slovenly, read during meals, and resent changing for bed since it robbed him of precious moments for reading. His disregard for social norms drew comparisons to the stoic philosopher Diogenes and, less charitably, to "a savage."[24] We do not need to diagnose Magliabechi retrospectively to recognize that such behavior today would qualify him as a savant of some type.

Magliabechi's distinctive combination of genius and misanthropy suggests an alternative way of thinking about the rise to prominence of one of the nineteenth century's most misunderstood figures: the idiot savant. The emergence of behavioral sciences like psychology and psychiatry during the second half of the nineteenth century led to the identification of this figure combining the gifts of genius with what were understood as mental deficits. Physicians began using the phrase "idiot savant" in the late nineteenth century to describe patients with cognitive disabilities who nevertheless displayed remarkable talents. The distasteful phrase combined "idiot," then an acceptable scientific term for a person with a low IQ, with the French word for a knowledgeable person (derived from "savoir" or "to know").[25] In a lecture given to the New York Medical Journal Association in 1869, Édouard Séguin characterized this group by the "useless protrusion of a single faculty, accompanied by a woful general impotence."[26] What accounted for the public's fascination with this figure was the juxtaposition of two terms usually thought of as separate, if not antithetical, to one another—profound cognitive ability and disability within the same person. But whereas Magliabechi's society valued his talents, enabling him to become one of that era's premier knowledge workers, the medical framework predominating throughout the nineteenth century focused almost exclusively on deficits or what patients seemed incapable of doing for themselves.

Use of the phrase "idiot savant" can be traced back to an 1887 lecture in which the British physician John Langdon Down applied the term to a group of patients under his care at the Royal Earlswood Hospital (then known as the Earlswood Asylum for Idiots).[27] After three decades working with patients with cognitive and developmental disabilities, Down delivered a series of lectures to the Medical Society of London in which he described his encounters with "feeble-minded" patients who demonstrated exceptional abilities including lightning-swift mental calculations; prodigious memories; and striking artistic, musical, or mechanical aptitudes.[28] Most of the earliest reported cases involved math prodigies. The first known example in England was Jedediah Buxton, an illiterate farmhand in Derbyshire who could perform complex mathematical calculations in his head, including multiplying a thirty-nine-digit number by itself (the answer took him more than three months to complete).[29] But there were reports of prodigious memories, too. Séguin's *Idiocy* featured "a real simpleton" who could repeat entire pages from books about the Peloponnesian War.[30]

Down's patients showed equally impressive recall, sometimes remembering entire books after a single reading. One boy could recite Edward Gibbon's *The History of the Decline and Fall of the Roman Empire* forwards or backwards. Yet a perseverative error hinted that the boy's grasp of the narrative might be superficial, at least from Down's perspective, who described it as a case of "extraordinary memory" coupled with "very great defect of reasoning power."[31] During the initial recitation, the boy had accidentally skipped a line and then doubled back to reread the passage with the omitted line restored. He went on to perform this exact sequence of omission and correction in all subsequent recitations—as if the mistake were part of the original text. Consequently, Down discounted such feats of memory as "verbal adhesion" characteristic of someone in the curious position of not understanding the book despite knowing every word.[32]

Subsequent clinical examinations sought to understand this apparent disjunction between memory and comprehension. In 1908, A. F. Tredgold's *Mental Deficiency (Amentia)* described twenty patients with developmental disabilities as well as exceptional aptitudes. Many of these patients exhibited superior memories, repeating a newspaper after a single reading or recalling entire biographies. But, like Down, Tredgold (who would go on to become a prominent eugenicist) discounted these feats as rote memory without comprehension—again, mere verbal adhesion. After witnessing the performances of numerous "aments"—another outdated name for individuals with cognitive disabilities—Tredgold singled out the discrepancy between sound and sense as a defining feature of the literate savant: "Other aments will reel off poetry almost *ad infinitum*, yet without any understanding of the sense of what they are saying, or even of the meaning of the words."[33] Drawing on the work of Swiss psychiatrist Eugen Bleuler, who coined the term "autism," one psychiatrist characterized the savant's ability to recite entire texts as "memory without consciousness"—or, to adapt the phrase for this chapter's purposes, reading without consciousness.[34]

Medical accounts from the early twentieth century pathologized savants for being drawn to words for their own sake rather than as a means of communicating with other people. One case study observed that a nine-year-old boy named Gordon knew verbatim at least half of the stories from James Baldwin's *Fifty Famous Stories Retold* even though he still depended on other people for help getting dressed. This boy seemed to savor the sounds of the storytelling over other linguistic functions. When listening to prose or poetry, he would frequently interrupt to say, "Please read that over again. Do you mind? It is such a nice sound."[35] And yet the psychologists' evaluations discounted this sensitivity to language because conversations with

Gordon consisted largely of excerpts from the poems he had memorized—what might have been Gordon's attempts to communicate in his own way.[36]

Other savants were judged for focusing on subjects with no obvious practical value—what Hans Asperger had dismissed as "crackpot interests."[37] Their selective memory capacity—that is, the ability to remember vast amounts of information but only of certain types—might be used to store songs, poems, foreign languages, biographical records, newspaper columns, and, of course, pages and pages of books. But savants were equally likely to focus on statistics that many people would find tedious, if not pointless: railway timetables, locomotive numbers, budget figures, census totals, calendar dates, number cubes, and so forth. The psychologists who worked with these savants found it a mystery why anyone would devote so much time to memorizing information (say, an outdated population census) that was of minimal utility and stored more efficiently in reference books anyway.

Further devaluing these achievements, clinicians began to distinguish between innate genius and brute force after discovering that some savants committed facts to memory through sheer repetition. In one case, a racially prejudiced psychological profile of Eugene Hoskins—a Black man from Oxford, Mississippi, renowned for his capacious knowledge of locomotive engine numbers—deemed these feats to be less the result of a natural gift than a devotion to poring over railway timetables. Hoskins's notebook was filled with entries like the following one: "Northern Line Passenger Engine Number is 1140 1139 1008 1051 1108 1065 1080 1141. Run from Champaign to Centralia 130 Miles Illinois Division Champaign District."[38] The *Lancet* relegated such cases to the category of "mentally afflicted 'brain athletes.'"[39] That same decade, psychologists scrutinized the career of another notable savant, one who earned a living as a "memory artist" on the vaudeville circuit even though his education had not progressed beyond the seventh grade.[40] Having memorized the 1910 census for every town in the United States, the man known as "K." could answer population questions forwards and backwards; when given the sum 83,252, for example, he responded with the correct location: Savannah, Georgia.[41] Observing that K. retained information through systematic rehearsal, writing down statistics multiple times and annually reviewing his notebooks, a psychologist characterized these feats of memory as the product of "an atypically focalized habit system."[42]

The implication was that anyone could do this with enough persistence. As the modern-day psychologist Michael Howe would later remark, "Savants are extraordinary in *what* they remember, but not *how* they remember."[43] These accomplished specialists, whose technical expertise might have made valuable contributions to society, instead had their accomplishments downgraded for not being done in a certain way.

Differing conceptions of reading contributed to the misunderstanding of savants by scientists who relied on psychological evaluations designed for neurotypical minds. An influential study conducted during the Second World War attributed a gap between memorization and comprehension to the savant's inability to think abstractly. A neuropsychiatric consultation with an eleven-year-old boy referred to as "L." determined that he could recite Lincoln's Gettysburg Address verbatim but not paraphrase portions of the speech in his own words. From the researchers' perspective, basic questions about a book L. had studied on the president seemed to stymie him:

> Q. "Who was Lincoln?"
> A. "He was the man who was born in 1809. He died in 1866."
> Q. "What was the book on Lincoln about?"
> A. "The book was about Abe and Sally."
> Q. "Who was Lincoln?"
> A. "Lincoln was the 16th President; Hoover was the 31st President."
> Q. "What is a president?"
> A. "I don't know."[44]

But viewed from another perspective, L.'s adherence to factual information suggests that these questions were a poor measure of his knowledge. Other questions wrongfooted him by asking for words to be defined apart from their practical applications. When asked, "Why do we have books?" for instance, L. answered, "because I read books."[45]

Drawing conclusions from tests designed for neurotypical subjects, the examiners resolved that word definitions, analogies, and metaphors remained beyond the comprehension of savants without giving equal consideration to what drew these individuals toward the sensuous qualities of words—in short, to the kinds of surface reading discussed by the insider accounts presented later in this chapter. The study's authors nevertheless concluded that the phrase "idiot savant" was no oxymoron: Savant skills occurred not despite but *because* of cognitive differences. (Disability gain is now a key concept in the field of disability studies.[46]) In other words, the fact that savants had limited means of engagement at their disposal may be what drove many of them to use those faculties they did control to an exponential degree—the single-minded pursuit of special interests.

Today, the savant's behavior no longer appears unrecognizable. Audiences have grown used to seeing examples of savants in *Rain Man* and other popular fiction, television, and film representations of autistic characters.[47] In retrospect, many of the savants documented by the medical literature of the late nineteenth and early twentieth centuries would fit somewhere on the autism spectrum.[48] As Joseph Straus put it, "the quality of intelligence displayed by people classified as *idiots savants* can be likened to a distinctively autistic sort of intelligence."[49] The eventual replacement of the term "idiot savant" by "autistic savant" acknowledged their affinities: a preference for alternative means of communication, a disregard for social norms, and, most relevant here, the systematic pursuit of special interests.

Autism's diagnosis in the 1940s provided a new lens through which to view people whose behavior did not fit into existing categories. In fact, rote memory was among the symptoms singled out by child psychiatrist Leo Kanner's foundational essay applying the term "autism" to a distinctive cluster of behaviors including what he identified as the avoidance of social interaction, impersonal use of language, and fixation on rituals. Several of Kanner's case studies displayed a precocious ability to memorize texts at an extremely young age; for example, Donald Triplett, the first person in the United States to be diagnosed with autism, could recite the Twenty-Third Psalm by the age of two. (At nearly the exact same time, Hans Asperger identified "fanatical reading" as one of the characteristics setting autistic children apart from neurotypical ones.[50])

And yet, just like previous physicians and psychologists, Kanner expressed disapproval of children who used language for purposes other than communication. The seemingly impressive feat of memorizing an encyclopedia index or portions of the Bible, as another one of Kanner's patients had done, was dismissed as "a self-sufficient, semantically and conversationally valueless or grossly distorted memory exercise." (Autistic people today might ask: "Valueless to whom?") Thus, Kanner described such precocity as practically meaningless:

To a child 2 or 3 years old, all these words, numbers, and poems ("questions and answers of the Presbyterian Catechism"; "Mendelssohn's violin concerto"; "the Twenty-third Psalm"; a French lullaby; an encyclopedia index page) could hardly have more meaning than sets of nonsense syllables to adults.[51]

Kanner's patients seemed to find it easier to recite phrases than to use them to speak to other people. From a clinical perspective, then, the autistic's affinity for words represented little more than a symptom or social deficit—an inability to communicate—instead of a new category of savant talents that would come to be known as hyperlexia.

MEMOROUS WORDWELLS

A child known only by the pseudonym "Memorous Wordwell" has the distinction of being the first known hyperlexic reader. According to an anecdote told in 1833 by a former student from Wilton, New Hampshire, Wordwell learned the alphabet before the age of two. He was known at school as a "reading machine" for his ability to read books beyond his age level, fluently pronouncing the names of Russian nobles as a five-year-old.[52] As his mother observed, "He can read in the hardest chapters of the Testament as fast agin as I can." His father added: "I never did see nothing beat it."[53] Yet there was one thing this reading machine could not do: understand the words that he read. Wordwell's inability to match up sound and sense prompted classmates to call him "the most decided ninny in the school."[54]

Memorous Wordwell's behavior would seem less peculiar after the diagnosis of a reading disability applicable to children who read fluently without seeming to comprehend what they read. A study published in 1917, for example, singled out a boy's "over-attention to words and sounds" while reading Alfred Tennyson's "The Lady of Shalott."[55] Other studies likewise characterized precocious word recognition as a disorder rather than as a different way of engaging with language. As a professor at Columbia's Teachers College noted in 1923, "Cases where a generally stupid child is innately gifted with special ability to master the mechanics of reading, for example, are no doubt as frequent as cases where a generally capable child learns them with difficulty."[56] A subsequent study titled *Children Who Cannot Read* called attention to "the defective child who reads fluently although he is unable to deal intelligently with the material read."[57] Wordwell's condition appeared to be dyslexia's inverse.

Psychologists eventually came up with a diagnosis for readers like Wordwell: "hyperlexia," a term introduced in 1967 to describe children whose ability to recognize words exceeded their ability to comprehend them.[58] From the clinicians' perspective, these children could "read" only in the barest sense of the word. The teachers in one study expressed concerns about a fourth-grader who read at grade level phonetically without seeming to understand anything he read, for example, and eleven of the twelve children participating in a subsequent study appeared to be unable to paraphrase the text.[59] Clinical studies of hyperlexia undermined the presumed link between decoding and comprehension. Instead, these investigations proposed a continuum with dyslexia at one end, where children could not recognize words, and hyperlexia at the other end, where children recognized words without understanding what they meant. Similar to the previous century's treatment of savants, the discourse concerning hyperlexia emphasized what these readers couldn't do over what they could do—a perspective disregarding any potential benefits this style of reading might hold for autistic people.

Hyperlexic children begin to read at an exceptionally young age—as early as eighteen months. Of the twenty children who participated in the study coining the term "hyperlexia," at least five began reading at preschool age; one of them began at the age of two years and four months. In a subsequent study, the pattern was strikingly consistent: All twelve children had started to recognize words by age four. These precocious readers usually began with labels or signs, then spelled out words with alphabet blocks, before proceeding to recognize letter groupings as words that could be read using a combination of visual and phonetic decoding. A case has even been reported of a hyperlexic child reading aloud in three languages.[60]

Hyperlexic children frequently read before they can speak (for neurotypical children, it is the other way around). Only one out of twelve hyperlexic children participating in a 1972 study used conversational speech (far more common was echolalia, the repetition of another speaker's words), and witnesses unfamiliar with autism were struck by the monotonous tenor of the recitations, whose cadences were described by one neurologist as "reminiscent of a primitive Gregorian melody."[61] Many of these children had shown no sign of language use before the abrupt emergence of their literacy skills; one boy who communicated through grunts, squeals, and rumblings (said to resemble an animal's roar) nevertheless read aloud fluently. These children read school texts several years beyond their age levels, too; most handled material from the *New Yorker* with 60–70 percent accuracy.[62]

For some children, sensory contact with books could itself be stimulating. The author of *When Babies Read* recalled of her son Isaak:

> He would sit and look at books for hours. He would turn the pages so gently. He would look at the words on the page more than the pictures. He was only a year old.[63]

Isaak went on to read words at age two and within a short time almost anything else, even if, like most hyperlexic children, he showed little grasp of texts above the second-grade level, a point at which narratives become increasingly abstract, require inferences, or use metaphor, irony, and other figurative language.

Parents who took their child's precocious fluency as a sign of high intelligence were often less enthusiastic about the emerging signs of autism. (There is an entire genre devoted to parents' complex feelings about having an autistic child.) Hyperlexia nearly always coexists with developmental or learning differences, and most children who show signs of it fall somewhere on the spectrum.[64] In fact, Treffert defines hyperlexia through its unique combination of reading proficiency and learning disabilities that can make understanding speech difficult.[65] There is a good reason why so many hyperlexic children are more comfortable with books than people.

Hyperlexia is considered to be a savant skill since no one teaches these children to read. One day they simply start, spontaneously, and often to the surprise of their parents. One mother discovered her four-year-old son's nascent literacy when he sounded out the word "SNOINO" on an upside-down can.[66] This spontaneous literacy resembles that of older autistic children who appear to be impervious to literacy instruction until one day something clicks and they're reading Shakespeare—less hyperlexia than what one autistic teenager called "can't-read-then-suddenly-starts-to-lexia."[67] An early reader may simply be precocious, of course, since children learn to read at different ages. The advanced word recognition skills associated with hyperlexia should be distinguished from those that are part of the precocious child's development.[68] Whereas most children begin to recognize letters around age four, when they already speak fluently, before then building up to decoding at age seven, precocious readers start earlier. As the young Francis Galton boasted, "I am four years old and I can read any English book."[69]

Biographies of child prodigies are filled with examples of children whose reading abilities surpass those of adults. William James Sidis read the *New York Times* when he was eighteen months old. He carried around a red tin bucket filled with alphabet blocks, which he used to spell out "physiological psychology" and other phrases imprinted on the spines of his father's medical books.[70] The precocious three-year-old taught himself Latin and then enough Greek to read Homer, becoming proficient in eight languages by the time he started elementary school; when asked by a teacher whether he could read, he recited the opening scene from *Julius Caesar*. Other prodigies likewise mastered foreign languages before peers had learned their own. John Stuart Mill famously began learning Greek at the age of three; raised on a curriculum of utilitarian thought rather than children's literature, he had worked his way through writings by Herodotus, Isocrates, Lucian, Xenophon, and Diogenes Laërtius by age eight. The ten-year-old Mill read Plato "with perfect ease."[71] Similarly, the German scholar Jean-Philippe Baratier could read Greek, Latin, French, and Dutch fluently at age five; three years later, he knew all the Hebrew psalms by heart.[72]

A few accomplished writers showed their aptitude for letters at exceptionally early ages (at least according to anecdotal evidence). Samuel Taylor Coleridge, who would grow up to become a self-described "library-cormorant," read chapters from the Bible at age three.[73] Similarly, Margaret Fuller began earning her reputation as "the best-read woman in America" at three and a half, when her father started teaching her to read; the following year, this child made her way through Maria Edgeworth's *The Parent's Assistant* on her own.[74] Psychologists would eventually differentiate between precocious and hyperlexic readers on the basis of comprehension. Whereas the hyperlexic child seems to view words as ends in themselves, the precocious reader treats them largely as means to an end. Thus, Harriet Martineau described reading *Paradise Lost* at age seven as a pivotal moment in her childhood.[75]

Parents, take note: Most children cannot be taught to read before the appropriate age—with a few notable exceptions. In 1918, for example, the Stanford psychologist Lewis Terman interviewed a two-year-old girl described as "a child prodigy who was able to read like a school child."[76] Martha's performance surpassed what he had thought possible at that age, for she read fluently from primers with "babyish" pronunciation.[77] But Martha's literacy had hardly been spontaneous. To the contrary, her father had trained her to read using a version of what would come to be known as applied behavior analysis: tacking red cardboard letters throughout the living room before pointing them out in picture books; incentivizing reading by applauding, cheering, or tossing his daughter in the air every time she finished a page; and even placing candy on the table as a reward for reading instead of playing with dolls. When all else failed, Martha's father spanked her. Needless to say, educational psychologists did not endorse using these methods to teach children to read.

The initial psychological assessments of hyperlexia focused almost exclusively on deficits as measured by an instrumental conception of reading. Such studies highlighted the difficulties these children had in responding to "wh-" questions ("what," "where," "why," "when," and "who") without considering other ways in which reading might be useful or pleasurable. Many of these studies implicitly condemned hyperlexic children for reading stories like *The Ugly Duckling* in the "wrong" way; as one concluded, "The activity of word-reading itself was the focus of interest rather than a search for the meaning of the story."[78] Clinically trained observers struggled to understand a form of reading that showed little regard for neurotypical expectations of what reading should be. Such studies were written from a clinical perspective that gave minimal attention to the individual needs being met by hyperlexia or to the ways printed words might be suited to the autistic neurocognitive profile. What is usually missing from these accounts is any attempt to understand the benefits children got from staring for hours at the CNN news crawler or putting themselves to sleep by reading a soap bar wrapper instead of a bedtime story.[79]

Society's normative conceptions of reading ensured that families were acutely aware that their hyperlexic children were "different" from other children.[80] As clinical studies noted, the hyperlexic child's preoccupation with the printed word seemed to go beyond a childish enjoyment of storytelling and even to be responsible for neglect of other typical childhood activities; one boy preferred looking at books in his playpen instead of playing with toys, for example, while another inspected the words printed on a box of blocks instead of playing with them.[81] In other words, these children were deemed to be playing in the wrong way. Other children drew scrutiny for reciting long sections of scripture or lengthy dictionary definitions of animals even though few of them enjoyed being read to by other people—a finding that is unsurprising since, as we now know, the hyperlexic reader derives satisfaction from the coding of words rather than from their decoding.

A psychiatric case study from the 1970s illustrates how readily the hyperlexic child's interest in words could be converted into a pathology. By the age of one, Sam was absorbed in print. Even before Sam could sit up, he spent long periods of time separating the pages of books and, later, peeling apart the layers of cardboard boxes in search of serial numbers or other markings. Sam would happily spend the entire day with a phone book. He continued to repeat lines even when walking around, observed one psychologist, "as though reciting the print no longer available."[82] Sam found books so engrossing that he did not blink when someone clapped their hands behind his head; even a forceful blow leaving a red mark on his arm failed to disrupt his concentration. But behavior that might be praiseworthy in other readers was treated as the sign of a disorder for readers like Sam.

In most cases of hyperlexia, medical professionals saw only indiscriminate readers who cared less about what they were reading than whether they were reading at all. Hence, neurologists described one six-year-old's reading as "a compulsive ritual" since the child showed minimal concern for the nature of the content.[83] Anything composed of words represented a potential source of pleasure: advertisements, menus, nametags, packaging, traffic signs (anticipating a proclivity toward certain types of factual literature to be documented later in this chapter). As pediatric neurologists observed of a four-year-old boy who wandered around a hospital clinic in search of something to read, "He appeared to enjoy the act of reading and to be quite unconcerned whether what he read had any meaning."[84] Outside observers hardly knew what to make of readers who showed little interest in going beneath the surface—in short, in reading like a neurotypical person. It would take the insider perspectives of autistic people themselves to rethink the experience of hyperlexia not in terms of deficits but as a different way of engaging with words.

SURFACE READING

The prevailing theories of reading seem inadequate when talking about readers on the spectrum. What good is reader-response theory when those responses barely relate to the story at all? Turning to the reading practices of the autistic majority (the norm is developmental level–appropriate literacy skills, after all, not savant syndrome or hyperlexia), the rest of this chapter will use the term "surface reading" to designate autistic styles of reading that give inordinate attention to a book's surfaces—its cover, binding, paper, texture, typefaces, ink, and so forth. If theories of reading generally focus on interpretation, then this style of reading stands out for its refusal to delve beneath the surface in search of deeper meaning.

Literary critics will recognize the phrase "surface reading" from recent conversations about a very different kind of textual interpretation privileging surface over depth.[85] This echo deliberately emphasizes the relevance of autistic ways of reading to ongoing conversations about other ways of reading, as critics like Savarese have done in comparing autistic engagement with texts to the practice of close reading performed by literary critics.[86] Use of the phrase "surface reading" should not be taken to imply that autistic readers can only read superficially, but rather that their distinctive cognitive skills (especially those with hyperlexia) predispose them to appreciate aspects of textuality neglected by most other readers. As we will see, autistic people are surface readers par excellence who stretch the boundaries of what counts as reading.

If parents of some autistic children worry about getting them to stop reading, other parents fret just as much about getting their autistic children to start. The latter group may be thought of as "hypolexic" readers for whom sensory processing difficulties push independent reading out of reach. In fact, the very concept of reading may come later to children on the spectrum, who sometimes find it useful for the unwritten rules of literacy to be made as explicit as the written ones. It took years for Alison Hale to figure out what she was supposed to look at in a book about pirates: "Is it the shapes of the black areas I should read, or should I look at the spaces between the black i.e. read the white? It is just completely baffling."[87] The fact that teachers wrote in white letters on a black chalkboard made the concept seem all the more perplexing.

Being forced to pay attention might feel overwhelming or even threatening to children whose brains require time to process information. "I have

terrible trouble sitting down for any length of time," explained David Miedzianik. "That is why I don't do much reading."[88] Autism memoirs are filled
with tales of children losing interest, zoning out, or disrupting recitations.
One set of parents told a psychologist that their goal was to read an entire
children's book to their son before he ran away.[89] Other children found the
best defense to be a good offense: A boy named Justin assaulted anyone who
tried reading to him. When Justin eventually began to enjoy reading, his
father pointed out that "This is the same little kid who used to beat me up
when I tried to read to him—I mean, hurt me, bruise me."[90] Reading could
be overwhelming even when children did sit still. Whenever classmates
read aloud, Donna Williams would either watch the speakers or listen to
their voices; either way, auditory processing deficits made it impossible to
follow what they were saying.[91]

Noncompliant bodies prevent many children from reading independently, or responding to books with what one parent called "forward motion."[92] Since Tito Rajarshi Mukhopadhyay found it difficult to keep his
eyes on the page, facilitated reading with his mother and a speech thera-
pist enabled Mukhopadhyay to keep his eyes fixed on sentences until his
concentration improved to the point that he could do it by himself—and
eventually go on to write numerous books of his own.[93] Similarly, modest
(and sometimes not so modest) interventions enabled Lucy Blackman to
read her first book when she was fifteen. To maximize Lucy's competency,
her mother, Jay, wrapped an arm around her shoulders (the same position
used by her nonspeaking daughter to type on a keyboard) before gripping
Lucy's wrist with a finger extended toward the book. This maternal embrace
ensured that Lucy read the sentences of *Storm Boy* in sequence instead of
snatching paragraphs here and there. On another occasion, Jay turned
the pages of *Wuthering Heights* to prevent Lucy from flipping them back
and forth. In cases like this one, interdependence facilitated independent
reading: Jay once helped her daughter complete the opening pages of John
Marsden's *So Much to Tell You* by sitting on top of her.[94]

Autistic children face different challenges than other children when
learning to read. Jim Sinclair learned to read at age three—and then again,
after those words vanished from his mind, at ages ten, seventeen, twenty-
one, and twenty-six.[95] But, once a child starts reading, it can be equally
challenging to get them to stop. George spent most of his waking hours
with dictionaries or encyclopedias, repeating items from them either to

accumulate information or perhaps to block out unwelcome stimuli.[96] Sparrow Rose Jones's parents took her books away in an attempt to force her—unsuccessfully—to play with other children.[97] It is not uncommon for autistics to spend the entire day reading. Mary-Ann Tirone Smith's brother sometimes read for twelve hours a day.[98] One boy found being apart from books so distressing that he ran away from school to find a shop with something to read.[99]

Books might be so stimulating to the senses that children never get around to reading them. There are just so many other things that can be done with books besides reading. Some autistics may enjoy touching, tasting, and sniffing books as much as or even more than looking at them. In addition, people might alphabetize books; count their page numbers; fan through their pages; hide behind them; cover them with a blanket; throw them; mutilate, tear, or shred them. It is not uncommon for books to be subsumed into rituals that gratify the senses independently of reading. One girl repeatedly traced the decorative border encircling the Little Golden Books, for example, solemnly tapping each figure with the beak of a stuffed Big Bird doll until completing the "circuit" (a phrase commonly used within autistic communities).[100]

The practitioners of these elaborate rituals valued books for purposes besides reading, a preference easily pathologized if measured against neurotypical expectations about the "correct" uses of books. Bruno Bettelheim's *The Empty Fortress*, a discredited study that applied a psychoanalytic paradigm to autism, presents the case (here, stripped of its Freudian analysis) of a nine-year-old admitted to the University of Chicago's Orthogenic School for believing that he was a machine. Joey would ignore the outside world until whirring into motion, gyrating his hands, and walking around the ward like a robot before smashing lightbulbs and shouting "Explosion!" or "Crash! Crash!"[101] Joey's robot powered itself by converting the bed's headboard into an elaborate apparatus bound together with wire, cardboard, and masking tape to recharge his battery while sleeping. To read, he would lay down imaginary wires connecting the book and his body (itself an "e-reader") to a socket. Yet technical difficulties or complaints that "not enough power was coming in" persisted even after the elaborate preparations.[102] (Bettelheim interpreted this phrase to mean that "not enough emotional energy was coming in from us to risk the dangers of reading."[103]) Joey's robot could only decode one or two words at a time before needing to recharge.

Many autistic readers take pleasure in the sensory dimensions of books to an extent that can spur other readers to become cognizant of their own micro pleasures. Stephen Shore enjoyed running his fingers over the ink on a book's page.[104] D. J. Savarese could easily spend an hour paging through a phone book, pausing now and then to feel the paper's width or watch its crinkling surface.[105] The first thing Mukhopadhyay did with a book was sniff its pages in order to gain a sense of its previous owners.[106] Jen Birch could even identify the University of Auckland Library's German literature section by its aroma ("a sort of spiciness").[107] These sensory pleasures will be familiar to any book lover, if magnified here to an almost unrecognizable degree. Neurotypicals have sometimes found it difficult to comprehend the strong attachments some autistic people have to books. One couple protested that their son's book hoarding made their home uninhabitable.[108] Bibliophilia can easily be misunderstood as bibliomania, a condition embodied by Gustave Flaubert's fictional bookseller who stared at his books for hours—without reading them.[109]

Whereas most readers derive pleasure from physical contact with books—savoring their design, heft, or even odor—autistic readers immerse themselves in books to a degree that makes many neurotypicals feel uncomfortable. "In My Language," an eight-and-a-half minute video posted on YouTube in 2007 (and mentioned briefly at the start of this chapter), shows Mel Baggs ardently rubbing their entire face—forehead, cheekbones, nose—against a book's pages, behavior more akin to smothering than to what people usually think of as reading. Baggs appears truly "lost" in a book. Yet the video's ensuing commentary undercuts hasty judgments by characterizing this sensuous interaction as a form of cognition in its own right. Subsequent footage of Baggs looking at a book in the conventional way further complicates attempts to dismiss them as a nonreader, not to mention normative expectations of what counts as appropriate behavior when it comes to books. Tasting, smelling, feeling, and listening to books has the detrimental effect, notes Baggs, of inviting other people to call into question whether Baggs is "a thinking being."[110] Baggs may not be reading in the usual sense of decoding words. And yet the video montage undermines any firm boundaries between cerebral and somatic engagement with print by showing Baggs deriving pleasure from both activities.

Far from being nonreaders, autistics rank among the most devoted readers (recall Magliabechi's complaint that changing for bed took precious time away from books). Although plenty of kids know their favorite books by heart, they probably haven't read those books as many times as some autistic children have read their favorites: approximately fifty-five times in the case of Kenneth Hall.[111] Others have read Dr Seuss's *The Cat in the Hat* hundreds of times or *Dibs in Search of Self* until it fell apart.[112] Although a deep understanding of the narrative might be expected to emerge from so many readings, as we saw in the previous cases of hyperlexia, there is not necessarily a correlation between repetition and comprehension. George Moore read *The Puppy Book* nearly a hundred times without seeming to realize that it was about—as the title suggests—puppies (his guess: pigs).[113]

In what sense can someone be said to have "read" a book without seeming to know what it is about? Skeptics would deny that surface reading counts as reading at all. But another way to resolve this issue is by splitting the term into two dimensions: decoding versus comprehension. For example, Therese Jolliffe recalled being able to "read" books before she understood them:

> When I was on my own I read books—hundreds of them. At first I just read them from cover to cover. Something made me feel I had to read them from beginning to end, without missing a single word. It was a long time before I actually understood and began to get any enjoyment from what I was doing.[114]

For Jolliffe, reading had once meant decoding words, or converting them back into speech, not necessarily understanding or enjoying them (though she would eventually do both). Comprehension would come later. Her testimony still considers hyperlexia as a type of reading, though, one that might even evolve into other forms of literacy.

What a previous section called "reading without consciousness" has long perplexed psychologists. However, recent studies have turned from an exclusive focus on hyperlexia's downside—namely, limited comprehension— to its potential benefits, with some even treating advanced word recognition less as a disability than a superability.[115] Research teams now recognize how printed words may offer a reassuring sense of coherence or coping mechanisms for people on the spectrum.[116] Those for whom the world is too much have long taken refuge in books. As Dawn Prince-Hughes once noted of the printed page: "There we find a peaceful world of art and order, a land we can share."[117]

People on the spectrum might even prefer the company of books over people. Hans Asperger's original case studies included an eight-year-old boy who sat in a corner of the ward buried in a book.[118] Whereas human behavior can seem volatile and unpredictable, books remain stable and consistent. Mukhopadhyay felt more comfortable with books than with the other boys at school for this reason:

> I can handle books the way I want to which I cannot with human beings. With human beings, there is a two-way situation of interaction. Because of that, the probabilities of uncertainty becomes more than with the interaction with books.[119]

The fixed page offered stability amid a world in flux. Hence, Trevor Tao's teacher concluded that he liked books for one simple reason: "The words didn't change like people."[120]

READING IN PICTURES

Autistic ways of reading may not only differ from but even surpass conventional ways of reading—think of Peek and the other savants whose reading feats stand out as a superability. Autistics push the limits of what counts as speed reading.[121] The rate at which some readers absorb information can be startling to anyone who thinks of reading as a linear, cumulative process proceeding gradually over time. Merely glimpsing the page was enough for David Eastham to take in material. "He could read very quickly a paragraph or a page in a few glances!" noted his mother. "He would glance and look away, glance and look away, almost as if his vision ricocheted off the page!"[122] This image of intermittent attention to the book is at odds with the more familiar portrait of total absorption or losing oneself in a book. In fact, Eastman's parents initially doubted whether their nonspeaking son was reading at all because his behavior did not resemble reading as they knew it. Lucy Blackman's aide warned future caregivers about her reading habits for similar reasons: "Lucy reads *extremely* quickly, and you may be in doubt as to whether she has actually read the page."[123] They might otherwise miss this nonspeaker's gesture of running a finger down the page to signal that she had already finished it.

Photographic or near-photographic memories enable some autistics not only to read more quickly than other people but also to remember more than them. A boy named Todd once named the entire cast of *Roots* after watching the television credits roll by a single time, for example, and Lester, after walking past a row of boxes at the supermarket, repeated every word on the labels—including the ingredients listed in small print.[124] Many autistics do not seem to read the page so much as take a snapshot of it—what Barb Rentenbach refers to as a "mental picture" to be filed away for future reference.[125] This phenomenon is usually described in terms of a photographic image of the page that could be read on demand at a later point. Hence, Carly Fleischmann's parents likened her to a photocopier. When they asked her how long it took to read a book, she answered: "A moment."[126]

Temple Grandin, one of the world's most well-known autistics, presents a compelling model of the kinds of surface reading facilitated by a photographic memory. To convey her atypical perspective, a 2010 film based on Grandin's life cast aside stereotypical scenes of the reader lost in thought to show precisely what this reader saw in her mind's eye. When Grandin is asked to read from a French textbook, she glances at the page before announcing: "Read it."[127] The ensuing shot overlays her face with the memorized page's image, suggesting that Grandin has not so much read the page as replicated it. As she explains to her puzzled French instructor, "Well, I just looked at it. Then I have the page in my mind and can read off the page" (Figure 4). To rephrase the title of Grandin's autobiography: She is reading in pictures.

As is the case with many surface readers, Grandin's style of reading values the medium of expression as much as the meaning being expressed. Grandin, who epitomizes many potential strengths of neurodiversity, would later describe her reading process as a form of mechanical reproduction:

> When I read, I translate written words into color movies or I simply store a photo of the written page to be read later. When I retrieve the material, I see a photocopy of the page in my imagination. I can then read it like a Tele-PrompTer. . . . To pull information out of my memory, I have to replay the video. Pulling facts up quickly is sometimes difficult, because I have to play bits of different videos until I find the right tape. This takes time.[128]

Grandin reads partly to expand the inventory of what she calls her "video library."[129] Notably, these technological analogies—to photocopying, photography, video cassette recorders, CD-ROMs, computer monitors, and, most recently, Internet search engines—all refer to storage devices since

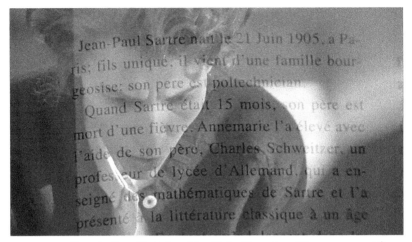

FIGURE 4. Temple Grandin (played by Claire Danes) reciting an excerpt from her French textbook.

Temple Grandin (HBO Home Entertainment, 2010).

processing the mental imagery comes at a later stage. Grandin's photographic memory reverses the usual sequence of reading: This is encoding followed by decoding rather than the other way around.

Photographic memories undermine any clean distinction between knowledge and knowing where to find something. In her memoir *A Real Person: Life on the Outside*, Gunilla Gerland recalls memorizing long texts almost effortlessly, for "the words just stuck."[130] She knew all her children's books by heart. Once she grasped a text's first word, she explained, "the whole word-snake uncoiled and came out through my mouth."[131] Her capacious memory absorbed everything from dictionaries to civil service regulations and National Food Administration tables. With a virtual bookshelf in her head, taking exams became a matter of information retrieval: "At the exam, I just turned to the right page in my head and read what was there."[132] This is a form of delayed decoding similar to Grandin's: Gerland does not so much read the homework as file it away for future consultation. "In some ways, I didn't really remember what was there," Gerland observed, "but I had a kind of copy of the page in my head, which I was then able to read off."[133] She, too, reads in pictures—a counterpoint to those aphantasic readers who do not visualize words in their minds at all (a condition addressed in Chapter 5). For Gerland, the term "read" applies equally well to material that she is reading for the first time as it does to material that, in a sense, she has already read.

For many autistic readers, the medium is as indispensable as the message. Photographic memories capture more than words—they capture entire surfaces, namely pages whose dog-eared corners and marginalia are as likely to be remembered as the story itself. One tell of the surface reader is a preoccupation with extraneous typographical marks disregarded by other readers as inconsequential. A clue to one child's hyperlexia came when he recited from memory not only the titles but also the page numbers of stories from his favorite book, *No Fighting, No Biting*.[134] Autistic adults have been known to entertain guests by describing from memory stray marks on the pages randomly called out from among the books on their shelves—an autistic slant on *Fahrenheit 451* that commemorates the books' pages as much as their plots.[135] Privileging token over type has its advantages: Jen Birch located books by their spines faster than other people could read the titles printed along them.[136]

For surface readers, presentation matters as much as, if not more than, plot. Tom Cutler found it tiresome reading Mark Haddon's *The Curious Incident of the Dog in the Night-Time* because the typeface lacked serifs to guide the eye horizontally across the page. The fact that an extraneous letterspace on page 82 distracted Cutler in no way meant that he failed to grasp the plot at a deep level, though; he simply noticed minutiae missed by most other people.[137] This hyper attention to detail makes surface readers natural proofreaders. Shore admitted to moving a document's object a single pixel (1/72 of an inch) on the computer screen, for example, until it looked just right.[138] Aspects of presentation to which other people would not give a second thought produced strong emotional responses in him. In fact, Shore found it so distressing to drop the letter "e" from the end of a word when adding the suffix "-ing" that he discussed the issue with a psychiatrist. When the psychiatrist tried to make a point by dropping a piece of paper inscribed with the letter, Shore rescued it. As he explains in his autobiography, "I truly felt bad for this letter that was cast aside and dropped to the floor."[139]

Surface reading—as the name suggests—need not involve decoding or comprehension at all. In fact, autistics frequently apprehend letters as shapes rather than symbols, focusing on their sensuous qualities instead of their signifying capacities. These individuals are in a privileged position to appreciate easily overlooked aspects of textual presentation since, as Ralph Savarese observed while working with autistic readers, "the medium of communication refuses to disappear."[140] For example, Jessy Park, who enjoyed viewing different type fonts for their own sake, quit looking at books with her mother to escape the pressure of having to recognize words. Punctuation simply gave her more pleasure than the plot. As a twenty-three-year-old proofreader, Park found the extra spaces between paragraphs and uncommon punctuation marks intensely satisfying—hyphens left her "shivering with delight."[141]

Other surface readers enjoy manipulating the shapes of words—again, recoding over decoding. Blackman would scan the print's shapes to make patterns in her head. For her, *The Collected Works of Shakespeare* and *The Penguin Book of English Verse* were less treasuries of wisdom than "word-pattern treasures."[142] Alberto Frugone likewise paid more attention to the verbal code's contours than to construing it, seeing words as a form of what he called "visual animations."[143] Playing with the word shapes in his mind involved arranging the consonants (all the letter "C's," for example) into symmetrical clusters. The shapes of Italian words like "aria," "aereo," and "letta" fascinated him even though he had no idea what they meant—one of the many consolations of surface reading underrated by psychologists.

Surface readers continually demonstrate just how many ways there are to read a book. As the preceding examples have shown, autistic readers aren't necessarily reading for the plot. These readers might be more interested, at a micro level, in individual words or, at a macro level, multiple books at once. First, the micro: Gerland resembled a magpie in search of shiny new words. While leafing through books, she would start reading whenever one caught her interest. Browsing Lennart Hellsing's books in this way added to her vocabulary the Swedish words for "coppersmiths," "croquembouches," and "Constantineapolitans."[144] Next, the macro: Autistics might jump around within a single text or across multiple texts at one time since the goal is not necessarily comprehension. "That's how he reads," a social worker remarked of a teenager who was looking at three books on butterflies simultaneously despite being officially classified as a "nonreader."[145]

One obstacle to writing a history of autistic ways of reading is that these interactions with books may be illegible to outsiders. As previous sections have shown, it is not always easy to tell whether an autistic person is reading—at least not in any sense of the word as it is used by neurotypical audiences. Although autistics have proven to be effective self-advocates when given the chance, their efforts to communicate how their minds work continue to be misinterpreted by people with preconceptions about activities like reading.[146] Asking autistic readers whether they enjoyed a book, for example, can be met with elliptical responses that go beyond small talk. "It seems to me that I liked the book, but I am really not sure," one teenager replied when asked this question. "The principle of reading is such that one is bound to be taken in."[147] Remarks like this one reveal less about particular books than they do about the nature of reading itself, a process over which people may have less control than they like to think.

Enjoyment is a relative concept for those who prefer the opposite of escapism—not so much realism as information about reality. John Elder Robison was in good company when declaring his favorite books to be *Automotive Technology* and *High Iron: A Book of Trains*.[148] It would be a gross generalization to claim, as neuroscientists and cognitive psychologists have been known to do, that autistic people take no pleasure in reading fiction.[149] (The Autism Spectrum Quotient includes the entry "I don't particularly enjoy reading fiction."[150]) As this chapter has repeatedly noted, autistic readers are perfectly capable of enjoying the same books as neurotypical readers. Thus Sean Barron identified with the narrator of Tobias Wolff's *This Boy's Life* for the same reasons as most of the novel's fans: "I was autistic and he wasn't, but his feelings were so very much like mine."[151]

Still, the risk of stereotypes should not stop us from appreciating that many people on the spectrum do show a marked proclivity toward factual writing. Aspergians have been known to proclaim to anyone who will listen that fictional literature is a waste of time (an attitude hardly restricted to people on the spectrum).[152] Such readers are more likely to curl up with a dictionary than a novel. This group includes savants like Christopher, a linguistic prodigy who could communicate in more than twenty languages and as a child avidly read dictionaries, telephone directories, and Ladybird Books about flags and foreign currencies—anything besides fairy tales.[153] Reminiscing about encyclopedias is practically a convention of the autism memoir genre. Even the supposedly dry act of reading reference books itself, though, can involve complex motivations that go beyond the acquisition of information. An autistic man named Jim recalled reading the

Encyclopedia Britannica when he was six not only for the facts but also to understand why he was different from other children.[154] Similarly, Gerland's motivation for preferring reference books resembles those driving many people who turn to fiction: self-knowledge. "I was searching for myself," Gerland explains. "Perhaps I would suddenly turn the page and find the story of myself there?"[155] Spoiler alert: The only thing she found by turning the pages of a medical textbook were melanomas and mutations.

Pleasure reading can be an ordeal for anyone used to taking things literally. Despite Peek's many talents as a reader, he sometimes found it difficult to distinguish between fact and fiction. "Everything was real to him," recalled his father, "no matter how farfetched the story."[156] But fiction can pose problems for those more comfortable with literal than figurative language. Sue Rubin attributed her preference for nonfiction to a "literal-mindedness" that made it difficult for her to grasp other people's humor and sarcasm.[157] Similarly, Shore found that "the meaning of the words were at the surface" in catalogues but not in creative writing, a genre whose ambiguity he found exhausting as a reader.[158] The famed opening sentence of Dickens's *A Tale of Two Cities* was difficult enough to comprehend at a literal level without trying to read between the lines at the same time: "[D]ecoding the meaning behind or between the words was impossible."[159] For Shore, the novel was less a tale of two cities than a tale of two codes.

From a neurodivergent reader's perspective, even a genre as seemingly straightforward as the comics was capable of being interpreted in multiple and potentially conflicting ways. Some autistic children found this genre to be refreshingly accessible. Daniel Tammet recalled enjoying *The Adventures of Tintin* because it reduced complex social dynamics to a form of graphic shorthand: speech in bubbles, emotions in bold type, and the emphatic use of exclamation marks. As he saw it, each frame seemed to contain a "ministory" in itself.[160] By contrast, Gerland found it easier to get through novels by Camus, Kafka, and Dostoevsky than to navigate comic strips. Unevenly sized frames thwarted her best guesses as to the correct sequence in which to read them, and the arrows directing the reader's attention in some frames only made those without annotation appear to be that much more mystifying: "I often went around thinking about things I had read but wasn't sure I had understood."[161] The implicit conventions easily intuited by neurotypical audiences remained illegible to her.

Autistics who go on to become avid readers of fiction might still pass through stages of development. Donna Williams used to prefer telephone books over novels because fictional discourse seemed to have no connection to the real world: "It was as though the meaning got lost in the jumble of trivial words."[162] It made no difference how hard she concentrated on the page; she saw only "disjointed strings of black print on white paper" or "useless little words."[163] In fact, Williams got more out of a novel's pages by scanning for key words evoking what she called "the feel" of a book.[164] Of course, none of this stopped Williams from going on to write multiple books of her own—including four autobiographies.

The choice between books and people is itself a misleading one, for many autistics turn to decoding language as way to help with decoding people's behavior. Grandin, whose recreational reading used to consist largely of science and livestock publications, once claimed to have little interest in novels because she found it difficult to make sense of their complicated personal relationships. As Grandin told Oliver Sacks, she had never been able to "get" Shakespeare's *Romeo and Juliet* ("I never knew what they were up to").[165] But the luxury of scrutinizing people's behavior on the page, without the pressure and unpredictability of in-person social encounters, is precisely what makes fiction attractive to so many other people on the spectrum. With books, you can spend as much time as you want trying to decipher the vagaries of social etiquette.

The novel of manners may be an especially daunting prospect to anyone who's been accused of lacking them. "I was afraid of this kind of fiction," confessed Tammet, who once offended the host of a dinner party by reading a book when the conversation did not interest him.[166] A key breakthrough came from realizing that books preserved dialogue in aspic, granting the reader time to inspect how people spoke in everyday life without the pressure of needing to respond. "So this is how people talk, I would think, as I read," Tammet recalled. "This is what conversation looks like."[167] Thumbprints, creases, and coffee stains on the page could even bring autistic audiences into contact with an imagined community of readers. In some cases, the annotations found in a book's margins held valuable clues to interpreting a character's behavior.

To bring to a close this list of neurodivergent reading practices (my nod to autistic ways of organizing information), there is no reason to think of surface readers as static and unchangeable in their tastes—at least no more so than other readers. Factual books might even act as a gateway to fictional ones, as they did for Tammet, who moved from dictionaries and encyclopedias to histories, biographies, and memoirs to, at last, novels. Following a similar arc, Tim Page memorized huge chunks of the *World Book Encyclopedia* as a schoolboy before eventually being moved to tears by *Goodbye, Mr. Chips*. As an adult, he found consolations in literature nowhere to be found in encyclopedias: "I had begun to trace in literature some emotional pathways that would fulfill me infinitely more than the road map of a Connecticut town or a list of names and dates from the back of an old recording."[168] It would no longer be possible to distinguish between the tastes of these lapsed encyclopedia-memorizers and anyone else. They have gone from being surface readers to just plain readers.

It would be a mistake to think of surface reading as an inferior version of reading. This chapter's panoramic (though hardly systematic) view of autistic reading practices, from clinical accounts of savant syndrome and hyperlexia over the past two centuries to contemporary accounts written by autistics themselves, has sought to present forms of textual engagement that privilege some aspects of books over others—namely, their sensory gratifications, captivating shapes, soothing grooves, extractable data, and reassuring stability amid a messy, unpredictable world. The preceding examples show autistic readers taking pleasure in contact with books even if it is not exactly the same pleasure taken by non-autistic readers. Autistic ways of reading thus invite other people to reflect on where the boundaries separating reading from other activities should be drawn and, more important, underappreciated aspects of their own textual pleasures— some of which might even fall outside those boundaries.

What all this chapter's readers share is an abiding interest in print. In *Pretending to Be Normal: Living with Asperger's Syndrome*, Liane Holliday Willey, who began reading before her third birthday, provides one of the most compelling accounts I have come across of what makes reading pleasurable even when people do not understand what they are reading:

> I did find solace in the dark print so neatly typed on the white pages. I enjoyed the rhythmic pattern and the flow that moved the eye from left to

right, from top to bottom. I welcomed the routine that insisted I stop for periods and break for commas and new paragraphs. I loved the way most words played on my tongue. I loved the way they caused different parts of my mouth to move.[169]

Willey's account distills the experience of reading into its most elementary form. The delight she takes from the eye traversing black letters across a white page in accordance with the punctuation and other cues, along with her body's subvocal physical responses to that script, convey how stimulating printed words can be even for readers who stick to the page's surface. Willey's fondness for print should nevertheless be familiar to all readers, even if it is not what they might have in mind when using the term "reading."

3   Alexia

"Inability to read has always been my horror."

—George Gissing, *The Private Papers of Henry Ryecroft*

SAM MARTIN KNEW THE PROBLEM was serious when he tried reading a novel. Although he had initially dismissed the pain above his left eye as a migraine, opening Matthew Glass's *Ultimatum* revealed the full extent of his injury. "I found to my horror that I could not read at all," Martin recalled in his memoir. "The scramble of letters on the page meant nothing to me, no matter which eye I used."[1] The brain hemorrhage responsible for this sudden illiteracy would not be discovered until he reached the stroke ward of Belfast's Royal Victoria Hospital. The seventy-five-year-old retiree felt relieved after hearing the diagnosis that the stroke's damage was not more severe. Yet as a former professor at Queen's University Belfast and an avid reader, he worried that he might never be able to read again: "I realised that a large chunk of my life style had been lost—would I ever regain it?"[2]

Martin was fortunate to have experienced reader's block in an era that understood the brain's influence over the reading process. By the time of his stroke in November 2011, medical professionals were trained to recognize neurological disorders that interfered with the ability to decode letters. In Martin's case, the hospital staff determined that there was nothing wrong with his eyes; he could see letters perfectly well, just not make sense of them. A computed tomography (CT) scan, a magnetic resonance imaging (MRI) scan, and other tests mapped the cerebral damage's extent before his discharge to the care of speech and occupational therapists for rehabilitation. In the months to come, daily exercises using an online therapy program enabled Martin to resume reading, starting with Dickens's *A Christmas Carol*, at the rate of between 7 to 30 words per minute (well below the average reading speed of 250 words per minute). He would eventually reach 90 words per minute and, with effort, could finish an entire novel—including Glass's *Ultimatum*—in about four months. From a therapeutic point of view, this represented enormous progress over previous centuries, when reading deficits were poorly understood by the medical profession and considered by many to be untreatable.

Martin's reading disability now had a name, at least: "alexia," a neurological syndrome in which a person can no longer read written or printed language but can still do many other tasks (for example, see and speak). Literally, the Greek-derived term means "not word" or "without word." Losing the ability to read is one potential consequence of brain damage, usually caused by a stroke (as in Martin's case), tumor, head injury, or degenerative disease.[3] In contrast to dyslexia, which disrupts the process of learning to read during childhood, alexia affects literate adults. It is sometimes referred to as acquired illiteracy since patients who have read books for their entire lives can suddenly find themselves no longer capable of making sense of them at all. This form of reader's block imparts a painful lesson: Literacy can be acquired, but it can also be lost.

Unsurprisingly, most of the earliest cases of acquired illiteracy were diagnosed during the first era of mass literacy. Literacy rates rose dramatically during the nineteenth century throughout much of Europe and the United States, and, by the century's end, Britain was essentially a literate society in which the adult literacy rate surpassed 95 percent, and nearly everyone—men and women alike—could read to some degree.[4] Whereas illiteracy's prevalence had once meant that reading deficits were unlikely to be noticed after a brain injury, rising literacy rates combined with neurology's development into a distinct medical discipline began to make them more visible. People who couldn't read now stood out from the crowd.

More people than ever before had begun to define themselves as readers, too. Literacy's benefits extended well beyond the ability to access information. Reading would come to be thought of as a crucial step to personal development and was often aligned with a rhetoric of moral, intellectual, and economic progress.[5] One has only to recall the emphasis in Samuel Smiles's 1859 book *Self-Help* on reading as "a source of the greatest pleasure and self-improvement."[6] Today, our understanding of the nineteenth century is inextricably bound up with reading, literacy, and print. What should we make, then, of those individuals who have lost the ability to read?

This chapter examines over a century's worth of case studies documenting patients with brain injuries, starting with anecdotes and reports in nineteenth-century medical journals before proceeding to longer, occasionally book-length accounts published in the twentieth- and twenty-first centuries, in order to show the profound impact alexia has had on people's lives, well-being, and sense of identity in societies increasingly defined by the ability to read. These cases reveal the full extent to which people struggle to adjust to life after reading—what this chapter will refer to as *postliteracy,* since we lack the terminology to describe literacy's loss—along with the numerous coping strategies devised to preserve their identities as readers even after they have stopped being able to do it. As we will hear from patients themselves, losing the ability to read means far more than the loss of a learned skill; it could also mean a loss of dignity, expressed through a rhetoric of partial or incomplete personhood. If "Reading maketh a Full Man," as Francis Bacon memorably declared, then such people no longer felt themselves to be a "Full Man."[7] (As the psychologist Scott Moss admitted after a stroke made it difficult for him to speak, read, or write: "For a long period of time I looked upon myself as only half a man."[8])

Worse, people with alexia know what they are missing. The end of reading might initially feel like a death sentence to anyone subscribing to Flaubert's advice: "Read in order *to live.*"[9] Whereas individuals deemed illiterate typically have only a distant notion of the republic of letters—Socrates and other voluntary exiles from literacy are rare animals—formerly literate ones know all too well what privileges have been revoked. The social, cultural, and economic benefits of reading and literacy have been well documented by historians and laypeople alike.[10] In modern societies, reading is widely perceived to be a source of communication, entertainment, and knowledge—especially the spiritual wisdom considered by many to be essential to a meaningful life. Helen Keller, for instance, spoke of reading as her "Utopia."[11]

These same societies commonly associate illiteracy with ignorance, by contrast, and stigmatize it accordingly. Consider the way Samuel Johnson defined "illiterate" in exclusively negative terms as the antithesis of Enlightenment values—"Unlettered; untaught; unlearned; unenlightened by science."[12] Illiteracy would come to be thought of less as the absence of a mechanical skill than as a personal deficiency linked to low intelligence or other failings. "Illiterates" were casualties of the war on illiteracy. The consequences for joining that group were felt to be especially profound after a lifetime of literacy and the benefits entailed by that distinction—a demotion from "men of letters" to merely "unlettered." The following accounts of alexia therefore convey how people since Johnson's time have coped, or failed to cope, with their newfound status as nonreaders.

UNLEARNING HOW TO READ

In "First Steps Toward a History of Reading," Robert Darnton observed the need for neurological evidence in order to understand the "inner process" by which readers decipher words.[13] Subsequent research by book historians has presupposed a socially diverse group of readers with nearly identical cognitive abilities. Yet there is more diversity among readers (and their brains) than is usually recognized among conventional histories of reading. In place of "the ideal reader" envisioned by literary theorists, as this book's introduction suggested, room must be made for "the unideal reader" whose disabilities make encounters with books uncomfortable or even intolerable. Alexia's diagnosis in the late nineteenth century represents one starting point from which to undertake such an investigation.

Incidents of reader's block can be traced all the way back to ancient times. The earliest mention in Western literature is by Pliny the Elder, who described a learned Athenian forgetting how to read after being struck in the head by a stone.[14] More detailed descriptions followed. In 1651, a Swiss physician recorded the case of an obese, red-faced nobleman who woke from a coma to find that he could no longer read Latin.[15] Fifteen years later, a stroke-survivor in Danzig recovered from impaired speech, partial paralysis, and epileptic convulsions only to discover that

> A final evil remained to be overcome. He could not read written characters, much less combine them in any way. He did not know a single letter nor could he distinguish one from another.[16]

Physicians across Europe reported numerous other cases involving a sudden loss of literacy in the following centuries, too, usually attributing these incidents to partial memory loss caused by injury or disease.

Clinicians' self-diagnoses played a prominent role in documenting what would come to be known as alexia. Whereas ordinary patients lacked the wherewithal to articulate their health problems, physicians were in a privileged position to observe their own symptoms and, equally important, mental state. Jacques Lordat, a professor of physiology at the Montpellier medical school, stopped reading after a stroke in 1825. "When I wanted to glance at the book I had been reading when my disease declared itself, I found it impossible to read its title," he recalled. "I will not allude to my despair—you yourself can best imagine it."[17] Lordat's account of "deep melancholy and resignation" established the link between reading and mental health discernable in nearly all subsequent cases.[18] His attitude improved dramatically, however, after he was able to recognize the title of one of his books, *Hippocratis Opera*: "This discovery made tears of joy come to my eyes."[19]

Lordat's melancholia demonstrates the perverse capacity of alexia to deprive its victims of a favorite source of consolation at the very moment when it is most needed. Other stroke survivors could at least take refuge in books. When former Lord Chief Justice Thomas Denman lost his speech, for instance, literature provided sustenance. According to Denman's memoir, "He found his chief solace in reading and being read to," including daily excerpts from the Bible, along with Shakespeare, Corneille, and Racine, whose writing gave him "infinite pleasure."[20] (Nearly a century and a half later, stroke survivors continue to seek refuge in books. Alberto Manguel, author of *A History of Reading* and other bibliomemoirs, consoled himself after a stroke with a line from Virgil's *Aeneid*.[21])

Medical knowledge of reading disorders improved during the second half of the nineteenth century as neurologists took increasing interest in cerebral pathology and the attribution of unusual behavior to damage in specific areas of the brain.[22] Paul Broca's clinical investigation into aphasia, the loss of the ability to speak or comprehend speech, led to the identification of the brain region governing speech production (later known as Broca's area) and, eventually, to reading deficits aligned with speech loss.[23] Subsequent research aimed to determine whether reading, writing, and other activities could be linked to distinct cortical areas, too. In 1869, H. Charlton

Bastian, a professor of pathological anatomy at University College London, produced one of the earliest reports of alexia based on clinical observation when he noted that an aphasic patient in his care could no longer read a book: "[T]he *sight* of the words seemed to convey to her no meaning."[24] It would take years of clinical observation, though, before physicians were able to identify the various types of alexia.

Progress was slowed by the fact that most adults experiencing reading difficulties sought out an ophthalmologist, not a neurologist, since the problem appeared to be a visual one. Patients affected by amaurosis, or partial sight loss resulting from damage to the optic nerve, for example, reported being able to read for only a few minutes at a time before the book's printed letters turned misty, blended into one another, and eventually dissolved into an indecipherable "black mass."[25] Shutting their eyes for a few minutes usually enabled these patients to resume reading, however. A doctor's survey of stroke survivors indicates how difficult it could be to tell the difference between ocular and cerebrovascular damage. According to that account, "Mr. I.," a gout-prone Liverpudlian distressed by business dealings, complained of pain in his head and arm, along with diminished reading ability; although these symptoms appeared to have been caused by a brain hemorrhage, his literacy was restored by the simple solution of a new pair of eyeglasses.[26]

Any number of illnesses could interfere with reading. A physician at St. Bartholomew's Hospital in London observed that something as common as migraines could interfere with word processing. "They look at a book, but they cannot read," he noted of these patients; "the lines waver like the air over a field on a hot summer's day."[27] Dementia also affected aging readers and their ability to make sense of the page (as we will see in Chapter 6). One mechanic's inability to comprehend books was judged to be the first symptom of "mental overthrow" or "brain-wasting." As that patient's case history noted, "the words seemed to have no meaning, or one so obscure that he had to puzzle over it some time before he could compass it."[28] Reading deficits could be difficult to disentangle from other neurological problems, too. A clerk admitted to the National Hospital for Epilepsy and Paralysis confirmed there to be no direct correlation between fluent speech and one's ability to read aloud. "I was surprised to find how badly he read," observed a physician, "after hearing him talk glibly and well."[29] When given a passage from Oliver Goldsmith's *The Vicar of Wakefield*, the clerk mistook numerous words (all of which verge on Freudian slip), including "lady" for "labour," "popery" for "poverty," and "cheerlessness" for "cheerfulness." For "superfluities," he ventured "seppertition," "sepperist," "sepperit," and "sepperistis" before giving up on the task. Conversely, other patients stopped comprehending anything read aloud. Following a head injury, a man who had once enjoyed listening to books found that he could no longer bear them; he complained, "cannot understand properly" or "cannot calculate what is said" before asking his wife to cut short the evening prayers.[30]

William Henry Broadbent was among the first to document reading deficits, which came to his attention while working with aphasic patients at St. Mary's Hospital in London. According to case studies published in 1872, some of these people could no longer read at all. "Charles D.," a fifty-nine-year-old gas inspector and member of the Paddington Vestry, stopped reading after being struck by falling timbers while captaining a volunteer fire brigade. "I can see them," said Charles while looking at the words, "but cannot understand."[31] When asked to state in writing that he could not read, he wrote, "I can not do read."[32] Broadbent's patients struggled to articulate the workings of a process that they had never understood or even thought about in the first place. Pointing to the letters of the hospital's name, Charles explained that he could "not get them into his mind-box."[33] For some of Broadbent's patients, a lifetime of near-effortless reading made it difficult to take the problem seriously. A former carpenter who found it amusing that he could not read a test passage presented to him at the hospital would be dead within two months.[34]

The most baffling cases involved multilingual patients who forgot how to read one of the languages in which they had been fluent while still being able to read other ones. In an especially perplexing case, a stroke survivor forgot how to read ancient languages despite remaining literate in his native tongue.[35] It took eight years of relearning Latin before he could once again read Horace. His plight is reminiscent of George Eliot's Baldassarre Calvo, a fictional scholar who forgets how to read Greek (among other things) after an illness. Faced with a book's pages, the narrator explains, "no inward light arose on them"—no Horace (or at least the Greek equivalent) for Baldassarre either.[36] Consequently, he loses not only his literacy but also his social standing in Renaissance Italy; as Sally Shuttleworth observes, "Without

Greek, Baldassarre is without identity."[37] Standing before an open book, he can only hold his head and cry, "Lost, lost!"[38]

MAGICAL READING

How did people cope with reader's block? The clinical tone used in medical reports makes it difficult to gauge the social, psychological, and emotional toll endured by patients with reading disabilities. Written from the physician's perspective, these brief, impersonal accounts tend to focus on physiological symptoms that could be useful for diagnostic purposes. Yet eccentric behavior here and there occasionally provides a glimpse into the anxiety and discomfort patients felt about their changed status amid the "social stratification" that was one consequence of rising literacy rates.[39] In fact, many alexic patients sought to protect their social standing by pretending that they were still readers. Their deceptive behavior offers a revealing counterpoint to the longstanding interest among book historians in documenting the phenomenology of reading—or, in this case, the phenomenology of *not* reading.[40]

Most patients lost all interest in books after a brain injury. For example, Henri Guénier stopped reading altogether after a series of debilitating headaches; he would only handle books for a few minutes before casting them aside. In that case, the waning appeal of books was taken as a sign of cerebral damage.[41] Other reading deficits were equally obvious. One formerly omnivorous reader acted like a completely different person after being admitted for a stroke to Yorkshire's Royal Halifax Infirmary, where a physician likened him to "an uneducated deaf-mute."[42] On one occasion, the man turned the newspaper upside down before asking why it had been given to him. When told that he used to read books, he cryptically replied, "that sounded like it."[43] This former reader seemed to lose the ability not only to read but even to grasp the very concept. After noticing the letters on a coin, he asked a nurse "if these were what were contained in books."[44]

But, for less dire cases, pretending to read could be preferable to the alternative: a loss of control, dignity, and social standing. One newspaper confirmed the alexic patient's worst fear by noting: "The casual observer might imagine that he was an idiot."[45] Since aphasic disorders were commonly associated in the public imagination with other cognitive disabilities, passing as a reader could be a useful strategy to avoid further stigma.

Take the case of a seventy-five-year-old stroke survivor in Dublin who woke from a coma to find that he was no longer literate. "Only a little could read the words," he explained to the physician, "but not take in the meaning."[46] The patient nevertheless continued to read newspapers and the Bible—or at least act like he was reading them—until an impromptu quiz exposed the sham. The man's physician noted afterward that "he read, as it were, but the words, unconnected and meaningless, had not even the most remote connexion with the text."[47] Understandably, the patient wished to maintain appearances in order to retain the rights of a gentleman. His concerns were justified, too, as the man's illiteracy contributed to the legal verdict that he was no longer capable of managing his own affairs.

Alexia frequently went unreported since patients who did not wish to be stigmatized as illiterate could easily deceive unsuspecting physicians. These impersonations raise the question: How can one tell the difference between reading and pretending to read? The two are practically indistinguishable to the naked eye. Patients exploited this ambiguity by continuing to go through the motions of reading in order to retain their status as readers. For example, a fifty-year-old French woman named Marie Keller was admitted to the Hôtel Dieu on April 1, 1862, after epileptic seizures, violent headaches, and loss of speech. No one mentioned alexia, though, since Keller spent much of the day reading—or at least mimicking it. She waited until after recovery to confess that "she only read with her eyes, not with *her stomach*."[48] The singular phrase seemed to mean that she did not understand—you might even say digest—what she read. If the typical reader pays more attention to *what* is read than *how* it is read, Keller reversed that ratio. Impersonations like this one suggest that being perceived to be a reader sometimes matters more than reading itself. Still, Keller's behavior is difficult to explain. Did she think that the ability to read would return? Was she reluctant to accept the situation? Or was the façade meant only to conceal her illiteracy from other people? We might refer to such instances as "magical reading," following Freud, since many alexic patients seemed to believe that wishing to read again would make it happen.[49]

Others continued to seek comfort in liturgical rituals despite no longer comprehending them. Adèle Ancelin read the *Month of Mary* nearly every day for over a year until her physician noticed that it was always the same chapter and sometimes even the same page. When asked whether

she understood it, she merely shrugged her shoulders.[50] Another patient at
St. Thomas's Hospital in London read the Lord's Prayer correctly but must
have been doing so from memory since he always added an extra line nowhere to be found on the page.[51] Unlike speech, reading could be faked.
Quizzes were often necessary to determine who could read since observation alone proved unreliable. In one case, a butcher who suffered a head injury after being thrown from a cart pored over a newspaper every day while
at St. Thomas's Hospital. To test his understanding, the patient was asked
to identify certain statements on the page; although he pointed to familiar
names, he showed minimal understanding overall. "It seemed to me," the
physician concluded, "that his condition was very like that of a person trying
to read a book in a foreign language, of which he only knew a few words."[52]

Certain patients seemed unwilling or unable to admit to themselves that
they could no longer read. Paquet was an educated man in his forties who
expected to be ordained after leaving the seminary until an accident left
him speechless and partially paralyzed. Although he continued to spend
entire days reading, following the book's lines with his eyes and even turning the pages at the appropriate moment, it was all a ruse: He resoundingly
failed the quiz given to him by a physician, who noticed that Paquet read
the same collection of tales over and over. The physician (no bibliophile,
to be sure) concluded that an ordinary reader could not sustain such interest: "[I]t would be an unbearable torture to be condemned to read the
same tale thirty times a day."[53] The gesture evidently fulfilled some kind of
psychological need to preserve Paquet's former identity as an educated man
or at least—like Dickens's Dr. Manette, who does nothing but make shoes
after being released from prison—posttraumatic adherence to his former
life's routines.

A few patients continued to insist that they were literate even when
faced with incontrovertible evidence to the contrary. In an especially striking case, a man who boasted about his literacy was asked to read a letter
beginning "My dear master," which he read aloud as "Sir" before abruptly
stopping and then mumbling a few incoherent words. Further examination quickly established that the patient was unable to read the *History of
Saint Geneviève* (after mistaking "preface" for "fasts," he failed to recite the
initial line). "It was evident that he could not read," the physician drily concluded.[54] Yet the patient did not seem to be knowingly faking it either, and,

even though he could not convince anyone else, he remained a reader in his own eyes.

WORD BLINDNESS

French neurologist Jules Dejerine is widely credited with establishing the neuroanatomic basis of reading through his pioneering research into alexia. Previously, the German physician Adolph Kussmaul had observed that word blindness (*wortblindheit*) could be treated as an isolated clinical condition rather than a symptom associated with aphasia or other language disorders, noting that "a complete text-blindness" might exist in patients whose speech, sight, and intellect were otherwise intact.[55] Dejerine's subsequent clinical work ushered in serious study of the brain's role in reading. He led a clinical neurology ward at Bicêtre Hospital, where he encountered a patient who, curiously enough, could not read but could still write—reader's block without writer's block—a condition that would come to be known as *alexia sine agraphia* or pure alexia. Anatomical evidence obtained from that patient's postmortem examination enabled Dejerine to connect alexia's symptoms to lesions on the brain. To this day, the case serves as a reference point in the scientific study of reading's cerebral basis.

On November 15, 1887, Dejerine interviewed a patient known as "Monsieur Oscar C.," a retired textile merchant who had experienced short bouts of numbness in the limbs on his body's right side and could no longer read the shop signs or street posters during his customary walks through the city. The case study notes: "Observation. Total word blindness—for letters and words—lasting four years in a man of 68 years, very intelligent and well educated."[56] Like most patients, Monsieur C. found the condition baffling. "I still know how to write the letters, there they are," he protested, "why can't I read them?"[57]

Monsieur C. used to read on a regular basis. Now, he still recognized the newspaper *Le Matin* by its familiar format, but unfamiliar papers appeared illegible. He could describe the shapes of individual letters ("A" resembled an easel, "P" a buckle, "Z" a serpent) without being able to name them. "He thinks that he has 'gone mad,'" noted Monsieur C.'s first doctor, "since he is well aware that the signs he cannot name are letters."[58] Still, he refused to come to terms with his illiteracy or rather postliteracy. As Dejerine notes of Monsieur C., "he has never accepted the idea that he cannot read, while remaining able to write."[59] It seemed to make little difference to his mental health that his wife continued to read to him. Acquired illiteracy left Monsieur C. depressed and even suicidal until his death on January 16, 1892.

Contemporaries initially found it difficult to grasp any split between the seemingly complementary processes of reading and writing. Jean-Martin Charcot, who established a renowned neurology clinic at Paris's Salpêtrière Hospital in 1882, observed patients learning of this phenomenon "in all its startlingness" after failing to read their own writing—incredulity was the inevitable result.[60] Following a hunting accident, one of Charcot's patients—a man who had been accustomed to reading novels and even moving his lips while doing so—discovered that he could not make sense of a letter that he had just written to a client. "I write," the patient explained, "as though I had my eyes shut, I cannot read what I write."[61] Writing with the eyes shut: The metaphor finds a way to reconceptualize an activity associated by most readers with vision. The experience of alexia led to an unusual form of impostor syndrome: Writing without being able to read no longer felt like writing at all.

Neurologists went on to report cases of alexia outside continental Europe after Dejerine published his findings. In Britain, James Hinshelwood led the way in documenting numerous cases of acquired illiteracy (a condition that would eventually be distinguished from "congenital word blindness" or what is known today as dyslexia, as documented in Chapter 1).[62] Hinshelwood developed an interest in the cerebral basis of vision while working as an ophthalmic surgeon at the Glasgow Eye Infirmary. Although his patients initially attributed their reading difficulties to eye problems, Hinshelwood connected them to brain damage. He was the country's first physician to treat alexia separately from aphasia. And instead of treating alexia as a single phenomenon, he distinguished multiple kinds of reading deficits in patients, some of whom were unable to read any words or letters, as we have seen, and others who were able to read letters but not words (word blindness without letter blindness) or even vice versa (letter blindness without word blindness). Hinshelwood published a series of articles about acquired illiteracy in the *Lancet* and the *British Medical Journal* that would later be reprinted in his 1900 book *Letter-, Word-, and Mind-Blindness*, a seminal work on reading differences.

Hinshelwood's first encounter with alexia took place on August 29, 1894, when a teacher of French and German discovered that a pupil's assignment was illegible to him. He could still see the letters, just not name them. The teacher's case reversed the usual trajectory from illiteracy to literacy: "The page of a printed book appeared to him exactly as it appears to a person who has never learnt to read."[63] Over the following year, the patient reverted from teacher to student, relearning the alphabet and even practicing with a child's primer. "His behaviour is exactly that of a child learning to read," observed Hinshelwood.[64] As this case suggests, physicians and patients alike spoke of alexia in infantilizing terms. It was as if losing the ability to read entailed losing one's standing as an adult, not to mention one's livelihood. Several tradesmen suddenly found themselves at risk of losing their jobs after a lifetime spent honing a craft. In one case, a forty-five-year-old tailor consulted Hinshelwood after reader's block cost him his job, for his reading inevitably came to an abrupt halt after the first few words of a sentence, when he "became stupid" while trying to make sense of the letters.[65] The process, though not painful, was mentally fatiguing, prompting the tailor to put his hands to his head during the trials, as if the pain of reading could be assuaged in the same way as other aches.

That tailor's case illustrates the distress and even revulsion felt by some people while reading—an impairment initially labeled dyslexia by Hinshelwood. Whereas most alexic patients felt no pain, others physically recoiled from words. A sixty-six-year-old German known as "Herr B.," for instance, cast books aside "as if to free himself of something unpleasant" after reading several words correctly.[66] Similarly, a Dublin surgeon described "a feeling of dislike or disgust which suddenly invades [the patient], and which he cannot overcome" after watching the man's head turn away from the book in almost theatrical fashion.[67] Patients like Herr B. could not help becoming profoundly aware of reading's physiological basis despite its longstanding phenomenological association with the mind's theater or even one's "innermost self."[68] Still other patients found reading too painful to try at all. James Simmonds's physician noted that he refused to read anymore after a blow to the left side of his skull because it makes him "very giddy, and causes great pain in the head."[69]

PSEUDOREADING

Case histories from Dejerine's time up to the First World War have preserved the ingenious and resourceful methods through which patients circumvented reader's block by using their full sensorium to continue reading.

Touch was one way to sidestep visual processing. Monsieur C., for instance, traced the shapes of individual letters that he could no longer recognize by sight—what one neurologist called "reading by the 'tip of the finger.'"[70] Similarly, a patient under Charcot's care traced letters on his thumbnail while holding his hands behind his back. Charcot's verdict: "one can say of him *that he reads only in the act of writing*."[71] Evidently, patients who could not read their own writing could at least write their own reading. (Subsequent clinicians have confirmed that patients frequently trace letters on the palm of their hand or other surfaces.[72]) Tactile-kinesthetic reading was hardly restricted to the hands; patients used their feet, too. One even traced letter shapes on the roof of his mouth. Oliver Sacks described the man as "reading with his tongue."[73]

Counterintuitively, the eyes themselves could be repurposed for tactile reading. A patient who could not make out letters visually managed to trace them instead using a series of minute head movements that followed the contours of each letter while keeping the eyeballs themselves still.[74] It was a sort of "visual Braille," in Sacks's words.[75] As neurologists concluded after watching the patient's eyes glide along the letter shapes, "The experienced movement constituted, to him, a letter, in the same sense as, for us, the seen letter."[76] With practice, educated guesswork based on partial letter shapes and contextual clues enabled the patient to increase his reading speed despite this labor-intensive way of doing it. Nonstandard forms of print introduced impediments, however. Minor variations in letter shapes, hardly noticeable to conventional readers, stymied this man's attempts at reading altogether, and words crossed by superfluous diagonal lines made no sense either since they disrupted the patterns registered by his head movements. The man could not read at all if someone held his head still—the kinesthetic equivalent to a blindfold.

Most patients who managed to retain some degree of literacy read slowly and laboriously, often proceeding letter by letter, at a fraction of their former pace. (According to recent studies, alexic patients can take over sixteen seconds to read three- and four-letter words; longer ones might not be decipherable at all.[77]) Predictably, patients who read in this way were treated like children rather than adults undergoing rehabilitation. One report noted that "G. L.," a robust shipwright in his fifties, could identify individual letters but not whole words (including his own name) unless he spelled them out "like a child learning its first lesson."[78] Saying "C-A-T" aloud was the only way for him to understand the word. Longer words were challenging, and very long words, such as "Constantinople" or "hippopotamus," beyond his grasp.

Word-blind patients were men and women of letters in the most literal sense. By contrast, letter-blind patients could read entire words, just not their constituent letters. A patient with spinal meningitis admitted to Glasgow's Western Infirmary failed to read a single letter of the alphabet except "T," which he called "Tom" (his own name). Yet he instantly recognized "electricity," "infirmary," "stethoscope," and other whole words. Furthermore, the word "JOB" was legible but not the rearranged letters in "OBJ."[79] The patient had no idea if words were misspelled or their letters reversed. Even those who could not read at all sometimes recognized words as visual pictures: their own names, perhaps, or brand logos. They read words ideographically or logographically, not phonetically—what the neurologist Kurt Goldstein called "pseudoreading."[80]

What hope do people have of regaining the ability to read? The prognosis remains gloomy: In many cases, reading will be remembered only as a paradise lost.[81] Those who do read again often do so through enormous effort and, even then, at a fraction of their former speed. For example, "D. S.," a thirty-four-year-old participant in recent clinical studies of alexia, eventually regained the ability to read. She resumed her former life as a homemaker and mother of two children, even enrolling in a typing course, but, crucially, she stopped reading for enjoyment.[82] Escapism is no longer an option when reading itself is such hard work.

Such cases of reader's block defy a neat story arc rewarding patients for their industry and perseverance (think back to the Samuel Smiles ethos quoted earlier). Derek, an eighteen-year-old soldier who vowed that he would learn to read again after being shot in the head, refused to become discouraged even though he could barely decipher a sentence after five years of rehabilitation. As he told the staff, "I'm a tenacious and motivated chap and I never get fed up with it [reading]."[83] Sounding out words letter by letter eventually enabled Derek to read at a thirteen-year-old level and even to resume reading for pleasure—especially military books. Yet, despite unusually high levels of motivation, Derek is still nowhere near his former reading level and now reads in a radically different way than he used to.

When asked how he feels about his current reading abilities, Derek replied, "It's a bloody miracle."[84]

BECOMING ILLITERATE

Surprisingly, there were only sporadic reports of alexia following the brutality of the First World War. The decline occurred largely because holistically oriented neurologists called into question whether activities such as reading could be linked to specific cortical locations.[85] Skeptics dismissed the work of previous neurologists including Dejerine and Hinshelwood for futilely attempting to design "brain maps" pinpointing the areas responsible for reading and other activities.[86] It was not until the 1960s that research on split-brain patients renewed interest in the links between behavior and brain structure. The behavioral neurologist Norman Geschwind led the way in defending his predecessors against the derisory charges of "diagram-making" and in rekindling interest in the role played by cerebral pathway lesions in producing reading deficits.[87]

The Second World War, by contrast, delivered no shortage of brain injuries for clinical scrutiny. By far the most revealing account came from the Russian soldier Lev Zasetsky, who went into a prolonged coma after being shot in the head during the Battle of Smolensk on March 2, 1943. When Zasetsky awoke, he could no longer read, write, speak, remember, or even recognize parts of his own body. Over the next several decades, the Russian neuropsychologist Alexander Luria compiled an account of Zasetsky's injuries, *The Man with the Shattered World*, which alternates between the neuropsychologist's analytical reporting and the patient's personal account. Such a protracted case study based on thirty years of observation allows for a level of detail and intimacy beyond the reach of the brief portraits found in medical journals. As a result, Zasetsky's testimony explains firsthand the brain injury's profound impact on his identity—especially the sense of being an entirely different person from the literate twenty-three-year-old soldier who went to war.

Acquired illiteracy came as a shock to Zasetsky. As is the case with most people who have not experienced a head injury, it had never occurred to him that literacy could be lost. Although he had been a trilingual student at a polytechnic institute before the war, Zasetsky could no longer read *Pravda* or even bathroom signs. The evidence before his eyes struck him as a cruel joke: "wrong," "ridiculous," "impossible!"[88] Hardly his most serious injury, Zasetsky's reading deficits nevertheless had a profound psychological impact by undermining his independence, competence, and ability to communicate. To make matters worse, the invisible disability invited little sympathy from people who might otherwise show respect for a war veteran. He met with disbelief instead: "What's the matter with you, can't you read?" "Can someone your age still be illiterate?"[89]

The Man with the Shattered World provides an intimate account of the psychological toll inflicted by alexia. It conveys the harsh lesson that the surest way to appreciate literacy is not to gain it but to have it taken away, for reading's power can only be mourned by those who have lost it. For Zasetsky, literacy represented empowerment:

> How awful it is not to be able to read. Only by reading does a person learn and understand things, begin to have some ideas about the world he lives in, and see things he was never aware of before. Learning to read means having some magic power, and suddenly I'd lost this. I was miserable, terribly upset by it.[90]

Although Zasetsky's reading slowly improved, anything more ambitious than children's books exhausted him. "It was such a strain reading," explained Zasetsky, "my head ached and felt like it was splitting."[91] Zasetsky's regression to children's books and a state of passive dependency—he compared himself to "a child who'd never seen a primer or an alphabet"—capped off the humiliation.[92]

It took Zasetsky nearly twenty-five years to write the 3,000-page manuscript excerpted in Luria's book. In it, he described feeling like a different person—even less than a person. "It was depressing, unbearable to realize how miserable and pathetic my situation was," he wrote.

> You see, I'd become illiterate, sick, had no memory. So once again I'd try to revive some hope of recovering from this terrible disease. I began to fantasize that I'd get over the headaches and dizzy spells, recover my vision and hearing, remember all I'd ever learned.[93]

The only imaginable future from his perspective depended on recovering the past—the memories, accumulated knowledge, and narrative of self that add up to a life. Luria suggested that the brain injury had spared Zasetsky's awareness of what it meant to be human. The tenacity with which the disabled veteran pursued literacy, then, must be understood alongside his determination to fight for recognition as a fellow human being—as Bacon's "Full Man." The manuscript's original title was changed from "The Story of a Terrible Brain Injury" to "I'll Fight On!"[94]

THE POSTLITERATE CONDITION

Whereas nineteenth-century medical journals diagnosed the most common types of alexia, twentieth- and twenty-first-century reports tend to identify the uncommon ones: children who lose the ability to read books; blind people who can no longer read braille; musicians who cannot read music anymore; and one patient who stopped reading after damage to the brain's right hemisphere (nearly all cases involve the left one).[95] Such reports document the breadth of acquired reading disabilities, if not the depth (unsurprising, considering that most of these patients could no longer write). Yet changing publishing conditions over the past half century have enabled patients to tell their own stories instead of relying on medical professionals to tell their stories for them. Whereas case histories based on clinical observation frequently reduce a patient to an impersonal set of physiological symptoms, a patient's own account is far more likely to address a brain injury's psychological toll.

Memoirs written by people with alexia bring to the foreground the affective dimension of reading, a focal point of recent scholarship.[96] Paradoxically, testimonies of reader's block can help audiences to understand what reading feels like in the first place. They do so by dwelling on the complexity of a process taken for granted by most adults, for how reading works is something to which people pay scant attention after passing the literacy threshold as children. Literate adults may worry about losing access to books, interest in them, or the physical capacity to hold them, but they are unlikely to contemplate losing the ability to read itself. For most people, the progression from illiteracy to literacy is a one-way street. This mindset helps to explain why suddenly becoming illiterate after a lifetime of literacy can feel traumatic—a distinctive form of suffering associated with the postliterate condition.

Reader's block offers an unwelcome reminder of the cerebral complexity of the reading process, even though, for most, it feels effortless. By forcing us to look inside reading's black box to determine what has gone wrong, these blocks underscore the degree to which the visual recognition of letters is merely one component of a multistep operation taking place inside our skull. As Hinshelwood announced at the start of his pioneering study on reading disabilities, "We are apt to forget that we see with our brains as well as with our eyes."[97] In this sense, alexia highlights the extent to which reading is as much physiological as intellectual, an embodied behavior for which countless minute but decisive physical exchanges must function correctly. Disruption at any stage of the reading process—whether to one's attention, vision, or linguistic processing—can interfere with reading efficiency or even bring it to a halt. Reader's block therefore cannot help but make people aware of what it feels like to read. Perversely, ex-readers might have a more sophisticated understanding of "the mysteries of what reading and writing are all about"—a phrase taken from an alexic patient's memoir—than the people who spend their days reading books.[98]

Reader's block can disrupt anyone's life. But the consequences will be more severe for some professions than for others. In fact, it would be hard to imagine a more perverse affliction for writers. After a stroke in 2001, Howard Engel worried that his career as a novelist was over. As a self-described "reading junkie" and "addict of the printed word," alexia stopped him not just from reading fiction but from writing it, too (since he could no longer edit his manuscripts).[99] Engel was hardly a casual reader; before the stroke, a cerebrovascular accident seemed less probable than being crushed by his bookshelves à la E. M. Forster's Leonard Bast. Engel's memoir, *The Man Who Forgot How to Read,* expresses what it feels like for wordsmiths to lose the words fundamental to their personal and professional identities alike. There is something about the experience of not being able to read your own writing that makes people want to write about it.

Phenomenological accounts of alexia face the unique challenge of trying to make readers understand what it feels like to become illiterate. Consider the following description of Toronto's *Globe and Mail* newspaper through the eyes of a stroke survivor:

> [T]he letters of the words appeared as though I was trying to make them out through a heat haze; the letters wobbled and changed shape as I attempted to make them out. What looked like an *a* one moment looked like an *e* the next and a *w* after that. It was like astigmatism on a drunken weekend.[100]

Engel's humorous account of the elusive, shapeshifting alphabet stands out within the largely impersonal archive of medical case studies. His description of letters that stubbornly refuse to come into focus draws on the same climatological metaphors of fog, mist, and haze that have been used by be-wildered patients since the nineteenth century (one medical journal de-scribed the disruption as a passing "cloud"[101]). More seriously, Engel aligns his efforts to show the world from a stroke survivor's perspective (the print "going fuzzy," "the strange, twisted look of letters on a page") with Temple Grandin's *Thinking in Pictures: And Other Reports from My Life with Autism* and other disability memoirs seeking to raise awareness about neurodiver-sity and the ways cognitive differences can shape perception of the world.[102]

For all of Engel's levity, though, reading is not just something one does; reading is an identity. For him, the stroke feels "personal," less a random biological accident than a perverse targeting of his love of books (like many other patients, he picks up immediately on the physician's use of the term "insult" to describe brain injuries).[103] Engel's self-identification as a reader, despite being neurologically incapable of reading, lays bare the term's as-pirational pull; he even continues buying books after becoming what he bluntly refers to as "an illiterate."[104] In fact, despite making a career out of imagining alter egos, the writer finds it impossible to conceive of a postliter-ate identity:

> I was still a reader. The blast to my brain could not make me otherwise. Reading was hard-wired into me. I could no more stop reading than I could stop my heart. Reading was bone and marrow, lymph and blood to me.[105]

The denial tells us everything we need to know about the postliterate con-dition. What more revealing link between reading and identity could there be than a self-proclaimed reader who can't read? Neurologists would dis-pute this definition, of course; a blast to your brain certainly *can* make you otherwise. But Engel's riposte to the brain localizers holds forth an ideal of reading as something extending beyond its cortical coordinates. What En-gel is expressing through corporeal metaphors is the sense familiar to book lovers everywhere that reading is irreducible to neurology and cannot be explained in physiological terms alone.

"I refuse to accept my status as a *former* reader," Engel tells us.[106] Yet *The Man Who Forgot How to Read* nevertheless confirms that willpower is no match for neurology. Literacy narratives are generally uplifting, cul-minating in the life-changing benefits of access to books. Alexia narra-tives defy such satisfying arcs, however, progressing instead from illiteracy to a sort of literacy limbo, a partial ability to read that is provisional and time-consuming, lacking in the near-effortless pleasure that allows other people to lose themselves in books. Postliteracy makes one acutely aware of reading, once a smooth, automatic process, as an intricate and unwieldy combination of different neurological activities—from visual recognition to decipherment and meaning-making—each of which can misfire at any given moment. The postliterate reader is a perpetual beginner, doomed to flounder in the early stages of literacy acquisition associated with child-hood, without any assurance of ever reaching adulthood.

Engel's identification with his fellow readers (and, by implication, the memoir's audience) explains the doggedness with which he tries to learn to read again using the letter-by-letter method. Whereas less fanatical readers might conclude that books aren't worth the effort, Engel persists with the lessons in order to conserve his identity as a literate adult—in short, as a reader. Six years after the stroke, though, he is still no speed-reader. The "snail-like" pace with which he sounds out syllables undercuts any hope of a Samuel Smiles-esque reward for perseverance.[107] That admission would seem to affirm the memoir's guiding question: "Was I doomed forever to sound out my words like a beginning reader?"[108]

As if writing a memoir about *alexia sine agraphia* were not enough for someone who found books challenging, Engel wrote a novel about it, too (a more accurate diagnosis of Engel's condition might be *alexia cum grapho-mania*). *Memory Book*, the eleventh novel in the Benny Cooperman detec-tive series, takes up the challenge of representing an alexic patient's "mental condition" using a genre not ordinarily associated with cognitively disabled protagonists.[109] After a blow to the head, Cooperman wakes from a coma to find himself in Toronto's Rose of Sharon Rehabilitation Hospital with no idea how to read. From the patient's inability to decode the newspaper to his suspended driver's license, the plot is a thinly fictionalized version of Engel's own experience—all the way down to the mention of Oliver Sacks (who makes a cameo in Engel's memoir and supplies the afterwords to both books). The novel's gimmick: a detective with neurological deficits who solves a murder while confined to a hospital trauma ward. Letters remain purloined in this novel: "Not only was I an amnesiac," laments Cooper-man, "I was illiterate to boot!"[110] Cooperman's appeal had always been a soft-boiled nature setting him apart from hard-boiled predecessors like Lew Archer and Sam Spade. *Memory Book* ensures that the hospital-bound invalid is physically incapable of walking down those mean streets.

The novel (itself a sort of memory book) takes its title from the note-books used by amnesic patients to record personal information, appointments, and musings that would otherwise be forgotten. Cooperman's memory book stands in for the detective's notebook, too. To make use of it, however, Cooperman must first relearn how to read. Inevitably, his attempts lead—as they do in the other memoirs examined by this chapter—to reflections on the nature of reading itself. Yet the focus shifts from Cooperman's tedious rehabilitation to his inspired use of compensatory strategies to decipher clues, if not words, leading to the crime's solution. Little is at stake in Cooperman's literacy (he is no man of letters, unlike the novel's author); the murder's solution does not even hinge on the illegible textual evidence in Cooperman's possession. No, this wheelchair sleuth solves the murder despite, or perhaps because of, not being able to read the paperwork. Cooperman relies instead on signs missed by the narrative's neurotypical observers. Shorn of the author's anxiety toward postliteracy, the novel reassuringly suggests that patients with alexia can resume their former lives by conceiving of reading merely as a tool, not an identity. As an impressed police officer asks, "Where can *I* get hit on the head like *that*?"[111] If only reading disabilities were so simple.

The study of alexia has particular resonance at a time when it is feared that people might cease reading altogether. Engel's detective invokes a very different version of postliteracy, introduced by Marshall McLuhan and taken up more widely by the field of media studies, according to which reading is becoming an obsolete skill in today's multimedia world.[112] McLuhan's postliterates give up reading voluntarily—no head injury required. Former readers should be able to stop worrying about stigma once everyone's postliterate or at least aliterate (that is, capable of reading but, like Herman Melville's Bartleby, preferring not to). Medical intervention will hardly be necessary, either, when there are numerous ways of accessing information that bypass conventional literacy, from audiobooks to assistive technologies such as text-to-speech screen readers. Alexia no longer entails being cast out from the world of letters. In short, there has never been a better time to experience reader's block.

But as this chapter has shown, people who value reading print as an essential aspect of their identity may still find alexia traumatic, the above workarounds notwithstanding, so long as reading is felt to be connected to selfhood. Consequently, their mental health depends on finding ways to reconcile alternative methods of reading with their sense of what it means to be a reader. The postliterate condition may even represent a new phase of literacy rather than its abandonment. The problems confronting individuals with reading differences thus have as much to do with the brain as with the attribution of meaning, by individuals or society at large, to those deficits. The testimonies shared here suggest that the best way to understand the value of reading in people's lives is to examine those instances in which it has been lost.

If Engel's detective points toward one way for alexic individuals to move on with their lives, others have not found it so easy. A final case study from 2014 brings home alexia's continuing impact on the inner life even in an era in which we have supposedly moved beyond the need to read. "M. P.," a forty-year-old kindergarten teacher who described reading as "her life's passion," found out that she had had a stroke after failing to decipher the school's attendance sheet.[113] As one might expect from a reading instructor, she worked diligently to restore her reading abilities, supplementing occupational therapy with flash cards, writing exercises, and other remedial techniques. But nothing worked. She missed reading books and the sense of fulfillment she got from reading to children. More than anything, she missed being a reader. In fact, M. P. refused to accept that she was not a reader anymore until it could no longer be denied:

> One day my mom was with the kids in the family, and they were all curled up next to each other, and they were reading. And I started to cry, because that was something I couldn't do. I could be there, but I couldn't pick up the book and read it. That's something that I'd always done, and it's something I had a lot of pleasure from. And I couldn't do it.[114]

Countless others affected by brain injuries have learned similarly painful lessons. M. P. is not thinking here about access to information, employment prospects, or even her standing as a literate adult—a "Full Woman," in this case. She is mourning the loss of a pastime that had always given purpose and meaning to her life. Today, reading is no longer part of that life. M. P. works in sales at the local fitness center since she cannot read to children. One day she hopes to write a memoir about her experience of postliteracy.

4 Synesthesia

"The relationship I have with a language is quite an aesthetic one."
—Daniel Tammet, *Born on a Blue Day*

"**WHAT COLOR IS A?**"[1] If you find this question puzzling, then you're not alone. Ludwig Wittgenstein noted that many people find it incomprehensible.[2] But the notion that letters have distinctive colors makes perfect sense to one group of people: synesthetes, or those affected by the neuropsychological condition synesthesia.[3] A small percentage of the adult population, estimated at a little over 4 percent, report experiencing unusual mental responses, such as the perception of colors, during otherwise ordinary activities like reading.[4] These individuals instinctively know the answer to Wittgenstein's question and may even find it surprising to learn that others see the alphabet without colors. The synesthetes among us direct attention to the disconcerting fact that people apprehend the world in startlingly different and even incompatible ways. When it comes to perception, all readers are not created equal.

"Synesthesia," a term derived from the Greek roots "syn" (together) and "aesthesis" (perception), occurs when the stimulation of one sensory modality spontaneously and automatically evokes a sensation in another sensory modality.[5] Vivid bursts of color or "photisms" might be experienced by someone listening to music, for example, as when the former member of the French Resistance Jacques Lusseyran heard an orchestra: "It flooded me with all the colours of the rainbow."[6] The term encompasses a diverse assortment of sensory experiences, of which there are currently over sixty-five variants, ranging from relatively common ones, such as colored hearing, to rare and unusual ones, including colored pain and even colored orgasms.[7] Intrasensory variants of synesthesia affect different dimensions of the same sense. One of the most common forms involves the perception of color in response to achromatic printed letters; for example, the black letter "A" might be perceived in the reader's mind as a red "A"—voilà, an answer to Wittgenstein's question. For synesthetes, the page is a virtual kaleidoscope.

The most exquisite account of synesthesia is surely in Vladimir Nabokov's *Speak, Memory: An Autobiography Revisited*, where the author describes, with characteristic precision, what he called "this rather freakish gift of seeing letters in color":[8]

> The long *a* of the English alphabet (and it is this alphabet I have in mind farther on unless otherwise stated) has for me the tint of weathered wood, but the French *a* evokes polished ebony. This black group also includes hard *g* (vulcanized rubber) and *r* (a sooty rag being ripped). Oatmeal *n*, noodle-limp *l*, and the ivory-backed hand mirror of *o* take care of the whites. I am puzzled by my French *on* which I see as the brimming tension-surface of alcohol in a small glass. Passing on to the blue group, there is steely *x*, thundercloud *z*, and huckleberry *k*. Since a subtle interaction exists between sound and shape, I see *q* as browner than *k*, while *s* is not the light blue of *c*, but a curious mixture of azure and mother-of-pearl.[9]

Nabokov's confessions of a synesthete (as he called them) flaunt the arresting beauty of language encountered first and foremost as a spectrum of color. It's hard to read about his polychromatic alphabet—an aesthete's ABCs—without experiencing pangs of color envy for those of us forced to settle for monochrome. What most audiences perceive in black and white, Nabokov and his fellow synesthetes experience in Technicolor. This brand of aestheticism is hardwired too, not a cultivated sensibility. We are talking about a group for whom the connoisseurship of color is the default setting—they are less aesthetes than neuroaesthetes.[10] Experiences of this sort—apprehending language in shades of color, textures, and even dimensions imperceptible to everyone else—suggest that more is going on inside other people's heads than meets the eye. This brings us to synesthesia's relevance for literary criticism: What impact does perceiving the alphabet in luminous color have on the experience of reading?

In 1881, Francis Galton's first published account of synesthesia urged readers not to assume that other people's minds work in the same way as their own.[11] Decades of neuroscientific lab work have since confirmed that people do experience the world differently. Synesthetes, who inhabit qualitatively different perceptual worlds, frequently report moving between their reality and those of other people.[12] Books, in particular, may exist in distinct realities. This dual perspective poses a conundrum to those critics who have assumed that audiences apprehend in identical ways the page's visual features or "bibliographical codes," including everything from typeface and ink to page layout.[13] Approaches of this sort presuppose a mind acting like a camera. But, as phenomenologists have long insisted, there is a fundamental difference between the world and perception of that world.[14] The cognitive neuroscientist Stanislas Dehaene calls the sense of immediacy felt while reading an "illusion" masking an elaborate series of cerebral operations.[15]

Synesthetes expose the shortcomings of the camera model by introducing sensations nowhere to be found in the manuscript itself; the synesthete's experience of reading differs from other readers due to contact with surplus "qualia"—the philosophical term for one's subjective experience of what it feels like to perceive the color red or other phenomena.[16] The examples of neurodivergent readers presented here emphasize the degree to which the page is a product of the brain as much as the eye.[17] The fact that two readers can perceive an identical book in starkly different ways is a challenging concept for anyone interested in aesthetics. Readers are not all on the same page, so to speak, when it comes to synesthesia.

The following accounts of neurodivergent reading illustrate the extent to which an individual's cognitive makeup influences textual reception and should therefore be taken into consideration by historians of reading, literary critics, and anyone else investigating the psychology of reading. Although we may still be far from recovering textual evidence of what the book historian Robert Darnton once described as the "inner dimensions" of the reader's experience, this chapter proposes that we can nevertheless begin to formulate the synesthete's phenomenological experience— what might be called, following Nabokov, the confessions of a synesthetic reader—through personal testimonies, press reports, medical case studies, and other textual evidence of what it feels like to read in color.[18] These accounts of synesthesia point toward a double aesthetic experience: the conventional one largely shared among audiences as well as a private one transpiring in the synesthete's mind alone. The physicist Richard Feynman, whose synesthesia led him to see tan "J's," violet "N's," and brown "X's" in a widely used mathematical equation, expressed this sense of difference with characteristic bluntness: "And I wonder what the hell it must look like to the students."[19] Literary critics must reckon with a similar question when it comes to the book: what the hell it must look like to the synesthetes.

PSEUDOSYNESTHESIA

Synesthesia's history begins with an act of reading. The first documented medical account of what would come to be termed "synesthesia" appeared in 1812, when a German medical student named Georg Tobias Ludwig Sachs published a dissertation containing a brief description of seeing the alphabet's letters in color.[20] Subsequent physicians proposed numerous names for the phenomenon—*hyperchromatopsia, hyperesthesie, pseudochromesthesia*—before the term "synesthesia" came into common use by the century's end.[21] It had yet to be determined whether the effects were caused by the eye (one researcher proposed that it might be the opposite of color blindness), other sensory organs, or the brain.

Psychology's establishment as a scientific discipline toward the end of the nineteenth century generated further reports of atypical perception. Notable among these studies was Francis Galton's 1883 *Inquiries into Human Faculty and Its Development*, which presented cases of synesthesia drawn from several hundred questionnaires on the nature of mental imagery (Figure 5). For example, one of Galton's respondents described the letter "E" as "a clear, cold, light-gray blue."[22] Although the initial studies primarily treated incidents of *audition colorée* or "colored hearing," subsequent ones singled out the peculiar relationship between color perception and literacy. As the French psychologist Alfred Binet noted, "There are also persons who do not perceive the color except while they are reading."[23] These accounts of reading, though heavily influenced by medical discourse of the time, provide valuable supplements or even counterpoints to those obtained by historians from more conventional sources.

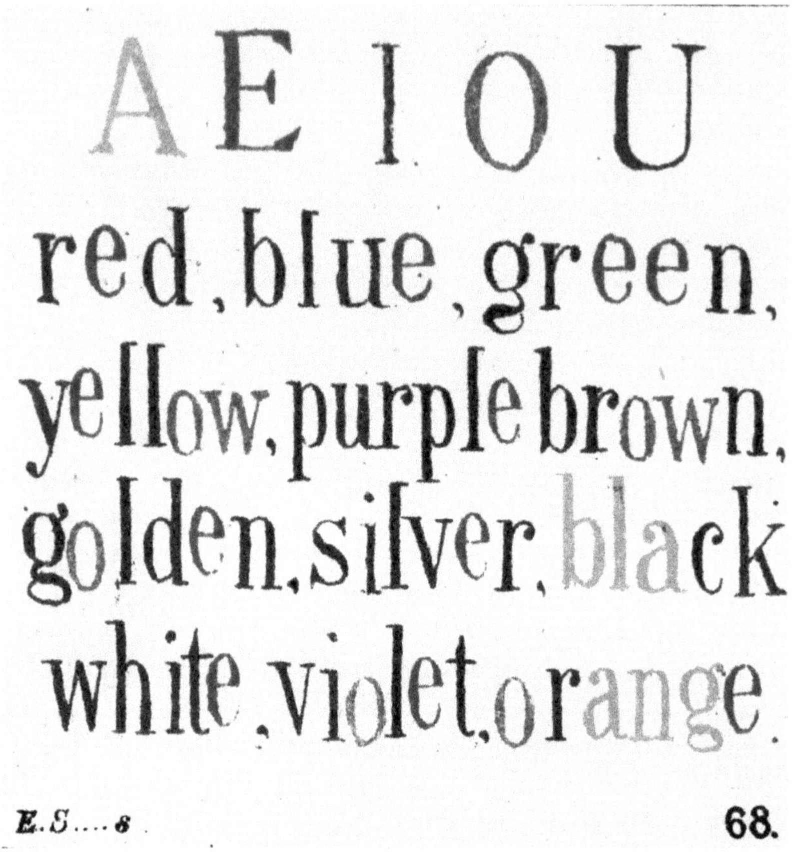

A E I O U
red, blue, green,
yellow, purple brown,
golden, silver, black
white, violet, orange.

E.S.... 8   **68.**

FIGURE 5. Colored letters from the "Colour Associations and Mental Imagery" plate in Francis Galton's *Inquiries into Human Faculty and Its Development* (1883).

Galton Papers, GALTON/2/11/5, UCL Library Special Collections.

Scientific interest in the condition declined from the late 1920s onward, however, with the rise of behaviorism and its skepticism toward subjective reports of mental states. After all, to the naked eye, people who see colored letters do not appear to behave any differently than other people. It was not until the shift toward cognitivism that scientific interest was renewed in mental imagery and states of mind.[24] The development of cognitive neuroscience—along with advances in neuroimaging techniques, psychophysical experiments, and statistical approaches—has enabled research teams to confirm through experiments that synesthesia is indeed a genuine perceptual phenomenon with a neurological basis, not a product of an overactive imagination.[25] Indeed, lab work has shown that people with synesthesia—which was once dismissed as hallucination, illusion, or some kind of memory trace—demonstrate patterns of neural activity distinguishing their brains from those of other people.

A provocative series of artistic experiments during the second half of the nineteenth century first brought synesthesia to public attention.[26] Writers sought to exploit synesthesia's mixing of the senses on the page before clinicians had even agreed on a name for it. Charles Baudelaire's "Correspondances" notoriously mixed perfumes, colors, and sounds ("Odours there are, fresh as a baby's skin, / Mellow as oboes, green as meadow grass") in pursuit of a transcendent reality unifying all the senses.[27] Then Arthur Rimbaud's "Voyelles" gave voice to the synesthetic reader's distinctive sensory experience by reporting colored letters ("*A* black, *E* white, *I* red, *U* green, *O* blue") and intense subjective associations ("*A*, black hairy corset of shining flies").[28] The Symbolist movement later turned to synesthesia as an exalted form of consciousness providing glimpses into a world beyond our own, a tradition culminating in Joris-Karl Huysmans's decadent aesthete who, through artfully combining different liqueurs, created symphonies on his tongue.[29]

Yet an artistic movement justly celebrated for its use of cross-sensory metaphors to intensify aesthetic experience turns out to have little to do with actual synesthetes. Many of these experiments were conceived by people without firsthand experience of the condition—perhaps even Rimbaud himself. It is unclear from the poet's boast whether he based his iconic poem on personal experience or merely fabricated his color scheme: "J'inventais la couleur des voyelles!" ("I invented the colours of the vowels!").[30] The experimentation at this time expressed interest in the use of sensory fusion for artistic ends—what scientists refer to as "pseudosynesthesia"—rather than the perceptive states of people who observe color in response to external stimuli.[31]

Nor did everyone welcome the nascent idea of neurodiversity, whether on or off the page. It was met with outright hostility by some cultural critics. With characteristic vehemence, the physician Max Nordau disparaged artistic uses of synesthesia as a symptom of "diseased and debilitated brainactivity."[32] Literary critics were scarcely more tolerant in their dismissals of synesthesia as irrelevant to the study of literature. William Empson described it as "an obscure physiological perversion" of little value to serious readers of poetry, for instance, and Irving Babbitt insisted that efforts to blend the senses concerned only "the student of psychology and medicine, and in some cases the nerve-specialist."[33]

Later generations of critics have shown themselves to be far more receptive to synesthesia's aesthetic potential. Some literary critics have scrutinized the use of imagery describing one sense in terms of another: Rudyard Kipling's "the dawn comes up like thunder," Edith Sitwell's "The light is braying like an ass," or F. Scott Fitzgerald's "yellow cocktail music."[34] These critics' primary interest lies in the exploitation of cross-sensory metaphors to heighten aesthetic experience; Shelley was credited by one study with transforming synesthetic imagery into "a complex, powerful artistic instrument."[35] Other studies have focused on fictional representations of synesthetes, like Nabokov's Adam Krug, for whom the word "loyalty" calls to mind "a golden fork lying in the sun on a smooth spread of pale yellow silk."[36] Critics have also sought to distinguish artists affected by the neurological condition of synesthesia from those who merely imitate it for the purposes of what the psychologist June Downey called "literary synesthesia."[37] (In fact, most of the writers who have experimented with synesthetic imagery—Nabokov excepted—did not have the condition.[38]) Moving from literary representations of synesthesia to the testimonies of actual synesthetes, as this chapter does next, illuminates how this unusual form of perception influences the reading experience itself.

PHENOMENOLOGY OF SYNESTHETIC PERCEPTION

What do synesthetes see when reading a book? Testimonies reveal the extent to which their phenomenological experiences diverge from those of neurotypical audiences. Most publishers pay scrupulous attention to aspects of visual presentation such as layout, typeface, and font size—all elements of what the bibliographer D. F. McKenzie referred to as the book's "expressive" form—since these elements affect a text's reception.[39] Yet the book's form may be even more expressive than predicted since synesthetes overlay this ensemble with a unique color palette of their own—reader-response theory gone wild.

Obviously, the major difference is the perception of colors that no one else can see. Color might appear in a synesthete's mind when a word is read, heard, or merely thought of. The group is notoriously precise when it comes to describing these hues. One of Galton's correspondents described the letter "O" not simply as black but as "the colour of deep water seen through thick clear ice."[40] To complicate matters, every individual's color scheme is different (though everybody insists that their scheme is the "correct" one). As early as 1893, a survey by Théodore Flournoy found that only 2 out of 250 synesthetes shared the same vowel colors.[41] Even similar shades may vary slightly in terms of hue, luminosity, texture, or other characteristics—as intimated by Nabokov's hyper-specific analogies to weathered wood and vulcanized rubber. Such colors might be imperceptible not only to others but even to oneself. While looking at graphic symbols, a color-blind man with synesthesia perceived what he called "Martian colors" that were nowhere to be found in the real world.[42]

Synesthetes grow up assuming that everyone sees books in the same way they do. But reading is hardly a uniform activity: People not only *interpret* texts in different ways; they literally *see* different scripts. Nearly all synesthetes can pinpoint the moment when they realized that other people read differently than they do. Most assume polychromatic alphabets to be the norm until a moment of Augustinian discovery, frequently at school. The artist Carol Steen regretted saying that "The letter 'A' is the most beautiful pink I've ever seen" after a classmate replied: "You're weird!"[43] Fear of stigma prevented her from mentioning colored perception again until the age of twenty. Other pupils learn to conceal unorthodox ABCs to avoid being laughed at, ridiculed, or shamed. A minority remain blissfully unaware of their exceptionality (what Galton called the "blind unconsciousness of our own mental peculiarities").[44] A Swiss woman reached her sixties before Nabokov's *Speak, Memory* alerted her that colored alphabets were rare.[45]

No one knows where the colors come from. Childhood toys have always been a prime suspect since the condition typically emerges at an age when children are learning the alphabet. This is an enduring idea: One of Galton's respondents attributed the phenomenon to the picture books he played with as a child.[46] Although correlations between toys and colored letters have largely been debunked, exceptional cases do suggest that letter–color pairings can be imprinted in childhood. (Eleven cases of synesthesia have been traced back to the same set of Fisher-Price refrigerator magnets.[47]) Experiments have even attempted to cultivate letter–color pairings in neurotypical adults by means of associative training procedures such as reading books printed in colored letters.[48] (Sorry, synesthete wannabes, but the experiments were unsuccessful.) Synesthetes will know from experience that there is no link, for toys often clash with their individuated color schemes. Nabokov's family learned of his synesthesia when the seven-year-old boy casually remarked that the colors of his alphabet blocks were "all wrong."[49]

Synesthetes see the same letters as other readers while at the same time perceiving chromatic effects perceptible only to themselves. These colors might take the guise of a halo, outline, wash, or background. One synesthete compared the coloration to "a mini aura surrounding each letter."[50] Whereas some hues remain stable, others flare up before then fading out. A retired language teacher found that occasionally "the printed word will leap out from the page in color."[51] And, for reasons not yet understood, certain letters outshine the rest, whereas others appear pale, washed out, or even colorless—what other readers would consider an ordinary letter. Colors might also fluctuate depending on the letter combination. For the writer and savant Daniel Tammet, a word's initial letter can shade the entire word, making "at" a red word, "hat" white, and "that" orange, for instance, or maybe the vowels of a diphthong will blend together. Color and content need not match, either: "raspberry" may be a red word, like the fruit, whereas the green word "geese" looks nothing like the bird.[52] Even a sentence's punctuation might be tinted. One boy despised question marks because of their "awful bricky red orange" appearance.[53]

A letter's coloration usually, but not always, remains stable no matter whether it appears in upper- or lowercase, italics or boldface, different fonts or sizes, or other variations ("Q," "q," and "*q*," for example, will all be the same shade of purple). There have even been reports of seeing equivalent colors in response to signed letters or fingerspelling, the use of hand movements to spell out words between deaf people.[54] Still, a minority responds to variations in visual form; for example, common fonts, such as Arial and Times Roman, occasionally elicit more vivid coloring than rare ones.[55] Other people see colors when merely *thinking* about letters. For them, a letter's concept, rather than its shape, triggers the experience of color, and imagined ones often outshine the real thing. One synesthete with whom I corresponded knew that she was losing concentration when letters reverted to ordinary black.[56]

Synesthesia's hues can travel across language barriers. In one case, a multilingual professor saw both Roman and Cyrillic letters in color. Russian appeared in a "parasitic color code" derived from that of the English alphabet, her native tongue, according to which letters that looked similar shared the same color.[57] These colored photisms served as aides-mémoire when studying foreign languages. While reading Russian, the woman occasionally remembered a word's meaning using the following technique: "It was a red word. Paintbrush the rest of the word, and then it'll just pop up."[58] Synesthesia facilitated her use of language to an extent. Yet the photisms interfered with her acquisition of other languages in which the letter sounds all blurred together. "I mean my whole recollection of French is in light blue," she explained. "Just everything seemed to be sort of light blue and sort of vague."[59] Even more confusing, the Polish letter colors got mixed up with the Russian ones.

For synesthetes, everything is illuminated: Who needs the richly decorated manuscripts of the Middle Ages when ordinary scripts appear embellished? A German woman described black-and-white vowels "shimmering in their colours."[60] Many synesthetes feel as if a spotlight were shining on the letters to which they direct their attention.[61] Others report letters shining through the page or even taking on colors "so that a printed page seems to be illuminated" in its entirety.[62] Colored letters have been known to seep into the page itself. "The paper grows orange-pink as I look at *a* on a page," reported a woman with one of the earliest documented cases of synesthesia.[63] The tints may even arise independently from the letters. A synesthete who associated books with a particular color (green for Dickens's *A Tale of Two Cities*, to take one example) felt compelled to match her reading material to the color of her mental background.[64] Similarly, a graduate student at the University of Oregon projected colors onto her visual field according to the emotions she felt. When she read about a neighbor's death, the newspaper suddenly turned green. "As I read the details the color faded somewhat," she reported, "but for several hours my imagery took on a greenish cast."[65] An acquaintance's mention later turned the green tint into rose, orchid, and cream-yellow—hues associated with happiness.

Such striking phantasmagoria might give the misleading impression that synesthesia is a strictly visual phenomenon. But the experiences of blind readers underscore the extent to which reading takes place in the mind as much as the body. Thomas Cutsforth, who lost his sight at the age of eleven before going on to enroll as a psychology student at the University of Oregon, perceived colors beneath his fingertips while reading braille.

These photisms vaguely resembled printed letters or took the shape of a figure made by connecting the braille character's points.[66] Recent accounts have confirmed instances of color perception following sight loss. "When I read Braille with my fingers," reported Sabriye Tenberken, cofounder of Braille Without Borders, "I see colours moving past beneath my fingertips."[67] An engineer who lost his sight in his forties as a result of retinitis pigmentosa reported that the tactile sensation of reading with his fingertips evoked patterns of tiny colored dots lit up "like an LED display."[68] "Lightish yellowish-orangey-pink" is how he characterized the braille letter "E" (whereas touching Roman letters had no effect).[69] Even people born with restricted vision are capable of reading in color. For one woman, each of the sixty-three braille dot combinations possessed its own hue. "Some letters seem to emit light or, perhaps, to reflect light from another source," she explained.[70] These tints remained the same even if she converted the braille word into Roman characters.

Synesthesia lacks clear boundaries since the phenomenal experience of color takes place both on and off the page. Distinctions made between "projectors" and "associators" (or "localizers" and "non-localizers") have tried to locate photisms in relation to the body: on the page itself, outside one's body, or in some kind of inner space.[71] Those who experience color internally use phrases like "the mind's eye" or "internal screen"; one woman reported viewing colored letters on a screen inside her forehead.[72] Some synesthetes observe a clear separation between the tangible and the phenomenal page. "I read in black and white and THINK in color," explained a woman named Rosemary. "The word 'Scotland,' for instance, is visible to my eyes as black, but is sensed as color in my head."[73] But, for others, the sensation of color feels diffuse and lacks precise spatial coordinates, in one case taking the form of a "color vapor" permeating a woman's entire body.[74] For many synesthetes, colors simultaneously seem to dwell inside of them and to hover in space. Nearly everyone experiences mental imagery of one sort or another while reading, of course; for many, that is the point of reading. The color sensations triggered by graphemes reportedly feel more vivid than conventional mental imagery, though, and different from the products of the willed imagination or those called forth by imaginative literature alone.[75]

When it comes to books, synesthetic readers experience a bibliographic double consciousness in which they perceive the page's original typeface overlain by an array of colors. "As I look at the page, I see the colors there even though I see the color of the REAL ink that's before me," explains a woman known by the initials "MT." "I know it [the color] isn't there for real, but I still can't help seeing it. There is still a sensation that the color is there."[76] This dual perspective is akin to "an optical illusion that *never* goes away."[77] Most synesthetes read fluently despite the distraction. Like other readers, they can focus their attention on decoding the meaning of words without dwelling on the appearance of individual characters or, unlike other readers, losing sight of the "Technicolor on the page."[78]

Various metaphors have been used to convey the phenomenological experience of seeing colors superimposed onto monochromatic surfaces. "I know the ink is black in my newspapers and books, but I see much more than that," writes Maureen Seaberg. "If you placed a sheet of cellophane on top of this page, with a different color for each of the letters, the result would be a pretty close approximation of what I see."[79] Similar analogies include a "clear overlay," "plastic transparency," and "heat shimmer."[80] For Patricia Lynne Duffy, reading print resembles watching black-and-white films onto which spectators impose their own color palettes.[81] Comparisons have also been made to the experience of gazing through a shop window in which both the merchandise and one's own reflection are visible at the same time.[82] Each of these metaphors seeks to convey the presence of extra dimensions or mental filters to which neurotypical audiences would remain oblivious in the absence of personal disclosures.

Synesthetes may visualize the entire alphabet differently than other people do. A subset of them habitually scan mental images of the alphabet arranged in space or what are known as alphabet forms, similar to the calendar and number forms drawn on by math prodigies. These phantasmal alphabets usually run in a straight line from left to right, sometimes bending or breaking at certain points corresponding to the midpoint of the alphabet or to conventional ways of reciting it, especially chunks of the Alphabet Song (ABCDEFG / HIJK / LMNOP).[83] More complex configurations have been reported, too. One synesthete's alphabet took the shape of a three-dimensional loop anchored by the letters "A" and "Z," for example, and then emerging from a dark background against which the other letters gleam as if lit up by a spotlight.[84] These virtual alphabets can be inspected from multiple vantage points. "In my mind's eye, I see the colored alphabet letters as a place I go to get the letters I need," reports Duffy. "The letters are side by side on an upwardly sloping pathway, which I 'glide' along in order to find the ones I need when spelling a word."[85] Like many synesthetes, she describes her alphabet in spatial terms as a landscape of colored letters. (Tammet finds it soothing to walk around the numerical landscape in his mind when he can't sleep.[86]) Standing between an orange "A" and a green "B," Duffy can see the rest of the trail's alphabet receding into the distance.

Historians of reading will need to go beyond the library archive, and perhaps their comfort zone, to document traces of a neurological condition that exists solely in people's minds. The page itself is no longer a prerequisite to reading for those who visualize speech as print—let's call it synesthetic "mindreading" to designate a form of literacy that takes place only in one's head. Galton recorded one of the first cases:

> Some few persons see mentally in print every word that is uttered; they attend to the visual equivalent and not to the sound of the words, and they read them off usually as from a long imaginary strip of paper, such as is unwound from telegraphic instruments.[87]

So-called ticker tapers resemble other readers with the exception that the scripts are virtual, which may be the brain's way of converting auditory input into a more accessible form. "I see the words scrolling across," Harry says of conversations. "It's as if I'm reading an autocue."[88] Other ticker tapers visualize their *own* thoughts in this way—a peculiar instance of reading one's own mind instead of someone else's.[89]

Ticker tapers sometimes describe themselves as acting as a conduit or even a prism for multicolored speech. "When I read or listen to a conversation," explains Jean Milogav, "color just flows through me."[90] She compares herself to the news tickers used to display scrolling text:

> You know on Times Square how they have that electric band with the news? That is exactly how it is in my head. Any word that comes in flows right though me in color.[91]

And while many ticker tapers read speech off a screen in their heads, others visualize the words streaming directly from a person's mouth. Synesthetes have been known to see noises spelled out onomatopoetically just like in the comics—as if graphic novels were unfolding before their eyes.[92]

CHROME READING

Colored perception might seem to be little more than a quirk when it comes to the history of reading—the bibliographic equivalent of a bad acid trip. Maybe Empson's generation of literary critics was right to dismiss synesthesia as frivolous. Yet actual cases of synesthesia should not be discarded too hastily, since a text's visual appearance—phantasmal or not—influences its reception. One implication is that aesthetic judgements can be influenced by criteria having little to do with the manuscript itself. Consider them aesthetic side effects or, as the case may be, side affects: anomalous responses that demonstrate color perception's potential influence over textual interpretation. Although few readers would cite the tedious list of names in the Book of Matthew ("Abraham begat Isaac; and Isaac begat Jacob; and Jacob begat . . .") as the Bible's most riveting section, for example, the painter Elizabeth Stewart-Jones saw in that list forty-two splotches of color that would form the basis for one of her first portraits.[93]

Seemingly neutral words elicit unaccountably strong responses among synesthetes. The engineer Robert Cailliau agreed to the cumbersome name "World Wide Web" because the three "W's" emitted his favorite green hue.[94] Color clashes can just as easily generate distressing feelings. As one synesthete explained, "I get frustrated by advertisements because the letters and numbers are always in the 'wrong' color."[95] Miscolored lexicons made other people feel as if they had walked into a room with the chairs turned upside down.[96] The arbitrary link between appearance and affect meant that a publisher's choices might have unintended consequences. Barbara Ryan has always avoided the Ladybird Books, a popular series of children's books in Britain, because she found them "a synaesthetic nightmare."[97] The lowercase letters and rounded fonts, designed to be visually appealing, struck her as bland instead ("a," "d," and "p" were practically indistinguishable). "The letters *did* take on individual colours," she explained, "but the way they were typeset rendered them impotent and without sensation."[98]

What's in a name? Color, if you're a synesthete. Synesthetes relate to names at a chromatic level, apparent to them alone, and may find it difficult to separate a word's literal meaning from their idiosyncratic emotional responses to it. "How could anyone tell whether a name was pretty or not except by its color?" asked a student who found the name Myrtle beautiful and Alice hideous.[99] The names of people and places with attractive letter sequences can trigger peculiarly intense responses. One woman chose to live in Catonsville after seeing the town's name on a map because she loved its combination of browns and greens alongside a nice shiny "n."[100] Naturally, the pleasure taken by synesthetes in harmonious letter sequences will be lost on everyone else. It has been surmised that Nabokov chose the name Ada for the title character of his family saga, for instance, because the letter sequence elicited the same alternating colors—black-yellow-black—as his favorite butterfly, the yellow swallowtail.[101] The challenge facing literary critics confronted by neurodiversity can be summed up by the made-up word: "kzspygv." That seemingly nonsensical string of letters had the effect of generating the colors of the rainbow in Nabokov's mind.[102]

What might come across as whimsical responses to arbitrary letter combinations could nevertheless influence personal relationships. A mother chose the name Benjamin Morgan for her son "because it looked right," whereas the colors clashed in Benjamin David.[103] Another gave her son a yellow name (Adam) to match those of his parents because a child with a blue or purple name would have felt to her "like having a stranger in the family."[104] As maternal misgivings intimate, color clashes could escalate into personal ones. One woman admitted being "unfairly biased" against anyone with weak-colored names like Phil or Lydia, and another facetiously described her preference for harmoniously colored names as "linguistic racism."[105] Not everyone finds it easy to separate distasteful names from the name-holders. Despite knowing better, a woman confessed to disliking anyone named Paul: "The name probably isn't that bad, but in my mind it's very awful. And that influences how I feel about people."[106] Conversely, attractive names had disproportionate impact on how she felt about them. The woman changed her own name (not uncommon among synesthetes) to Alexandra because of its pretty blue color.

As the previous encounters suggest, synesthesia plays an unacknowledged role in textual reception, triggering responses ranging from delight to disgust. Synesthesia warrants attention, then, because of its capacity to enhance or disrupt the reading process. In many cases, color helps synesthetes concentrate on the text. Christine Leahy saw a "polychromatic mosaic" when she looked at the page, enabling her to "savor" individual words and their distinctive color array—chromatic reading as a form of close reading.[107] Not everyone is as fortunate as Leahy, however, in being able to move at will between literacy and luminosity. Color can be equally disruptive when sensations overwhelm sense. As the neurologist Richard Cytowic observed, "Very rarely, the sensual experience is so intense as to interfere with rational thinking."[108]

Overassociative minds illustrate the potential risk of involuntary imagery leading to reader's block. Tito Rajarshi Mukhopadhyay's account of listening to a psychologist read aloud while undergoing tests at an autism research laboratory shows how some readers prioritize color over content:

> Who knows what he was reading about? I was aware that I was supposed to hear what he was reading. I was aware that I would be asked questions from the passage he was reading. And I was also aware that I did hear him. The difference is that I heard his voice more than I heard his words.
>
> Claude read. I heard his voice fill up the spaces between the files and dig behind the computer monitors. I saw the voice transform into long apple green and yellow strings, searching under the tables for who knows what? Threads like raw silk forming from Claude's voice.
>
> Claude read. I watched those strings vibrate with different amplitudes as Claude tried to impress the silent beholders and serious researchers of autism with the varying tones of a near-to-perfection performance.
>
> Claude read. I watched those strings with stresses and strains, reaching their own elastic limits and snapping every now and then, when his voice reached a certain pitch. I saw those snapped strings form knots like entangled silk, the color of apple green and yellow.
>
> Claude read. I heard his voice, and saw its vibration blowing away those silk threads all over the floor.[109]

Words can hardly compete with the sensuous imagery of vibrant, multicolored silk strings conjured by Mukhopadhyay's mind. The repetition of the phrase "Claude read" at the start of each paragraph makes us insistently aware of the recitation while at the same time replicating Mukhopadhyay's susceptibility to the sounds of the speaker's voice. The result is that our attention drifts along with Mukhopadhyay's, beguiled by the silk threads, until neither of us knows—nor cares—what exactly is being read.

The polymodal synesthete Solomon Shereshevsky faced a similar predicament since words, for him, summoned up splashes of color accompanied by graphic images. Neuropsychologist Alexander Luria's *The Mind of a Mnemonist* notes that Shereshevsky struggled to comprehend simple stories because of the sensory overload. Reading became a "Sisyphean" task, "a tortuous procedure for S[hereshevsky]," observed Luria, "a struggle against images that kept rising to the surface in his mind."[110] As this book's introduction proposed, Shereshevsky is one of many readers who find themselves not so much reading against the grain as reading against the brain.

LITERARY TASTE

So far this chapter has presented the cases of individuals who read in unconventional, neurologically driven ways that set them apart from other readers. But colored letters may seem downright ordinary compared to the variants of synesthesia introduced by this chapter's final section. The following cases are meant to compound the difficulties historians and literary critics face in speaking about reading as anything like a consistent and transferrable behavior shared across different groups. Instead, we should think of reading as an activity that is just as cognitively diverse as it is socioeconomically complex.

Book historians have documented numerous sensory responses to books: the way they look, feel, smell—even the way they taste. But, understandably, most of those accounts have missed the peculiar sensations evoked by books in neurodivergent readers. Take the case of gustatory synesthetes, for whom reading induces specific tastes and textures felt on the tip of the tongue, the roof of the mouth, or the back of the throat. Flavors experienced by this group go well beyond generic categories like sweet and salty. In the case of college student "TD," the word "chairman" tastes of maraschino cherries, "suggestive" of iceberg lettuce coated with Italian dressing, and "attendant" of a chicken nugget dipped in sweet-and sour sauce.[111] For gustatory synesthetes, a book is akin to a tasting menu. "Some words are a complete 'experience' in that they have flavor, texture, temperature, and are sensed in a certain place in my mouth, i.e., back of throat, tip of tongue, etc.," explained one of these synesthetes. "Richard tastes like a chocolate bar, warm and melting on my tongue."[112] It would hardly be surprising if this woman responded differently than other people to Shakespeare's *Richard III*.

Talk about distractions: How do gustatory synesthetes manage to pay attention to the words in their mind instead of in their mouth? In many cases, they don't. For James Wannerton, a forty-three-year-old businessman, various tastes traversed his tongue when his eyes scanned a page. The sensory crossover enabled him to engineer artificially pleasant flavor combinations, like eating toast while reading newspaper reports about New York (a name tasting of runny egg yolks).[113] Yet taste sensations, which persist in Wannerton's mouth until being "overwritten" by other flavors, can be distracting while reading—and not just when he is hungry.[114] If words like "absolute" (tangerines) or "acrobat" (chocolate cookies) are pleasant, the entire process is brought to a halt by the taste of "six" (vomit).[115] Other synesthetes avoid what they call "ugly words" triggering disagreeable tastes; two women reported intense aversions to seemingly innocuous words such as "novice," "yeast," and "Cincinnati" that other readers would hardly notice.[116] These idiosyncrasies underscore the futility in trying to determine through speculation alone how readers respond to texts. To paraphrase the old saying, synesthetes and neurotypicals are two peoples divided by a common language.

Those synesthetes for whom the experience is conceptual, and not just sensorial, face the greatest challenges to concentration. Mary Whiton Calkins, who established one of the first psychology labs in the United States in 1891, documented the phenomenon of grapheme personification in which people endowed letters with personal or psychological attributes, and sometimes even distinct personalities. Calkins's questionnaire included prompts like "Do the letters seem to you to have mental and moral characteristics?" and do they "seem like persons?"[117] One of her subjects responded, "T's are generally crabbed, ungenerous creatures."[118] Another went a step further by observing personal relationships between individual letters: "K seems like a young woman, a friend of L, which seems like a daughter to M. N seems to be a sort of maiden aunt, sister to M. O is a young man connected with M as a nephew."[119] Not all letters of the alphabet got along, either: "Q is odd and stands by himself as rather an eccentric middle-aged man."[120] Needless to say, these personalities sometimes became a distraction for readers. Calkins noted how letters "often become actors in entire little dramas among themselves" that, if too animated, risked upstaging the script.[121]

Subsequent studies have confirmed that individuals affected by this variant of synesthesia—or what some clinicians prefer to call "synaesthesia-like phenomena"—attribute gender, physical traits, personality traits, mental states, cognitive abilities, social relationships, occupations, interests, attitudes, and even moods to graphemes.[122] The mini-biographies may come across as surprisingly detailed and specific to anyone who thinks (as most people do) of letters as inanimate. For instance, one subject described the letter "G" as a "rather old-fashioned" woman, "O" as a man who "likes to be at the centre of a crowd, a bit showy," and "E"—literally a man of letters—as an "even-tempered male who can be scholarly or bookish."[123] Even ostensibly neutral letters can still provoke feelings of affection or distaste; one high school student reported finding "M" pleasant but disliking "S."[124]

Keep in mind that the attribution of personal traits is not a consciously adopted mnemonic technique but a form of hyper-mentalizing over which synesthetes have little control. (When one woman was asked why she attributed gender but not personalities to letters, she replied, "well—I don't know them well enough."[125]) Instead, they are spectators or even alphabetic anthropologists observing the behavior of a community with its own protocols and hierarchies. Rich psychodramas can play out in the minds of synesthetes independently of a book's plot. One person described encountering different assortments of letters as "like viewing people at a dinner party"—and, like a dinner party, the viewing could go on longer than anyone wants.[126]

If synesthesia can enhance reading in many ways, such as by intensifying sensory pleasure or boosting memory recall, vivid personifications make it all but impossible to concentrate on the text. In 1897, a nineteen-year-old student reported associating words with psychological profiles that bore little relation to their meanings. In that case, the word "bottle" evoked the image of "a large woman, laughing, sitting on a little backed bench, with a table in front of her, but no other suggestion of a bottle in the vision."[127] Some imagery adhered closely to the original word; for example, the word "cat" brought to mind the image of a cat with a twist to its mouth, as if it were laughing. Yet other images conflicted with the word's meaning; "shark" brought to mind the image of a large horse. The Swiss psychologist who reported the case described the imagery as an impediment to the patient's reading—especially when the book was dull.

The preceding examples may give the impression that synesthesia takes place solely in the theater of the mind, inaccessible to onlookers and historians. But a rare audiomotor variant suggests that people may even respond physically to words—synesthesia as kinesthesia. In one memorable instance, a Hungarian teenager automatically performed movements with his body in response to names. Hearing the name József, for example, prompted him to go through the motions of tightening a bow tie. Other names compelled him to mimic the gestures of shaving with a straight razor, tucking a handkerchief into the cuff of a sleeve, or pressing a piano pedal with his foot.[128] Every book risks turning readers affected by this form of synesthesia into René Magritte's *La Lectrice Soumise*. Bear this precedent in mind the next time you judge a fidgety reader.

Historians face a daunting task in putting together anything close to a comprehensive history of reading. How can something as complex as a book's reception be adequately documented when even its smallest constituent units evoke a perplexing range of meanings? A seemingly ordinary reader might turn out to be a polysynesthete who associates the letter "A" with the color green, a sensation of coldness, and an unpleasant taste all at once.[129] And yet, alien as those responses may at first seem, synesthesia merely represents an extreme version of the mental imagery perceived by almost everyone. Understanding what takes place in the mind of the synesthetic reader, where perception acts as a form of interpretation, can therefore guide us toward a more refined understanding of what happens in the mind of all readers. Tammet's account of the beauty he finds in language should resonate widely: "Sometimes I will read a sentence in a book over and over again, because of the way the words make me feel inside."[130] You do not need to see letters in color to know what he is talking about.

The cases of synesthesia featured throughout this chapter suggest that historians and literary critics need to acknowledge the role played by neurodiversity in the history of reading, while at the same time becoming alert to its influence over current and future readers, too. Testimonies gathered from neurodivergent readers reveal the breadth of reading experiences beyond the neurotypical spectrum and offer an enriched understanding of the sensorial and cognitive complexity of the act of reading. The lesson imparted by these testimonies is that readers identical in nearly every respect can still experience the same page in radically different ways—in one case, as black ink against a white background; in another, as a collage of shimmering color. The evidence from over a century of neurological investigation invites us to rethink fundamental convictions about what happens when someone reads a book—or, to go back to Wittgenstein's question, "What color is *a*?"

5 Hallucinations

"I was lying in bed reading a book by Italo Svevo, and for some reason, looked down, and there they were: a small pink man and his pink ox, perhaps six or seven inches high."

—Siri Hustvedt

IN 1879, THE PSYCHOMETRICIAN Francis Galton began sending out questionnaires seeking information about the nature of mental imagery. By gathering hundreds of personal accounts describing what individuals saw in their mind's eye, Galton sought to confirm statistically the substantial variations among people's abilities to visualize objects. The original questionnaire contained the following prompt about reading: "6. Printed pages.—When recalling passages in a book, is the actual print clearly conspicuous? How much of a page can you mentally see and retain steadily in view?"[1] Galton already knew that individuals visualized in strikingly different ways. Even so, the response from the novelist Mary Eliza Haweis stood out:

> Printed words have always had faces to me; they had definite expressions, and certain faces made me think of certain words. The words had *no* connection with these except sometimes by accident. The instances I give are few and ridiculous. When I think of the word Beast, it has a face something like a gurgoyle. The word Green has also a gurgoyle face, with the addition of big teeth. The word Blue blinks and looks silly, and turns to the right. The word Attention has the eyes greatly turned to the left.[2]

Haweis's animated alphabet (Figure 6), a concoction of synesthesia and fantasy that stretched credulity, proved to be an outlier among the responses,

FIGURE 6. Mary Eliza Haweis's sketches of the mental imagery associated with the words "beast," "blue," and "attention."

Galton Papers, GALTON/2/7/2/5/8 f.18 and f.20, UCL Library Special Collections.

most of which differed from one another only by degrees (and certainly did not mention gargoyles). Galton concluded from the survey that mental imagery exists on a continuum ranging from the almost total absence of images—a condition known today as *aphantasia*—to ones so extravagant that they could only be understood as hallucinations.[3]

The term "hallucination" refers to the experience of seeing, hearing, or sensing something that does not exist outside of an individual's mind. Whereas illusions account for an object's misperception, hallucinations apply to situations in which there is no object in the first place. The psychologist William James memorably defined the experience as sensing an object that seems to be there but isn't.[4] Hallucinations range in visual expression from elementary shapes (lines, dots, geometrical patterns) to complex ones (faces, objects, animals, landscapes). They occur in other sensory modalities, too—as anyone who hears voices will tell you. The stigma associated with voice hearing points toward a longstanding link in the popular imagination between hallucinations and mental illness. But, as this chapter maintains, everyone is susceptible to hallucinations.[5] In fact, consciousness itself may be thought of as an elaborate form of it. The brain gathers sensory data from the world around us in order to construct our sense of reality, and most of the time our internal estimations match those of other people. When they don't, we call that hallucinating.

Reading and hallucinating are natural bedfellows since both acts involve seeing something that no one else can see. Northrop Frye recognized as much in crediting the page with "the glittering intensity of the summoned-up hallucination."[6] You might think of reading as a form of guided hallucination.[7] Seeing pink spiders crawling over the page of your book would qualify as a hallucination, for example, unless one did so as a result of reading this sentence.[8] Seeing pink spiders would even be the expected outcome of reading the following line: "Don't think of pink spiders!" In most cases the proximity between hallucinations and pseudohallucinations is mutually beneficial. Trouble only arises when a reader cannot tell the difference between them.

This chapter investigates the intimate relationship between reading and hallucination in order to demonstrate how easily—and unwittingly—the boundary separating these two forms of mental imagery may be crossed. As we will see, there are readers for whom close reading is perpetually on the verge of tipping over into too close reading. The risk is especially high for people affected by mental illness, for if books allow most readers to glide between real and imaginary worlds, mental illness makes it difficult to tell the two apart. Classic fiction from *Don Quixote* to *Madame Bovary* has long warned against over-immersion in fiction lest one confuse that world with real life. Of course, these metafictional accounts remain safely confined between a book's covers—hence reading's appeal as a form of simulated reality. The real-life cases of *bovarysme* presented here, by contrast, show how hazardous it can be to lose contact with reality outside of books. There is nothing romantic about the life of the young woman who purchased a train ticket to Orlando, Florida, because that is what she believed Virginia Woolf's *Orlando* was instructing her to do.[9]

My inquiry into where reading and hallucinating intersect turns our attention from readers who understand too little to those who understand too much. Whereas previous chapters focused largely on decoding, or the conversion of graphic symbols into meaningful information, the one you are reading now (*or are you?*) contends that everyone is potentially capable of what Roland Barthes called "overcoding": the superimposition of meaning onto a text.[10] The readers presented here detect meanings imperceptible, and at times incomprehensible, to other people. Accentuating the mind's role not only in receiving but also in transforming narrative imagery, hallucinatory readings cover everything from the idiosyncratic perception of words (as with Haweis's gargoyles) to visualizing letters, words, sentences, books, and even other readers that no one else can see—what this chapter calls seeing "things."

BIBLIOTRAUMA

Scientific investigations carried out in the nineteenth century introduced the unsettling idea that seeing things happens more commonly than supposed. Galton's study of mental imagery helped shift attention from the hallucinations of insane people to those seen by supposedly sane ones. In "The Visions of Sane Persons," Galton enumerated instances of hallucinatory imagery experienced by individuals with no history of mental illness in support of his claim that hallucinations were more common than suspected—even if people did not always feel comfortable divulging those visions.[11] A number of responses to the study seemed to corroborate Galton's viewpoint. For example, the *St. James's Gazette* reprinted several accounts from people who had seen "mind-pictures" of illuminated faces, figures, animals, landscapes, and even books. One of these correspondents described watching bibliographic imagery materialize before his eyes: "Out of the fleecy cloud emerges an enormous book, closed, and held by two hands; the hands open the book, and the pages lying exposed are covered with curious written characters; then it disappears."[12] It was becoming apparent that hallucinations were seen not only by people in need of psychiatric help. Anyone could see them.

The modern understanding of hallucinations emerged in the 1830s along with the advent of clinical psychiatry. The French physician Jean-Étienne Dominique Esquirol laid the groundwork for future medical investigations by clarifying the concept's meaning and distinguishing it from related mental states such as illusions and dreams. Notably, Esquirol was among the first to identify hallucinations as a symptom of insanity—or what was still known at that time as "madness"—and even as a potential consequence of exposure to books.[13] "Lecture de romans" ("reading novels") ranked high on his list of behaviors that caused insanity since books had a reputation for overexciting the brain.[14] Caveat lector: Esquirol's cautionary tales include a woman driven to suicide by the specter of a bloody head that she saw everywhere after merely reading about a criminal's execution.[15]

There was little agreement among Esquirol's successors over whether reading should be considered a benign or pathological category of hallucination. The prevailing view among members of France's Société Médico-Psychologique held hallucinations to be pathological.[16] But Alexandre Brierre de Boismont broke with the consensus by insisting that sane and insane people alike were capable of hallucinating. Brierre de Boismont stood out as the most vocal critic warning against retrospective diagnoses of historic figures—writers like Goethe and Balzac among them—who trafficked in hallucinatory imagery. If the relationship between writing and "madness" has been thoroughly documented, less attention has been given to its equally strong ties to reading.[17] The episodes of hallucinatory reading noted by Brierre de Boismont's *Des Hallucinations* (1845) can be divided into two categories: phantom books and book-ish phantoms. The first covered sightings of unreal books. For instance, a young engineer described reading a pamphlet titled *Project for Opening a Canal Through the Plain of Sologna* before its sudden disappearance from view—it turned out that the pamphlet had existed only in his imagination.[18] The second type of hallucinatory imagery arose in response to real books. Hence, Colonel Gardiner's spiritual conversion came while leafing through Thomas Watson's tract *The Christian Soldier, or Heaven Taken by Storm*:

> Whilst [Gardiner] held the book in his hand, God vouchsafed him a vision, which bore the happiest and most important results. He perceived an extraordinary light fall on his book, which he at first attributed to the lamp, but, raising his eyes, he saw, to his great astonishment, our Lord Jesus Christ on the Cross, encircled with a glory. At the same time a voice uttered these words: "O, sinner! see to what a condition thy crimes have reduced me!"[19]

The prevalence of divine revelations among these accounts suggests that the reading mind is especially vulnerable to imagery blurring the line between reality and unreality. In fact, the conjunction of books and religious visions featured prominently throughout nineteenth-century medical treatises. Forbes Winslow's *Obscure Diseases of the Brain and Mind* (a work dedicated to Brierre de Boismont) cites the case of a minister who could not read the Bible to parishioners without blasphemous and obscene thoughts entering his mind.[20]

Books were thought to be capable not only of nurturing fantasies but also of nullifying them. Consequently, they played a key role in the therapeutic care provided by mental asylums from the nineteenth century onward. Changing attitudes toward mental health across Europe and the United States led to increasingly humane treatment regimens, many of which considered reading to be beneficial to the well-being of people with poor mental health—what today would be called bibliotherapy.[21] In the United States, Benjamin Rush was one of the first physicians to promote the benefits of reading novels, which, in his view, diverted attention away from morbid concerns and helped to regulate the operations of the mind. Consequently, Rush urged every mental institution to appoint someone whose duties included reading aloud to patients and, in turn, being read to by them.[22] Similar logic underpinned an 1844 report produced by Britain's Metropolitan Commissioners in Lunacy, which advised: "No Asylum should be without a library."[23] It was in this context that a Bethlehem Hospital patient agreed to have her photograph taken on the condition that she be portrayed holding a book—no matter whether it was upside down (Figure 7).[24] Yet books were hardly thought to be without risks of their own. In 1853, an influential report titled "On the Reading, Recreation, and Amusements of the Insane" cited concerns among asylum superintendents that novels, newspapers, and even the Bible could be used by patients to substantiate their psychotic delusions.[25]

Bibliotherapy risked turning into bibliotorture for readers who were susceptible to hallucinations. In 1860, James Frame's firsthand account of life inside the Glasgow Royal Asylum confirmed how distressing reading could be for patients affected by mental illness. "No one whose mind is much distracted can settle down to read," he observed.[26] Sentences conveyed hidden meanings to patients during manic episodes, according to Frame, under the influence of which the religious zealot "will find damnation written in every line of a child's toy book."[27] At the height of his own psychosis, Frame believed there to be a demonic spirit lodged in his belly. His memoir recalls being forced to listen to that demon read from what turns out to be *The Bible of the Damned*, "the words of which alternately fell cold as haildrops on my brain, or flowed upon it like a stream of molten fire."[28] Imaginary books could still have a very real impact on their readers.

Seeing things made it all too easy to lose sight of the page—a pathological form of reader's block. The medical literature of the nineteenth century records numerous instances of visual hallucinations interfering with people's ability to focus on books. These phantasms varied in terms of their

Plate I

RELIGIOUS MANIA.

From a Photograph by Dr Diamond

FIGURE 7. A patient at Bethlehem Hospital holding a book. The image appeared in the *Medical Times and Gazette* in 1858.

Wellcome Collection. Public Domain Mark.

intensity and impact. At the mild end of the spectrum, a woman at a mental asylum in Scotland reported seeing a halo around whatever she happened to be reading.[29] At the severe end, noises filled the ears while sparks, stars, and moving circles of light filled the eyes of the Russian physician Victor Kandinsky, who somehow managed to resume reading despite these distractions:

> At first it was difficult, for the hallucinations of hearing disturbed me, and those of sight stood between the book and the eyes, but in time I succeeded in continuing my reading without paying any heed to the hallucinations.[30]

For readers on the verge of a psychotic episode, reading merely introduced a competing set of hallucinations.

Bizarre imagery of this sort makes it easy to understand why, toward the century's end, many investigators attributed hallucinations to supernatural agencies instead of psychosis.[31] When the founders of the Society for Psychical Research (whose members included William James) began investigating apparitions, ghosts, and phantoms (at a time when many people believed in the spiritual realm's existence), scenes of reading figured prominently among the eyewitness testimonies as entry points to another world—not an imagined one but an actual one. Many of the paranormal experiences documented by the society would seem to fit the rationalist understanding of hallucinations as arising from grief, fatigue, stress, trauma, social isolation, sensory deprivation, or plain old drowsiness. Yet these scientifically plausible visions of otherworldly beings, ranging from deceased loved ones to demons, had the opposite effect of reinforcing many people's beliefs in the existence of the supernatural.

After the Society for Psychical Research was founded in 1882, the experimental psychologist Edmund Gurney and his associates began compiling evidence of hallucinations for *Phantasms of the Living*, a collection based on the testimonies of over five thousand participants who claimed to have seen apparitions of people at the exact moment of their deaths. The prevalence of reading among these testimonies suggests that, at the very least, absorption in imaginary worlds played a role in priming the reader for imagery of an altogether different order: Dead parents, spouses, siblings, relatives, classmates, and even pets all appeared before readers upon raising their eyes from the page. To take one example, Kate Bolland saw the specter of a dead soldier she had once known:

I was lying down in my drawing-room on a bright sunshiny afternoon, reading a chapter on Chalk Streams in "Kingsley's Miscellanies," when I suddenly felt that some one was waiting to speak to me. I looked up from my book and saw a man standing beside an arm-chair, which was about 6 feet from me. He was looking most intently at me, with an extraordinary earnest expression in his eyes, but as I walked forward to speak to him, he disappeared.[32]

Imagining the presence of a fictional character was one thing; sensing the presence of a real person (dead or alive) another. Such visitors would eventually disappear without a trace or confirmation from other witnesses—one more way in which they resembled the fictional characters found in books.

Where should the line be drawn between reading and hallucinating? Scientific investigations at this time flagged the risk of the one form of mental imagery turning into the other. The *Census of Hallucinations* (1894), a follow-up survey of paranormal encounters commissioned by the Society for Psychical Research, compiled numerous testimonies reflecting the proximity between the words "read" and "dread." Consider the following incident reported by a young man whose earliest memory was of a childhood storybook featuring a hideous animal on the front cover. "Of this animal I was much afraid," he recalled, "and one day, on going alone into a room, I suddenly saw this animal (about the size of the picture) standing on the carpet."[33] The boy's refusal to reenter the room confirmed that any line separating fact from fiction had been crossed. A more commonly reported hallucination was the sensation of another human being or what psychologists refer to as a "felt presence." For example, "Mr. H." sensed the presence of a woman looking over his shoulder while he read Cicero's *De Senectute* late one evening. Henceforth, this specter would frequently read over his shoulder until the man finally lost patience and shouted at it, "Oh, go to the—!"[34]

The episodes documented by the Society for Psychical Research confirmed how difficult it could be to draw a sharp line between real and imaginary worlds. They also point toward a growing awareness that the source of much of this imagery lay not in the supernatural realm but in the mind itself. Whereas reading words inside a book was usually treated as a sign of intellectual distinction, reading words outside of a book signaled a degree of cognitive dysfunction. To that end, the Reverend Robert Wilson knew something was wrong when he began seeing text everywhere:

One day, after having spent a considerable time in inspecting a village churchyard, what was my horror and consternation to find, on leaving it, that wherever my eyes rested I could descry nothing but monumental inscriptions. The dust on the roadside somehow seemed to form itself into letters. The macadamised highway seemed written all over with mourning, lamentation, and woe: and even when I turned my gaze to the stone dykes on either side of the way, it was only to find that, by some subtle chemistry of my brain, the weather-stains and cracks shaped themselves into words which I could plainly decipher, and found to be of the same nature as those which I had recently been reading in the churchyard.[35]

Wilson's phantom epitaphs offer a sneak preview of the sorts of text hallucinations to be taken up later in this chapter. For now, though, it is enough to note that such seemingly supernatural visions were already being attributed to the brain. If cognitive literary criticism has made huge strides in identifying the mechanisms by which narratives generate mental imagery, the field has yet to confront atypical instances like this one in which the generation of mental imagery bears little, if any, relationship to the text itself.

THE WRITING ON THE WALL

Everyone is susceptible to hallucinations. The difference is that some people see them at the appropriate times or in the appropriate contexts. While it may be unsurprising that mental illness can lead to a distorted view of the text, few realize how prevalent idiosyncratic mental imagery (think back to Galton's aphants and synesthetes) may be when it comes to the experiences of the average reader. This next section pivots from the textual hallucinations aligned with insanity to those tolerated as being within the range of socially acceptable behavior. The following examples of hallucinatory reading relate to three areas of life—divinity, dreams, and drugs—in which people indulge visions and voices that would almost certainly be pathologized in other contexts. These incidents further illustrate how easy it is to cross the line separating the real world from the read world.

To begin with the Word, the supernatural events within Christian scripture would hardly be credible outside that tradition. The Bible's most memorable theophanies include the writing on the wall beheld at a feast given by King Belshazzar of Babylonia. According to the Old Testament's Book of Daniel, guests look on as a disembodied hand inscribes the Aramaic

FIGURE 8. The writing on the wall as shown in *Belshazzar's Feast* (c. 1635–1638) by Rembrandt.

Purchased by the National Gallery with the support of The Art Fund.

words "Mene, Mene, Tekel, Upharsin" in glowing letters across the palace wall (Figure 8).[36] Everyone in the kingdom sees the words. But no one can read them except for Daniel, who correctly interprets the divine message to be a prophesy of the king's impending doom. The meaning is as much metaphorical as literal, of course, since the warning is addressed to everyone who will ultimately answer to God: "'Tis like the *writing on the wall*," as Jonathan Swift memorably expressed it.[37] And yet, outside of spiritual traditions, the ability to detect encoded messages from acousmatic or hidden sources—the writing on the wall, figuratively speaking—points not toward wisdom but mental illness (usually schizophrenia, as we will see in the next section).

Cryptic messages play an equally prominent role in the lives of saints, who express similar conviction that visionary experience derives from the grace of God, not their own mind. Within religious traditions, hearing voices is often prized instead of pathologized. We owe St. Augustine's conversion to Christianity to what may be literary history's most renowned auditory hallucination. At the pitch of a spiritual crisis, a voice tells him, "Tolle, lege" ("Pick up and read").[38] This divine commandment steers Augustine toward a biblical passage convincing him to devote his life to God. Instead of being taken as a sign that Augustine has lost touch with reality, as hearing voices would in most other contexts, the epiphany has sanctioned direct communion with divinity in succeeding generations of readers.

Reading contributed directly to the visionary experiences of previous centuries. During the Middle Ages, many forms of devotional reading encouraged the cultivation of otherworldly visions, which emerged out of a context of prayer, meditation, and spiritual training that made devotees acutely sensitive to manifestations of God's presence.[39] From the twelfth century onward, clerics produced a series of texts like *Meditations on the Life of Christ* designed to help readers visualize Jesus's life with a vividness verging on the hallucinatory. Yet if numerous visions emerged from the sacred manuscripts circulating throughout monasteries, convents, and other places of devotion, reading fell by the wayside once one reached the highest stage of intimacy with God. After entering an ecstatic trance, Saint Teresa of Ávila observed that "the letters, indeed, are visible, but, as the understanding furnishes no help, all reading is impracticable, although seriously attempted."[40] Divine plenitude makes the very need for media superfluous.

Celestial visitations are hardly consigned to the past, of course. The anthropologist Tanya Luhrmann's *When God Talks Back: Understanding the American Evangelical Relationship with God* elicits numerous testimonies of divine interventions into contemporary life. These manifestations range from the widely shared feeling of God speaking through the Bible to the extreme case of a man who saw words written on people's foreheads instructing him what to pray for. Many evangelical Bible study groups in the United States encourage participants to hear God's voice. One of the high school students interviewed by Luhrmann compared hearing God to "kind of remembering the words on a page," as if the one could simply turn into the other.[41] Luhrmann's other subjects heard directly from on high. One woman began waking before dawn to study scripture after being commanded by God to "*Read James*" (which she took to mean the Bible, not the novelist, as I would have done).[42] Tellingly, Luhrmann herself makes no pretense of being immune to the visions documented by her study. Once, after staying

up late reading about Arthurian Britain, she awoke to find six druids standing outside the window, beckoning her to join them. They had vanished by
the time she got out of bed.[43]

Dreams represent another realm in which readers may have trouble
distinguishing between reality and fantasy. Confusing daytime and dream
worlds is surprisingly common among people with no history of mental
illness. Galton's survey of mental imagery mentioned at the start of this
chapter revealed that an unexpectedly high number of people perceive images in the drowsy state just before the onset of sleep.[44] Hypnagogic imagery varies in intensity from faint kaleidoscopic patterns to full-blown
visual (faces and flowers, animals and angels) and auditory (voices, bells,
music) hallucinations.[45] Since at least the nineteenth century, writers have
sought to preserve the strange sights glimpsed within this threshold state of
semi-consciousness. Vladimir Nabokov, for instance, memorably described
being visited by a red-faced dwarf with swelling nostrils and ears while
drifting off to sleep.[46] Similarly outré imagery directly fed into the creative
output of other writers: Enid Blyton, Charles Dickens, Robert Frost, Johann
Wolfgang von Goethe, Nathaniel Hawthorne, Franz Kafka, Edgar Allan
Poe, Marcel Proust, Mary Shelley, Robert Louis Stevenson, Leo Tolstoy, and
Mark Twain all drew on hypnagogic states for source material.[47]

Readers turn out to be equally susceptible to these phantasms. Since
hypnagogic visions draw on activities happening before falling asleep, reading books at bedtime may even facilitate this imagery. According to one
study, subjects who read in bed are more likely than other people to experience hypnagogic hallucinations—including those of reading itself.[48] It felt
to the historian Robert Charles Zaehner, for example, as if he were reading
a book before losing consciousness: "I see the print clearly and distinguish
the words, but the words rarely seem to have any particular significance."[49]
Significance is in the eye of the beholder, of course. The entire Surrealist
movement can be traced back to a seemingly nonsensical sentence ("A man
is cut in half by the window") glimpsed by André Breton while dozing off.[50]
Imaginary scripts can still have a very real impact on waking life—assuming
anyone can read them.

The most famous (and disputed) instance of dream reading surely comes
from Samuel Taylor Coleridge's account of "Kubla Khan," a poem bearing
the subtitle "A Vision in a Dream." Although the poem was allegedly the

product of an opium-fueled dream, the details are too sketchy to confirm this origin story's accuracy or even whether Coleridge was asleep as he watched the verses unspool. Whatever the case, sometime in 1797, the poet stopped to recuperate at a Somerset farmhouse while out walking. According to one account, the stanzas rose before Coleridge's eyes "in a sort of Reverie" brought on by a dose of opium.[51] Other accounts describe the poet falling asleep while reading a collection of travel stories, from which flowed as many as three hundred lines of verse during one of literary history's most fertile dreams. After waking, Coleridge managed to write down fifty-four of these lines before allegedly being interrupted by an unnamed visitor who has been vilified ever since for the poem's incompleteness.

Skeptics have pointed out numerous holes in Coleridge's alibi and even raised doubts about whether he dreamed the verses at all.[52] The most likely explanation is that the dream provided material for the poem, not ready-made verses, or that he composed the lines in a semi-waking state of consciousness akin to hypnagogia. But Coleridge's reputation as a seer remains intact since no one disputes that he dreamed up verse on at least one occasion. His short poem beginning "Here sleeps at length poor Col." stands up to the test of biographical scrutiny, if not artistic merit.[53] Unsurprisingly, the genuine dream verses have proven to be less memorable than the fraudulent ones.

Dreams can be read, then, but can reading be dreamed? For most people, the answer is no. The psychiatrist Ernest Hartmann's study "We Do Not Dream of the Three R's" concluded from a survey of over two hundred participants that reading seldom occurs in dreams, perhaps because it is a recently acquired skill, at least in evolutionary terms, or perhaps because the regions of the brain responsible for language processing shut down during sleep. As Hartmann noted, even the researchers who reported reading in their own dreams were unable to make out actual words or letters. One study's author recollected a dream in which it felt as if he was reading even though the paper turned out to be blank.[54] Reader's block might even be a clue that you are in a dream.

Thinking of dreamscapes as reading-free zones may seem counterintuitive. Many people I have spoken to remain convinced at a gut level that they read in dreams, and it is certainly plausible they have experienced the sensation of reading if not reading itself. For on closer inspection texts in dreamscapes usually turn out to be gibberish. Dream texts are frequently compared to hieroglyphs—misleadingly so, since there is no key to these codes. The occultist Oliver Fox was among those to acknowledge this oneiric form of reader's block: "The print seems clear enough until one tries to read it; then the letters become blurred, or run together, or fade away, or change to others."[55] What dreamers see is not a book so much as the trappings of one.

Writers, however, represent an exception to the normal rules of dreaming. Individuals who think about language more than the average person have been known to read longer excerpts in dreams than other people. Writers may also be more inclined to find verbal hallucinations illuminating. Poets are especially prone to appreciating textual scraps found in dreams, seemingly meaningless strings of crypto-words unconstrained by grammar or syntax that would be discarded by others as nonsense. As every literary critic knows, one person's trash is another poet's treasure.

A lone word haunted the dreams of Edmund Gosse's 1907 *Father and Son*. In the memoir of the writer's stern religious upbringing, Gosse described a recurring dream in which a mysterious force propelled him toward an unattainable endpoint: "Far away, in the pulsation of the great luminous whorls, I could just see that goal, a ruby-coloured point waxing and waning, and it bore, or to be exact it consisted of, the letters of the word CARMINE."[56] The message's brevity and suggestiveness are typical of dreams. In Gosse's case, meaning arose less from this particular word than from the psychological associations it held for the author. As the narrative later revealed, carmine is the name of an expensive crimson paint that Gosse's father prohibited him from using—a luxury, in other words, and therefore the emblem of a forbidden lifestyle that privileged hedonism over religious asceticism. For the aspiring writer, a word glimpsed while sleeping represented an awakening.

By contrast, Robert Louis Stevenson encountered not just words in his dreams but entire stories. Stevenson led a double life as a student, one split between the waking world and a strange dream world in which he frequently spent time reading. Although these hallucinatory tales outwardly resembled the historical romances of George Payne Rainsford James, no living novelist could compete with the stories consumed while unconscious. As Stevenson reveals in "A Chapter on Dreams," the tales he read while asleep were "so incredibly more vivid and moving than any printed book, that he has ever since been malcontent with literature."[57] For Stevenson, imagined books would always be superior to real ones. To adapt a line from Keats: Those unread are sweeter.

Not all writers were beneficiaries of dreams about reading since these visions could easily turn into nightmares. The American journalist Fitz Hugh Ludlow suffered through excruciating dreams after he quit using drugs, a common side effect of substance withdrawal. In *The Hasheesh Eater*, the title page of which reprints verses from "Kubla Khan," Ludlow explained how whatever he saw before blowing out the lamp would end up pervading his dreams:

> Did I shut the pages of a book immediately before lying down?—the last sentence I had read was as distinctly printed on the dark as it could have been upon a scroll, and there for half the night I read it till it grew maddening.[58]

The distressing sentence "Depart, ye cursed!" kept him awake for the entire night.

Nightmarish visions of reading made it difficult to think of books apart from these disturbing sensations. One opium addict interviewed by Brierre de Boismont noticed the drug's impact on his dreams: "[A] theatre seemed suddenly to have opened in my brain."[59] The most terrifying of these nightmares involved a corpse—images of decay were common among the dreams of opium abusers—entering his chambers to embrace him. "At other times," the patient recalled, "it would lean over my shoulder, and read the book which I held in my hand. I felt its disgusting beard scrape my throat and my cheek."[60] The corpse turned the relatively mild discomfort of a stranger reading over one's shoulder into a nightmare from which the reader could not awake.

The prominence of opium in writers' dreams points toward a third source of hallucinations among otherwise sane people: psychedelic drugs. Narcotics provide a way of chemically inducing visions left to chance by communing with God or falling asleep. Reading under the influence (RUI) is easier with some drugs than others, of course. Alcohol inevitably leads to reader's block. Although Iraq War veteran Kevin Powers insisted that books saved his life, beer brought them to a halt. When intoxicated, he recalled, "my attempts to read anything became ridiculous, often resulting in a book held diagonally in a trembling hand, examined with one eye squinted and the other shut."[61] Reading happened during intervals of sobriety and, eventually, rehabilitation, for "The Big Book" promoted by Alcoholics Anonymous presupposes a sober mind.[62] Harder substances that do not block reading outright may simply make the alphabet's code undecodable. Music critic Tim Page learned as much after dropping acid:

> But now the print on the magazine pages kept jumping out at me, random words quivering and italicized, and suddenly there was red-flame graffiti racing around the walls like the newswire at Times Square.[63]

Psychotropic drugs turn the code itself into the main attraction: recoding without decoding.

Reading nevertheless figures prominently among the reports of hallucinogenic experiences accumulated over the last century. Perhaps the best example is mescaline, which has been used for millennia by Indigenous peoples and, since being synthesized in laboratories in 1919, sought after by psychologists, artists, and those seeking spiritual enlightenment for its reputed ability to call forth alternative states of consciousness. These experiments have bequeathed hundreds of firsthand accounts of mescaline-induced visions.[64] True to nature, the intellectuals who experimented with mescaline at the turn of the century did so while continuing to read, as if their routines would be unaffected by the psychotropic drug. Color enhancement was one of the more dramatic effects singled out by self-experimenters who turned their gaze on print. The physicians Silas Weir Mitchell and Havelock Ellis both noticed a violet haze on the page—a chemically induced variation on what the preceding chapter called chrome reading. As Ellis noted, "a pale violet shadow floated over the page around the point at which my eyes were fixed."[65] (Ellis titled his essay "Mescal: A New Artificial Paradise" as a nod to Charles Baudelaire's *Les Paradis Artificiels*, an account of the poet's experiments with hashish.) Their contemporaries had less benign reactions, however. Pharmacologist Arthur Heffter ingested mescal in an effort to pinpoint the chemical responsible for its dazzling color visions. When Heffter tried to read, green and violet patches spread across the paper, as they had for other self-experimenters, accompanied by a distressing nausea that could not be blamed solely on bad writing.[66]

The publication of Aldous Huxley's *The Doors of Perception* in 1954 helped popularize the transformative potential of mescaline not just for individuals but for society at large. Psychoactive drugs were an active research area among biomedical researchers (not to mention artists, bohemians, and thrill-seekers) when Huxley published his philosophical reflections on the hallucinogen. One of the first effects noticed by Huxley was that the books lining the walls of his study glowed with mesmerizingly bright colors:

> Red books, like rubies; emerald books; books bound in white jade; books of agate; of aquamarine, of yellow topaz; lapis lazuli books whose color was so intense, so intrinsically meaningful, that they seemed to be on the point of leaving the shelves to thrust themselves more insistently on my attention.[67]

Unfortunately, this attention to the books' casings came at the expense of their contents—the substance user's equivalent to judging books by their covers.

Self-experimenters who did manage to open their books seldom got much further. Performance-inhibiting drugs seemed to cause at least one of them to forget how to read. Although the mescaline taken by physician Philip Smith at the Veterans Administration Hospital in Topeka, Kansas, stimulated him to rethink conventional ways of doing it, his ambitions to optimize reading had the opposite effect: analysis paralysis. As Smith reported after the experiment:

> I had to decide anew, for instance, where to begin when I attempted to read. I knew accurately that one begins on the left, reads left to right and top line to bottom, yet it seemed as if this were not yet decided definitively. I toyed for moments with attempting to read in some different pattern. Nothing sprang from memory to inhibit this ignorant idea, nor to remind me of my well-learned habitual pattern of reading. I thought I would read backward just to see if the sentence still made sense. (I knew it would not.) I thought of reading every other letter, of choosing letters at random, of not attempting to read, of spelling the words "out loud," even of pressing the card with my hand to see if some message would "soak" into my hand without further effort.[68]

Fixating again on decoding, these thwarted attempts to read point toward an obvious conclusion: that the mental imagery generated by one medium can clash with those generated by another. Whereas the ideal reader will quickly forget the medium of transmission, the intoxicated reader becomes hyperaware of it to the point of distraction.

Plus, there is always the risk of terminal reader's block. The very substance that enabled Coleridge to compose verses in his sleep ensured that others would never wake up from those dreams. The final notes taken by Kandinsky (the Russian physician mentioned earlier) trace in real time the incapacitating effects of an opium overdose on the reading brain: "I swallowed several grams of opium, still able to read," then "hardly reading," then not another word.[69]

PARANOID READING

Schizophrenia can be a devastating mental illness—what anthropologists Tanya Luhrmann and Jocelyn Marrow have called "our most troubling madness."[70] Although there is disagreement over the condition's exact contours, symptoms include cognitive dysfunction, emotional withdrawal, and, most relevant to this chapter, hallucinations, all of which make it difficult to concentrate on the page.[71] As journalist Susannah Cahalan was told by a psychologist, "Schizophrenics don't read."[72] But schizophrenics *do* read, or at least some do, some of the time, even when psychotic episodes lead them to lose touch with reality, to see things that cannot be present or to believe ideas that cannot be true—the unwilling suspension of disbelief.

The most influential theoretical discussion of paranoid reading practices deliberately stops short of making comparisons to clinical manifestations of paranoia. According to Eve Kosofsky Sedgwick, the paranoid stance has become a hallmark feature of contemporary literary criticism devoted to exposing truths that other people are either unable or unwilling to see. Schizophrenics and literary critics resemble one another in suspecting texts of harboring hidden meanings awaiting exposure by a vigilant reader. In this sense, every reader is potentially a paranoid one. Yet there are crucial differences between figurative and pathological uses of the term since only one of these groups wields control over their interpretive strategies, whereas the other cannot help decoding (or misdecoding) every line toward the same end. Genuine paranoia makes it impossible to tell if you're being paranoid, in fact, taking all the humor out of Sedgwick's provocative line "You're so paranoid, you probably think this essay is about you."[73]

The paranoid reader may have trouble differentiating between reading and reality. As we saw earlier, hallucinations have been linked to mental illness since the nineteenth century. Shortly afterward, Emil Kraepelin, the

German psychiatrist responsible for distinguishing schizophrenia from similar pathologies, noted that auditory and visual hallucinations interfered with a patient's capacity to read.[74] Voices forced at least one of Kraepelin's patients to abandon his studies. "When reading I was disturbed by a voice on my left which read quickly along with me in an unpleasant way," the man explained.[75] Visual hallucinations proved equally disruptive. Another one of Kraepelin's patients saw strange faces grinning at him out of books.[76]

The disruptions faced by schizophrenic readers range from sensory disturbances to outright hallucinations. At the mild end of the spectrum, light sensitivity made reading unpleasant for a woman who complained about bright colors and print that seemed "excessively black."[77] Patients with hyperesthesia or heightened senses could find visual stimuli overwhelming. Whereas most brains screen incoming sights and sounds, malfunctioning ones must cope with a flood of sensory data, making cognitive activities all but impossible. Schizophrenics may also struggle to combine auditory and visual stimuli into a coherent whole. As one patient recounted, "I tried sitting in my apartment and reading; the words looked perfectly familiar, like old friends whose faces I remembered perfectly well but whose names I couldn't recall."[78] He shut the book after failing to understand a paragraph on the tenth attempt.

At the spectrum's severe end, false perceptions interfere with the reading process. The fixity of print cannot be taken for granted by patients with mental illnesses—a concept described in Chapter 1 as the fluid page. As a result, schizophrenics can never know for sure whether they are viewing the same page as other readers. One woman protested that entire sentences in her book had been replaced by hallucinatory ones. According to her testimony, "On these occasions, the passage which I have been seeing has dissolved while I have been looking at it and another and sometimes wholly different passage has appeared in its place."[79] Other patients saw messages that were imperceptible to anyone else. The Swiss psychiatrist Eugen Bleuler, who in 1908 introduced the term "schizophrenia" (literally meaning "split mind"), witnessed one patient assault another for blocking his view of the words formed by a window's iron bars.[80]

Hearing voices makes it difficult to tune into the voice invoked by the page.[81] This is especially true for patients who hear someone else reading along with them instead of just their own inner voice—a distraction known as echo reading. In most cases, the echo precedes or accompanies the reader's perception of the words on the page. As one patient said of these voices, "When I read, they read at the same time and repeat every word."[82] Voices that clashed with the speaker's customary inner voice were particularly distracting. "Little girls five years old repeat my thoughts," complained a woman in her forties. "When I'm reading, they just repeat after me sometimes. They say it the same as it is printed and their own way too."[83] The inner voice could easily be outnumbered. In one case, a German man who had always enjoyed reading books now found them echoed unpleasantly by a chorus of fifty to sixty women.[84]

Supernatural agents similarly interrupted any dialogue between author and reader, for better or worse. Whereas a Parisian curate who conversed with God took pride in hearing an angel's voice before he pronounced the words on the page, a compatriot gave up trying to read the Bible because demons sought to corrupt his understanding of it.[85] As the latter man said of these intrusive voices, "They sometimes say it wrong so I have to read it wrong, so I quit. They don't want me to have God with me."[86] Resourceful patients learned to pit the two sides against each other. A Ghanaian man drowned out the demonic voices by reading scripture, for example, which replaced the maleficent voices with the soothing one of the Holy Spirit.[87]

Competing voices made it difficult for even the most committed readers to concentrate. According to *Welcome, Silence: My Triumph over Schizophrenia*, Carol North considered her voices a minor distraction, doing little more than, as she put it, "mumbling softly while I was concentrating on my books."[88] But the voices annoyed or distressed many others, some of whom quit reading altogether. "I used to read, but I was so bothered. Too many try to help me. They were interfering, trying to keep up with me," explained a woman who was beset by voices when looking at the page. "They would change it if they could, but they'd say about the same words."[89] Thought broadcasting proved equally distracting to readers. A woman who claimed to "share a brain" with a famous conductor found it impossible to concentrate when she sensed that her other half was reading—reader's block by proxy.[90]

For many schizophrenic readers, the concept of authorial voice was hardly metaphorical. Print media offered some of them a respite from their voices. In the 1903 *Memoirs of My Nervous Illness*, the German judge

Daniel Paul Schreber explained how he relied on books and newspapers as his main defense against voice hearing; reciting Schiller's poems to himself proved effective at stilling these voices, perhaps because the technique inhibited sub-vocalization.[91] The same tactics used to stifle echoes (holding one's breath, pursing one's lips, reading aloud) were useful in damping the voices in one's head, too. To take a recent example, Kristina Morgan turned to books as a way of coping with voices urging her to self-harm. "Reading sometimes even keeps the Voices from the other reality away," she recalled, though the qualifier "sometimes" should not be overlooked here since this statement came shortly before her first suicide attempt.[92]

Schizophrenia gave new meaning to the hallowed Dickensian phrase "reading as if for life."[93] Ken Steele began hearing voices as a teenager. Voices transmitted through radios and televisions insisted that he was worthless and deserved to die. But not all media turned against him. The first-person narration found in *David Copperfield* and other books drowned out the hostile chorus. "The voices would then become muffled, like a radio playing in the background," Steele explained in *The Day the Voices Stopped: A Memoir of Madness and Hope*. "And so I read voraciously. I read everything I could get my hands on, while the voices waited in the wings, ready to surge onto the stage as soon as I turned the last page."[94] Focusing on stories diverted attention away from the voices urging him to kill himself. It made no difference what he read so long as he was reading something; once, Steele worked his way through an entire set of the *World Book Encyclopedia* to block out the voices in his head. Unfortunately, this meant that a book's ending brought to an end his peace of mind, too: "As soon as I stopped reading, the voices turned the volume up."[95] Other media such as radio and television had the opposite effect of books, turning the volume up to the max. For schizophrenics like Steele, the medium is the message in the worst possible way.

Schizophrenic readers risk becoming *too* absorbed in books. Whereas many people turn to books to escape from the real world, mentally ill readers face the opposite problem: escaping from books. While living at a commune in a remote part of Canada, Mark Vonnegut passed the time with *Anna Karenina* and *War and Peace*. But it was while reading Jack London's *The Sea-Wolf* that realism escalated into too-realism. "About halfway through, the whole thing started getting too real," he explained of this psychotic episode. Vonnegut could not shake the feeling that "it had to be more than just a book"—a common delusion held by paranoid readers who suspect that everything is somehow about them.[96] Such readers may never want a book to end, less out of enjoyment of the story than fear of the consequences:

> The pages and words would twist and blur in the really gruesome spots. I had to stop and catch my breath after every two or three pages. The closer I got to the end the worse it became. I was convinced that I really shouldn't finish the book, that if I did I would die or the world would end or worse.[97]

The suspense leaving him breathless has little to do with the book's plot, of course, pointing instead toward the hazards of overidentifying with fictional narratives or succumbing to magical thinking. Books may change the world—just not in the way schizophrenics think.

Paranoid readers may discern hidden meanings that stretch plausibility to the breaking point—what might be dubbed "the schizoaffective fallacy" to capture the psychotic reader's intense and usually incoherent subjective responses to a text.[98] Literary critics have debated whether there are limits to legitimate interpretations of a text, a problem encapsulated by the hypothetical "Eskimo reading" of a William Faulkner story that has nothing to do with Eskimos.[99] While Stanley Fish concludes that no reading, however outlandish, can be ruled out completely, even he agrees that extreme interpretations will prove unacceptable in the absence of the appropriate interpretive strategies to support them. Genuinely paranoid reading lacks any interest in persuading others of its legitimacy—either you see it or you don't. "Paranoid reading" in the literary-critical sense of the term, by contrast, still depends on persuasive tactics and an evidentiary basis that will be of little relevance to clinically paranoid minds, many of whom lack the resources or the inclination to justify their distorted worldview to other people—especially when those skeptics themselves may be suspected of being potential conspirators.

Paranoid reading suggests that readers may not always be in control of their interpretive strategies: Sometimes those strategies choose us rather than the other way around. Thus, delusional patients will frequently insist that a book is about themselves.[100] Clifford Whittingham Beers's *A Mind That Found Itself*, his 1908 account of being mistreated at various mental institutions, exemplifies the schizophrenic reader's ability to detect personal significance in impersonal texts, as if these narratives were merely an elaborate pretext for secretly communicating with that reader. During his first psychotic episode, Beers came to believe that family members have been replaced by sinister doubles, who used a magic lantern to project messages onto the bedsheets:

> Handwriting on the wall has ever struck terror to the hearts of sane men. I remember as one of my most unpleasant experiences that I began to see handwriting on the sheets of my bed staring me in the face, and not me alone, but also the spurious relatives who often stood or sat near me. On each fresh sheet placed over me I would soon begin to see words, sentences, and signatures, all in my own handwriting. Yet I could not decipher any of the words, and this fact dismayed me, for I firmly believed that those who stood about could read them all and found them to be incriminating evidence.[101]

In this passage reminiscent of the Book of Daniel, paranoia inverts the biblical narrative by making Beers the one person who *can't* read the accusations. This sense of persecution reinforced his belief in an all-powerful Secret Service monitoring his communications at the sanatorium and finding ways to contact him through coded messages. "During the entire period of my depression, every publication seemed to have been written and printed for me, and me alone," Beers recounted. "Books, magazines, and newspapers seemed to be special editions."[102] George Eliot's novels proved to be especially entertaining even though Beers suspected more than one passage had been altered by his persecutors. In this way, even the work of a novelist famed for empathizing with other people's lives could be converted into an opportunity for paranoid readers to continue ruminating about their own.

To paranoid minds, there is no such thing as an impersonal document. The "imagined communities" represented by the press, to use Benedict Anderson's phrase, brought distrustful readers into contact with the outside world only to confirm their special status within it.[103] Richard McLean used to scan the comic strips of Melbourne's newspapers for "magical messages," for example, whereas Anisha Chaturvedi presumed that she would be the next target of the crime section's perpetrators.[104] A Dutch professor who shared this view of the press as a source of personal communications admitted that reading news reports about babies with broken legs had convinced her that the local hospital's infant ward would be attacked if she did not obey an imaginary agency's commands.[105] Schadenfreude is no longer an option when other people's misfortunes threaten to become your own. In one case, a woman's taphophobia began after reading a news story titled "Man Put in Coffin Alive."[106] So consuming was this threat that she posted detailed notes around the house instructing anyone who found her body to take the precaution of dismembering it before burial.

All readers should be paranoid to some extent. The usual suspects (government agencies, communists, mobsters) of paranoid readings are not necessarily far-fetched ones; the average American citizen has only to consider the CIA's role in promoting creative writing workshops as one of the fronts in the Cold War to begin questioning where state power begins and ends.[107] A key difference is that genuinely paranoid readers may regard themselves as being the only ones capable of seeing the full extent of the conspiracy. A common delusion among schizophrenics is to suspect government agencies of trying to control their thoughts. For example, Kurt Snyder was convinced that the CIA was trying to communicate with him through magazines brought by a psychiatric ward nurse. Viewed through that lens, it seemed entirely plausible that an article offering advice on how to find a new career would be the agency's way of recruiting him.[108] Similarly, a woman who interpreted the philosophy in Iris Murdoch's fiction as a set of instructions to Soviet paymasters who covertly employed the novelist was simply being consistent in viewing any disputation of this fact as complicity in the scheme.[109]

All texts may be seen as ciphers by someone in a state of paranoia. Mira Bartók was warned by a schizophrenic parent to watch out for the hidden meanings contained in books, movies, and television shows. As her mother explained after finishing a book on the seemingly innocuous subject of plants, "What is said or written is often in code and not what is meant."[110] Similarly, Susan Weiner believed herself to be at the center of a conspiracy between the CIA, the NSA, and an evil dictator intent on terrorizing the United States. As she would later explain, those in the know were capable of discerning self-confirming messages that no one else could see: "The movies, TV, and newspapers were alive with information for those who knew how to read."[111] As one of those who did know, Weiner spent most of her days searching the newspaper for coded communications that might aid the imaginary resistance standing up to the corrupt authorities—at least until antipsychotic drugs put an end to the insurgency, throwing into relief the difference between plausible and pathological conspiracy theories.

Auditory hallucinations generate some readers' delusions of persecution—less close reading than host reading. Voices convinced Katsuko Miyanishi that she was the culprit behind nearly every crime (including assault, embezzlement, public lewdness, and even murder) reported by the *Hokkaido Shimbun*.

> When I read the paper, my Gencho-san voice tells me, "You did it. You must have done it." He whispers these things in my ear, and that's how I come to believe it.[112]

Yet she simultaneously maintained that the accusations had been fabricated by an imaginary gangster named Waruo, who controlled the security forces along with the voices in her head. She only spoke out to be exonerated before Waruo's assassination squad eliminated her, turning her into one of the very headlines that she had always suspected of implicating her.

And yet, just because you're paranoid doesn't mean that the book is *not* trying to get you. It is worth remembering that people with schizophrenia turn to books for the same reasons as everyone else. Sylvia Plath's *The Bell Jar* has been enormously influential to people affected by mental illness since it was published in 1963. The novel's heroine is at once an everywoman and a figure set apart by mental illness, one whose symptoms can be mapped onto Plath's own struggles with what was probably depression or bipolar disorder. Esther Greenwood's quest to find a satisfying role for herself in the stifling culture of 1950s America speaks to many women. But the heroine's symptoms of distress have meant something different to that subset attuned to signs of mental illness. For them, Greenwood's inability to concentrate on James Joyce's *Finnegans Wake* reflects more than taste. Fanning the book's pages before her eyes verges on hallucination and expresses a sense of depersonalization recognizable to those readers: "Words, dimly familiar, but twisted all awry, like faces in a funhouse mirror, fled past, leaving no impression on the glassy surface of my brain."[113] In Greenwood's case, reader's block reflects a mind unable to get outside itself. The only characters with whom this supposedly fictional character can relate, in fact, are the ones who are losing their minds. At one point, Greenwood confides to the audience that "everything I had ever read about mad people stuck in my mind, while everything else flew out."[114] The same might be said for Plath's most devoted readers.

More than one memoir written by women with schizophrenia has singled out Plath's novel for its personal impact. In many ways their identification with the novel's heroine is typical of young women: "*She's me!*"[115] Yet they go beyond the average reader by identifying with specific symptoms of mental illness, which can be taken literally as well as metaphorically. For example, Lori Schiller encountered *The Bell Jar* in a high school literature class the same year she began hearing voices. "I have never been so emotionally upset about a book before," Schiller wrote in her journal. "The symptoms of the crack-upped Sylvia Plath-Esther Greenwood are me. Of course not everything, but enough. Maybe I'm descending into madness myself."[116] That diagnosis was less a sociological than a psychiatric one. Whereas other readers compared their social lives to Greenwood's, Schiller compared their symptoms—namely, who went the most consecutive nights without sleep (Schiller won that contest by a margin of twenty-three to twenty-one).

Similarly, Elyn Saks (now an accomplished law professor) recognized that Plath's depiction of isolation, disengagement, and social anxiety has affected lots of teenagers, especially sensitive bookish ones. But Saks also sensed that the heroine's deteriorating mental health stemmed from the author's personal experience. Hence, Plath immediately came to mind when Saks began seeing hallucinatory messages projected onto the houses while walking home from school one day: "*Look closely and ye shall find.*"[117] This line might be the motto of the schizophrenic reader, whose confirmation bias is always on the verge of tipping close reading into too close reading.

SEEING "THINGS"

Text hallucinations represent the most extreme variation on what this book has been calling mindreading. If paranoid readers see in texts *things* that no one else can see, a psychotic version of Barthes's overcoding, one final class of hallucinators sees *text* that no one else can see. Hyperactivity within the brain's visual cortex, specifically the visual word form area (VWFA) involved in reading, can generate lexical hallucinations ranging from individual letters or words to entire sentences splayed across the walls in pathological sequels to Belshazzar's feast. Precoding instead of decoding, text hallucinations show that it is possible to read even when there is nothing to read—at least, nothing outside the reader's head.

Visual hallucinations impinge on reading with varying degrees of severity. In Monroe Cole's case, illusory dogs, horses, and people began entering his field of vision after a stroke, while thin blue diagonal lines cutting across the right visual field distracted him when he tried to read (a nuisance comparable to floaters, those tiny spots drifting across the aging eye's field of vision).[118] Other people's hallucinations seemed to arise from the page itself. Elderly patients have been known to treat the people featured in newspaper photographs as if they were real—parasocial interaction that's stopped being "para"—watching these figures move around the room, talking to them, even offering them a drink.[119] For others, merely opening a book invited company. Following a cerebral infarction, an eighty-year-old woman began having visions of a group of faceless men ("It was as if they were in shadows") wearing different outfits, from business suits to a cowboy suit.[120] This accidental book club met as soon as she started reading a book before disbanding the moment she stopped.

Neurophysiological experiments give the impression that fictional characters may be trapped inside our brains, as one woman discovered while reading Charles Perrault's fairy tale *Puss in Boots* as part of her epilepsy treatment. Stimulating electrodes attached to her brain elicited a hallucinatory cat that she identified from the fairy tale. According to the woman's testimony, this virtual Puss, who was as tall as a tea kettle and flat as a sheet of paper, emerged from the script held in front of her eyes before then moving to the side of the bed and darting away whenever she tried to get a closer look.[121] Bookish imagery emanates from other people's brains without so much as a nudge from lab equipment. Visual hallucinations during seizures usually consist of faces, objects, or scenes, though words may appear, too. After a head injury, one French teenager began to see isolated words written in black letters: "chameau" (camel), "ciseaux" (scissors), "voiture" (car), "magnetophone" (tape recorder)—all items that had been used or thought about before the seizure.[122]

Aging people worry that text hallucinations mean they are losing their mind. Gerda Saunders felt "stark, staring mad" after seeing columns of black and red Arial type scrolling across her eyelids.[123] Another woman with dementia began reading her thoughts as if they hung in the air—a form of mindreading reminiscent of the previous chapter's ticker tapers. "I can see my thoughts as sentences in front of me," the woman explained. "For example, when I thought about a conversation with my friend, I could see what I had said to her as sentences. I can read those sentences just as I read movie subtitles."[124] She had a habit of reading aloud in the middle of conversations.

The brain's primacy in mindreading is underscored by the fact that blind people can see tactile forms of print, too. An American woman known as "B. H." reported visualizing the phrase "defense plant" after thinking about a factory at which she used to work. As she said of the phrase, "It doesn't come out in handwriting or print. It seems to come out in braille lettering, like in front of my forehead, in front of my eyes."[125] The imagery offers yet another reminder that we read with our brains, not with our eyes—or even fingers. Counterintuitively, vision loss very often gives rise to visual hallucinations. One survey of patients with Charles Bonnet syndrome estimated that around 25 percent of them saw text hallucinations, which, in most cases, consisted of single letters, individual words, or nonsense strings of letters—less seeing things than seeing "things," as this chapter has put it.[126] Patients have been known to see forms of text ranging from rows of typed black letters to writing on the ceiling that changes shape every time the person looks at it. Typically, these scripts, like those glimpsed in dreams, will come across as meaningless language or undecodable codes. Hallucinatory words resemble the pseudowords glimpsed in dreams—what Oliver Sacks once called "letter-like runes."[127]

Sacks documented numerous reports of text hallucinations, ranging from people who viewed letters, words, and sentences imprinted on the walls to a woman who saw emails superimposed over her mother's face.[128] The words seen by one of Sacks's correspondents were not from any known language; whereas some of these words had no vowels, others ("skeeeekkseegsky") had too many. Although it was difficult to identify the individual words dancing around her field of vision, the woman glimpsed fragments or distortions of her name ("Doro," "Dorthoy," and so forth).[129] Another one of Sacks's patients involuntarily converted printed sentences into musical notation, turning the book's page into a score before his eyes. His efforts to "play" the newspaper fell flat, though, since, just as most verbal hallucinations turn out to be illegible, these hallucinatory composi-tions proved to be largely unplayable.[130] Sacks makes clear that hallucina-tions of this sort could happen to anyone—even himself. The manuscript incorporates tales of his own psychedelic experiences, including at least one verbal hallucination—a passage written by the historian Edward Gibbon that turned out to be a figment of the neurologist's imagination.[131]

The hallucinations mentioned to this point have scarcely been legible. But people do encounter coherent and grammatically correct sentences, too. One seventy-eight-year-old stroke survivor began seeing written mes-sages on the walls several times a week. These messages, which were ei-ther in black print or red handwriting, consisted largely of instructions and warnings: "Don't eat the fish"; "Don't take your tablet"; "They're after your money."[132] The visual directives resembled the auditory command halluci-nations associated with schizophrenia—the patient described them as "see-ing her own thoughts written down."[133] Although she recognized that the messages were not real, she did at one time believe that the messages float-ing in the air could be read by other family members and once had even obeyed a written command to pour hot tea on her daughter.

Severe cases of Charles Bonnet syndrome subject people to seeing text relentlessly—less escape reading than reading from which there is no es-cape. The neurologist Eric Nieman began to see increasingly distressing text hallucinations everyday as a result of progressive visual deterioration caused by glaucoma.[134] Whether his eyes were open or shut, Nieman saw dense, bright fogs accompanied by dazzling forms of print. Some days introduced a pale green fog along with lowercase print, whereas others brought a dark gray fog with white capital letters that changed with the ad-dition of new print. The phantom phrases derived from personal exposure to medical terminology, mentions of acquaintances, and speech heard on audiobooks or the radio. Knowing the hallucinations to be harmless (Bon-net described them as mere "playthings of the brain") did not make them any less distressing.[135] Once an enthusiastic reader, Nieman found himself trapped in a never-ending story.

READING AMONG THE ANGELS

This chapter set out to understand how hallucinations affect people's en-counters with books, instances in which reading operates less as a means of decoding words than of precoding, recoding, or overcoding them. What Saul Bellow calls "fictions which did not have to be invented," hallucinations represent an extreme form of the mental imagery generated by books, and, as we have seen, may even simulate the experience of reading itself.[136] Similar to the other conditions examined in *Reader's Block*, hallucinations should be thought of in terms of a spectrum applicable to the mental imagery perceived by all readers. The possibility of seeing "things" underscores the brain's influence over textual interpretation by making it difficult—if not impossible—for some readers to discern for themselves where the line is separating factual and fictional worlds. No readers can be certain that what they are reading is real, even though every reader must proceed as if he or she can. This thought is enough to make a reader . . . paranoid.

The cases presented by this chapter have ranged from people reading to save their lives to those reading themselves to death. But reading need not stop there—it may even continue in the afterlife, for it turns out that books are surprisingly prominent among testimonies of near-death experiences. Various sensations recur across survivor accounts: floating outside the body, traveling toward a light source, entering an otherworldly realm, meeting spiritual beings, and experiencing a sense of bliss.[137] Encountering books belongs on that list, too. It makes sense that one of the last things people see is a book since so many of these accounts draw on (or, as survivors insist, confirm) the New Testament's Book of Revelation, in which a prophet testifies, "And I saw the dead, small and great, stand before God; and the books were opened."[138] No need to read between the lines here: Names written in the Book of Life will be spared at the Last Judgment, while others will be cast into a lake of fire.

In reports brought back from the brink, the metaphoric books of the Christian apocalyptic tradition inevitably take the form of actual ones— culturally specific details that bring these otherworldly visions into alignment with an individual's background, beliefs, and expectations. According to some accounts, Saint Peter awaits the deceased at heaven's gates with an antique, leather-bound book; in others, angels turn the pages of a book that stands a mile high and three-quarters of a mile wide.[139] In one survivor's account, Gary Woods, a Texas minister who nearly died in a car crash, recalls being met at the celestial gates by an angel holding a book. His ensuing tour of the city, led by a deceased friend, suggests that life after death entails literacy after death:

John took me into a very large building that looked like a library. The walls were solid gold and sparkled with a dazzling display of light that loomed up high to a crystal, domed ceiling. I saw hundreds and hundreds of volumes of books. Each book had a cover of beautifully carved gold with a single letter of the alphabet engraved on the outside. Many angels were there reading the contents of the books.[140]

I'll confess that Woods's vision of paradise is remarkably close to my own. In any case, reports of near-death experiences confirm the persistence of reading among the angels—perhaps because of the Bible's influence, perhaps because bibliographic imagery is common among hallucinations, or perhaps because angels enjoy reading as much as the rest of us. If survivors' testimonies are anything to go by, there is no reader's block in heaven.

6 Dementia

"To write down one's impressions of *Hamlet* as one reads it year after year, would be virtually to record one's own autobiography."
—Virginia Woolf

TERRY PRATCHETT HAD THE HONOR of giving the 2010 BBC Richard Dimbleby lecture. Or rather, the actor known as "stunt Terry Pratchett" had the honor of giving the lecture in his place, for the beloved fantasy novelist had been diagnosed with a rare form of Alzheimer's disease that slowly eroded his ability to decipher words, a particularly harsh sentence for a writer.[1] Pratchett wished to give the televised lecture "Shaking Hands with Death" anyway—by proxy, if necessary—in order to raise public awareness about the challenges faced by people living with terminal illnesses. Since he would be unable to follow the teleprompter's scrolling type (and certainly could not memorize the speech), Pratchett agreed to deliver the lecture's opening section instead. "Regrettably I have to point out that the nature of my disease may not allow me to read all the way through this lecture," he explained to the audience before handing over the microphone to his stand-in.[2] Pratchett was hardly alone among writers in being suspected of having Alzheimer's (other prominent examples include Agatha Christie and Iris Murdoch).[3] But his case offered an unusually candid glimpse into the impact memory disorders can have not only on the ability to write words but also to read them (Figure 9).[4]

My final chapter brings us full circle from learning how to read at the start of life to unlearning how to read at the end of it. Literacy is one of

FIGURE 9. Terry Pratchett gets stuck midway through a live reading of
Nation: "You can follow a line easily enough. But the line below sort of moves
out of the way."
Living with Alzheimer's (BBC, 2009).

the many skills left behind by adults entering what Shakespeare famously
called a "second childishness."[5] The culprit turns out not to be age, however,
but neurogenerative disease. People with dementia and related conditions
like Alzheimer's usually find it difficult to concentrate on books or retain
information from them, one consequence of a progressive cognitive decline
characterized by short-term memory loss, waning concentration, and diminishing language skills.[6] Dementia's impact on readers is epitomized by
Jonathan Swift's senescent Struldbruggs, who "never can amuse themselves
with reading, because their Memory will not serve to carry them from the
beginning of a Sentence to the end."[7]

The foremost cause of disability among adults in later life, dementia describes a constellation of symptoms leading to overall cognitive decline.[8]
Although many conditions give rise to dementia (a term whose roots mean
"to depart from one's mind"), the most common cause is Alzheimer's, a
neurodegenerative brain disease whose unrelenting progression will eventually destroy all cognitive abilities.[9] Memory loss is the hallmark symptom of dementia and Alzheimer's, two terms that will be used almost inter-
changeably throughout this chapter. While cognitive decline is pathological
and not a normal part of the aging process—Thomas Carlyle read all of

Shakespeare in his eighty-fourth year—the main risk factor for dementia is advanced age.[10] Anyone may experience a modest decline in memory, including lapses like forgetting a character's name—less reader's block than what psychologists call "blocking."[11] The memory changes associated with Alzheimer's, by contrast, will be severe, worsen over time, and have a drastic impact on one's life. The gradual slipping away of the mind can be traumatic both for the individuals directly affected by Alzheimer's and anyone close to them.

Memory is necessary for just about every activity in our lives. Without it, we would not be able to speak, recognize objects, or, of course, read. Everything from remembering the meaning of words to recalling a novel's plot would be beyond our grasp. As a psychologist with firsthand experience of memory loss observed, "words lacked the richness of meaning they once had."[12] Assessments of reading ability can even be used to identify dementia's presence; in the simplest version of this test, physicians will ask patients what book they are reading or to summarize a story from *Readers Digest*.[13] At a more advanced level, clinicians have been known to use the National Adult Reading Test (NART) to measure cognitive decline.[14]

Memory disorders expose how much of our behavior depends on memory as well as how easily those abilities can be lost because of changes in brain function. Without memory, we would live in what Daniel Schacter and Elaine Scarry have called "an eternal present"—or what this chapter on the relationship between memory dysfunction and reading refers to as an eternal present tense.[15] Memory works by transforming what people sense, think, or feel into memories—a procedure known as encoding.[16] We remember experiences that have been encoded while forgetting the rest. For most people, then, reading a book entails decoding sentences as well as encoding them in our memories. But this chapter's readers may not be able to remember what they have read: decoding without encoding. They represent pathological versions of the novelist George Gissing's Henry Ryecroft, who vowed, "To the end I shall be reading—and forgetting."[17]

Forgetting what you read need not be a sign of senility. No one doubted the mental fitness of Michel de Montaigne or Charles Darwin, for example, despite their admissions of being unable to remember what they read (in "Of Books," Montaigne describes himself as "a man of no retentiveness").[18] Nor do you need a dementia diagnosis for realizing halfway through a book that you have read it before: déjà lu. Psychologists confirmed long ago that readers forget most of what they read, retaining only a loose approximation or the gist.[19] The novelist Milan Kundera documented in real time his own lack of retentiveness: "[T]urning the page, I already forget what I just read."[20] The examples taken up by this chapter, however, go beyond cognitive shortcuts and memory lapses. The readers featured here have reached the point of life at which, in the words of the psychologist William James, "forgetting prevails over acquisition, or rather there is no acquisition."[21] As we will see, pathological forms of memory loss eventually culminate in reader's block. Some people will spend their retirement reading Proust; others will spend it asking, "Proust who?"

A more intriguing question is why books remain part of people's lives long after they have lost the ability to read them. For people with dementia do not stop reading overnight so much as say a long goodbye to it. They are akin to the fictional characters in Gabriel García Márquez's *One Hundred Years of Solitude* who stave off a plague of memory loss with handwritten signs noting everything worth remembering: "chair," "cow," "God exists."[22] To put it schematically, the early stages of dementia permit reading without difficulty, besides occasional memory lapses. In the middle stages, comprehension gradually declines, making it increasingly difficult to understand what words mean, to grasp what a sentence is conveying, or to remember what was read. The late stages see people lose interest in reading altogether. And yet, even at this late stage, people still find ways to derive pleasure from books, even if doing so means forsaking closure.

My contention is that testimonies about living with dementia single out for attention aspects of reading that have been undervalued by a literary discourse invested in plot and the retrospective mastery of narrative. As we will see, reading with dementia ranges from comprehension of an entire narrative to mere continuance of it, dwelling on a single page, sentence, or even phrase instead. Those who cannot make out the words on a page may still find it satisfying tracing letters with their fingers or word-calling (pronouncing words without comprehension) or looking at a book's pictures. Or it may be comforting simply to have books nearby. This chapter is therefore as much about forgetting how to read as it is about finding ways to continue reading long after people have stopped doing it in the familiar sense of the word.

GRAPHIC READING

Before considering readers who can't remember, it is worth taking a look at those who can't forget. The antithesis to senility is the prodigy, children whose phenomenal memories make retention appear effortless. It took a young Samuel Johnson mere moments to recite a portion of the Book of Common Prayer after being instructed by his mother, "Sam, you must get this by heart."[23] Similarly, his precocious student Hester Maria Thrale was said to have "a little Compendium of Greek & Roman History in her Head" by the age of six.[24] Children have been known to memorize entire tomes. Elijah ben Solomon Zalman, known as the Vilna Gaon, reputedly memorized the Hebrew Bible by age four before going on to memorize 2,500 volumes, from which he could quote at will.[25] Prodigies were celebrated as much for their memories as their intellects. It was said of Johnson (as it was said of Hugo Grotius, Gottfried Wilhelm Leibniz, Blaise Pascal, and other wunderkinds) that he forgot nothing he had ever read.

Memorization was a prized skill in eras when books were precious. A classical education prioritized memory training using the techniques developed by Simonides and disseminated through the *Rhetorica ad Herennium* (c. 86–82 BCE) as well as other textbooks. Pliny's list of exceptional memories includes the names of people who memorized entire books, such as a Greek named Charmadas who "recited the contents of any volumes in libraries that anyone asked him to quote, just as if he were reading them."[26] Knowing every word of Homer and Virgil was not uncommon in earlier eras. For instance, Augustine claimed that his friend Simplicius could recite Virgil backwards.[27] Medieval scholars such as Thomas Aquinas and Francis of Assisi were renowned for their ability to recall entire books, as was the playwright Ben Jonson—at least until he reached his forties and started complaining about a memory "much decayed."[28]

Memorization has hardly become obsolete in the era of smartphones. The same mnemotechniques used to remember books in ancient times continue to be used today by professional mnemonists. Until recently, the World Memory Championships promoted their ties to the ancient world by requiring participants to memorize an unpublished poem (the inaugural tournament's verses were written by none other than Ted Hughes). Competitors were given fifteen minutes to memorize a poem of approximately fifty lines, and then half an hour to reproduce as many of those lines as possible, all spelled, capitalized, and punctuated in accordance with the original.[29] Most competitors used the same *ars memorativa* that enabled Peter of Ravenna—if we are to believe his boasts—to store in his mind a thousand texts by Ovid.[30] In Joshua Foer's *Moonwalking with Einstein*, a chapter titled "How to Memorize a Poem" explains how the journalist used the method of loci (commonly known as a memory palace) to work his way through the *Norton Anthology of Modern Poetry* in preparation for his first memory competition—before stumbling over how to convert the words "brillig" and "slithy toves" from Lewis Carroll's nonsense poem "Jabberwocky" into mental imagery.[31]

For centuries aspiring mnemonists have tested their memory capacity on Milton's *Paradise Lost*, an epic poem with more than ten thousand lines.[32] Thomas Babington Macaulay and Harriet Martineau both committed these lines to memory in their youth; Macaulay would even peruse Milton's verses in his head when circumstances prevented him from reading anything else.[33] A voracious reader, Macaulay was able to recite entire pages from hundreds of volumes that he had read a single time; a nephew recalled the historian's "extraordinary faculty of assimilating printed matter at first sight."[34] Similarly, the mathematician Alexander Aitken memorized Milton's epic as a teenager. This talent came in handy during the First World War when his platoon's roll book disappeared; brought into a state of near-hypermnesia by the stresses of trench warfare, Aitken was able to visualize the names and regimental numbers recorded in the lost roll book, which was "almost, as it were, floating" before the soldier's eyes.[35] Aitken's memory was far from indiscriminate, though. He could only recall material in which he took an interest: names, dates, locations, numbers, music, and literature. Strings of random digits and other information that he found "too repellent" refused to stick.[36] Aitken's selective memory exemplified what the experimental psychologist Frederic Bartlett called "effort after meaning," a phrase used to describe how subjective factors like personal interest, cultural expectations, and general knowledge influence a person's ability to remember a story.[37]

Memory loss makes reading difficult, maybe even impossible. But this does not mean that the reverse scenario is true: Exceptional memories can make reading equally difficult. The linguist John Leyden could repeat any document after reading it once. Leyden considered his capacious memory an inconvenience, though, since he needed to repeat the entire document to himself in order to locate a point—the mental equivalent to rummaging through a filing cabinet.[38] Nor should retention be equated with comprehension. A common criticism of mnemonists is that they elevate sense over spirit. Thus, the members of a group who memorized the entire Babylonian Talmud were suspected of understanding little about its meaning.[39]

Total recall might even harm one's ability to read. Jill Price has the distinction of being the first person diagnosed with hyperthymestic syndrome (derived from the Greek for "excessive remembering") after proving that she could recall every day of her life from the age of fourteen onwards—a condition now known as highly superior autobiographical memory (HSAM).[40] Whereas the individuals reported in Chapter 2 exhibited an extraordinary ability to recall impersonal information, such as long strings of words or numbers, Price only remembered personal information. Give her a date and she could tell you exactly what she did that afternoon. In fact, Price could not stop thinking about the past. These memories resemble scenes from home movies constantly playing in her mind—with no pause button. Ironically, Price's prodigious memory offered few advantages at school. Although superior memory would seem to be an asset within an educational system that rewards rote memorization, the relentless stream of memories made concentration on impersonal matters difficult. Like Aitken, Price struggled to remember anything in which she wasn't personally interested: arithmetic, sciences, languages. "Memorizing poetry was especially painful, if not impossible," she explained.[41] Her memory drew a bright line between literature and life.

Exceptional recall of impersonal information can make reading equally difficult. The Russian mnemonist Solomon Shereshevsky (who made a brief appearance in Chapter 4) used a combination of mnemonic devices, natural aptitude, and synesthesia to launch a stage career showing off remarkable feats of memory. Despite not speaking Italian, for example, he accurately reproduced cantos from Dante's *The Divine Comedy* fifteen years after hearing them read aloud. His ability to convert words into graphic imagery and his own idiosyncratic synesthetic responses ("splotches," "splashes," and "lines" of various colors) made it easy to remember seemingly endless series—a technique known among psychologists as perceptual chaining.[42] Yet the imagery generated by these words proved to be both an aid and an obstacle to reading. On the one hand, Shereshevsky's style of "graphic reading" (as it was called by the neuropsychologist Alexander Luria) summoned up images for each word on the page, making it easy to visualize events and spot contradictions missed by other readers—say, a Chekhov character wearing a cap in one scene but not the next. As Shereshevsky put it, "Other people *think* as they read, but I *see* it all."[43] On the other hand, the ceaseless generation of imagery focused his attention on details at the expense of meaning, sometimes bringing them into conflict: another example of someone recoding when they want to be decoding. The very techniques that enabled Shereshevsky to remember foreign words, mathematical formulas, and nonsense syllables made reading intolerable. "This is too much," Shereshevsky protested while listening to a story read aloud. "Each word calls up images; they collide with one another, and the result is chaos."[44] Poetry and other forms of figurative writing usually overwhelmed his mind; the parade of imagery called forth by the *Song of Songs*, for instance, made it almost impossible to understand its lines metaphorically.

Shereshevsky recognized that he was fighting a losing battle. He recalled losing track of the plot to George du Maurier's *Trilby*, for example, after the narrative's mention of an attic invoked childhood memories of a neighbor's room that he could not get out of his head. "What happens is that I just can't read," he lamented, "for it takes up such an enormous amount of my time."[45] His only recourse was to skim texts—a technique we will see used by people with dementia as well—in order to limit the number of images entering his mind. What would have helped Shereshevsky read was not a better memory but a worse one. As it was, the surplus imagery turned his mind into a real-life version of the Borges character who compared his photographic memory to a garbage heap.[46]

PERPETUAL PRESENT TENSE

People with dementia are not the only ones who forget what they read. So does anyone with amnesia (a term derived from the Greek for "without memory"). But whereas dementia entails deficits in multiple cognitive domains, amnesia affects only memory. A group of people who are unable to create memories might seem to be unpromising subjects for a book about reading. One study of transient global amnesia (a sudden but temporary disruption to one's ability to lay down memories), for instance, showed that patients affected by it had no recollection of a story read to them half an hour ago.[47] And yet, like other people with memory disorders, amnesics retain complicated relationships to print.

Amnesics sometimes forget not only what they read but also how to read in the first place. After a ceiling fan struck her head, Su Meck could no longer recall her name, much less what to do with books; according to *I Forgot to Remember: A Memoir of Amnesia*, the first book she remembers reading is Dr. Seuss's *Hop on Pop*—at the age of twenty-two.[48] Amnesia does not wipe out memory completely, however. As one of the earliest studies of amnesia observed, it usually spares the patient's ability to speak, write, and read.[49] Amnesics may forget personal experiences while still retaining factual information and skills; in other words, amnesia does not lead to alexia (a condition examined in Chapter 3).[50] Although Sheila Moakes stopped reading books because she could no longer follow the plot, for example, she continued to spend hours each day reading the newspaper.[51] Even profoundly amnesic patients may remain literate, as was the case with "E. P.," a retired technician in the aerospace industry who continued to read the newspaper after lunch as part of his daily routine.[52] And despite having no memory of completing a fine arts degree at the University of Michigan, Lonnie Sue Johnson still enjoyed reading and being read to (fables lasting under a minute worked best). A fan of wordplay, Johnson spent so much time browsing through the dictionary that its binding needed to be taped back together.[53]

Reader's block caused by memory loss will be temporary in some cases. One sign that Christine Hyung-Oak Lee had experienced a stroke was that she kept rereading the opening lines of Kurt Vonnegut's *Slaughterhouse-Five* without realizing that she had already read them: "'*All this happened, more or less*,' I read. And yet I did not realize what was happening."[54] Not until doctors informed her of the cerebrovascular accident more than a week later did Lee realize that she could not remember anything she'd been reading. According to her recollection of Vonnegut's novel, "It was just snippets of lines that faded minutes after being read, forcing me to read them over again and again, without even being aware of doing so."[55] Lee had once been the type of university student who visualized the page of a book in her mind's eye. Now she resembled Swift's Struldbruggs in forgetting a sentence's initial words by the time she finished it. Still, she resumed reading novels within a year, even making it to the end of *Slaughterhouse-Five*.

Others will never fully recover from reader's block. A teenager named Jack found it hard to remember things after a suicide attempt left him with carbon monoxide poisoning. When asked by a medical questionnaire to compare his ability to remember "What you have read" before and after the incident, Jack and his parents chose the rating "Very much worse."[56] A memory diary likewise included entries for "When reading a newspaper or magazine being unable to follow the thread of a story" and "Starting to read something (a book or an article in a newspaper or magazine) without realizing you have already read it."[57] Rehabilitation helped Jack compensate for amnesia by using mnemonic strategies. Yet he remained acutely aware of his limits, bluntly stating, "I don't read novels."[58] Jack believed reader's block to be one of the prime ways that memory deficits had adversely affected his life.

Still, even people with severe cases of memory loss may preserve space for reading in some capacity. Clive Wearing was an accomplished musicologist before contracting the virus that left him with anterograde and retrograde amnesia, a double whammy that prevented him from either recalling the past or preserving new memories. Wearing lived—and read—in a perpetual present limited to the last thirty seconds. As his wife, Deborah Wearing, explained in *Forever Today: A Memoir of Love and Amnesia*, "Clive could not remember the sentence before the one he was in."[59] He nevertheless scanned the *Times* every day in search of clues that might explain his baffling situation. The result was a form of paranoia that will be familiar from Chapter 5. Wearing suspected whoever appeared on the newspaper's front page of participating in a conspiracy against him: King Hussein of Jordan, the politician Geoffrey Howe, the social activist Victoria Gillick.[60] What set him apart from the previous chapter's paranoid schizophrenics was that Wearing had no way of knowing in advance what these conspiracies involved: Decoding compensated for lost memories rather than confirming them.

The scientific community's most famous amnesic is undoubtedly Henry Molaison, known from hundreds of experiments by the initials "H. M." Over half a century spent observing H. M.'s brain has transformed scientific understanding of how memory works, for a botched brain operation stripped H. M. of the ability to lay down new memories, leaving him with a memory span of roughly twenty seconds. Conversations, introductions, and experiences vanished from his mind moments after happening. He lived in what the neuroscientist Suzanne Corkin characterized as "a permanent present tense"—a tense ensuring that H. M., like other amnesics, could not follow a storyline.[61] Yet losing track of events did not stop H. M. from reading altogether. When he returned home after the catastrophic surgery, he continued to enjoy his rifle magazine, working his way through the same issue again and again without realizing it.[62] Reading remained one of his leisure activities during his time as a patient, too. He would read a newspaper, put it down, and then read it again twenty minutes later as if for the first time.[63] It is possible that daily exposure to the media might even have built up a sense of familiarity with events, boosting his cultural literacy if not his literacy overall.[64]

Amnesics need not give up novels altogether. It is certainly difficult, of course, to read long narratives when you cannot remember the plot. An amnesic patient named Jason was sometimes referred to as a modern-day H. M. because he could remember no more than a few seconds. But a crucial difference between the two patients was that Jason found a way to read novels—something H. M. never did. Specifically, Jason read Stephen King novels by jotting down in the margins compressed plot summaries every few pages.[65] This compensatory strategy enabled Jason to work his way through fiction in the perpetual present tense—less reading for the plot, as Peter Brooks would have it, than reading while forgetting the plot.[66]

If reading for pleasure is a luxury, functional literacy remains essential to people with amnesia. Nowhere is this more vividly portrayed than in *Memento*, a neo-noir film about an insurance fraud investigator named Leonard Shelby who has a memory span of roughly fifteen minutes. As Shelby describes his condition, it is "like you always just woke up."[67] (This is a distinctly cinematic conception of amnesia since he remembers that he has a memory disorder.) The question driving the film is this: How can an amnesic seek vengeance against the man who murdered his wife without remembering that his wife has been murdered in the first place?

The short story on which the film is based, Jonathan Nolan's "Memento Mori," shows literacy to be essential to the survival of someone who wakes up with no memory of the previous day.[68] The story originated in Nolan's psychology class at Georgetown University, where he studied examples of real-life amnesics like H. M. In Nolan's story, the first thing seen by "the ten-minute man" is a blown-up photograph from his wife's funeral—one of many memento mori from which the script's title derives.[69] The picture of the protagonist deciphering the headstone's epitaph is followed by the question: "But why bother reading something that you won't remember?"[70] One answer is that an amnesic cannot seek revenge without reminders. Hence the signs, Post-its, legal pads, and lists strategically placed around the protagonist's bedroom to focus his attention on the mission. (There are no books, of course, since those contents would require longer attention spans.) The mission's very goal is a note: To end the loop, confirmation of the execution matters just as much as the execution itself.

The trouble with relying on Post-its is that there is always a chance you might wake up in the wrong place. So the amnesic's solution is tattoos— or what Shelby calls permanent notes—steering his gaze from an arrow printed on his wrist toward the instructions along his forearm, shoulder, and chest before terminating in a police sketch of the culprit's face. We can still read our bodies even when we cannot be expected to read anything else. The film, which attempts to replicate Shelby's disorientation by telling the story backwards, dramatizes the otherwise undramatic act of reading by showing the protagonist's inked torso in the mirror emblazoned with the headline: "JOHN G. RAPED AND MURDERED MY WIFE" (Figure 10). There is no trigger warning for this amnesic: Shelby begins every day with a

FIGURE 10. Leonard Shelby (played by Guy Pearce) reading the instructions tattooed across his torso in Christopher Nolan's *Memento*.

Memento (Newmarket Films, 2000).

jarring reminder of his wife's sexual assault. The film may be more ambiguous than the story when it comes to Shelby's mission, but the tattoos tell the story straight. Shelby is the main character in a plot whose beginning he cannot remember and whose ending won't be remembered either. A revealing flashback shows Shelby teasing his wife for rereading one of her favorite novels even though she already knows what happens next. The joke's on him, of course, since amnesics read in order to find out what happened last.

LOSING THE PLOT

When a post titled "Many Alzheimer's Patients Find Comfort in Books" appeared on the *New York Times*'s "The New Old Age" blog in 2010, many caregivers were surprised to learn that dementia did not necessarily mean the end of reading.[71] To the contrary, dementia patients who have difficulty handling verbal exchanges might still understand print perfectly well. Some (though by no means all) maintain literacy until the final stages of dementia—even if their methods of deciphering sentences may scarcely resemble the way they used to read. As one person following the blog commented, "I think that one has to open up to different interpretations of the action of 'reading.'"[72]

Reading is hardly an obvious pastime for someone with memory impairments. The challenges facing people with dementia include flickering attention span, dwindling short-term memory, and difficulties following a conversation. None of this bodes well for reading. In fact, one way in which dementia can adversely affect people's lives is by driving them away from activities that they used to enjoy—including books. Yet psychologists who work with people affected by dementia insist that there are therapeutic benefits to taking part in reading groups organized around imaginative literature, and bibliotherapists point to the potential of these groups to improve participants' well-being by facilitating social interaction and enabling self-expression.[73] Poetry in particular may help to stimulate interest, maintain concentration, and even invoke memories, of life as well as literature, at least for those who grew up memorizing poetry at school.[74] The founder of the Alzheimer's Poetry Project recalls being surprised and delighted when a member of the group completed a line he had begun reciting from Henry Wadsworth Longfellow's "The Arrow and the Song."[75]

People affected by dementia might no longer be in a position to take on Proust's *Remembrance of Things Past*, of course. There are two schools of thought when it comes to reading and dementia. One approach takes Shakespeare's "second childishness" literally by steering adults who are adjusting to memory loss toward children's books. This regressive model presumes that the dementia patient's diminished reading ability will turn them into the equivalent of a child. As guidelines published by the International Federation of Library Associations and Institutions (IFLA) state, "Children's picture books with big and clear illustrations are appropriate" for patrons with dementia.[76] The rationale is that adult literature's sophisticated language—with its distinctive syntax, extensive vocabulary, and figurative speech—would be lost on people with memory deficits, for while the ability to read aloud may remain stable for some people, reading comprehension declines as dementia's severity increases.[77]

The most extreme version of the "second childishness" approach sets out to pare down words to an absolute minimum. A number of the most popular titles on the UK's Reading Well Books on Prescription list for people with dementia are Picture to Share books filled with captioned photographs on themes such as family, pets, and travel. Although pictures of seaside holidays may suggest escapism, the goal of books pitched to "memory-challenged" adults (to use the publishers' lingo) is captivity—holding the viewer's attention long enough to trigger reminiscences. Words play a minimal role here despite the emphasis on books—one of which recommends taking "a nonverbal approach" to its contents.[78] As the activities coordinator at a residential care home in Newcastle upon Tyne remarked, "I have never seen a book with so few words evoke such emotionally positive reactions."[79]

Publishers aiming to reach aging audiences may find it necessary to conceal from these readers that they are *not* reading Proust. Many dementia book titles are pitched to adult readers who want children's books without the stigma of being childish. The selling point of Emma Rose Sparrow's dementia series is that each volume comes "disguised as a 'real' book," for caretakers know from experience that adults who read children's books are still capable of taking offense at anything labeled for children. As Sparrow reassures customers,

You'll know that you're buying a book that is perfect for a dementia or Alzheimer's patient, but the reader will only know that he/she is receiving a beautiful book that is eye-catching and easy to follow. Neither the title nor any text on or in the book states that the book is for dementia or any type of memory/cognitive problems. It is truly concealed so that the reader is not insulted.[80]

In other words, dementia books want to make it possible for these adults to continue reading with dignity.

The genre's main benefit may be permitting aging parents to continue reading on their own terms. Eliezer Sobel's eighty-six-year-old mother could no longer hold a conversation after reaching the advanced stages of Alzheimer's disease. Sobel reasonably assumed that his mother could no longer read, either, since she had stopped retaining the meaning of con-secutive sentences and certainly of any storyline. And yet she continued to leaf through magazines while reading the captions aloud. Her residual literacy came as a revelation to Sobel: "My mother can still read, I realized. Maybe not a book; maybe not a paragraph, or even a full sentence; but she could still read individual words and short phrases."[81] The "adult picture book" that he designed with his mother's memory deficits in mind enables people to continue reading even when what they do with books no longer looks like reading.

Most dementia books are designed less for reading than for co-reading. As the name suggests, Two-Lap Books targets an audience made up of care-givers as much as patients, who will presumably read the books side by side, the one standing by as understudy should the other falter. Clinical psychologist Lydia Burdick wrote the first book in the series for her mother, whose speech had been reduced to monosyllables. As her mother picked up the manuscript, Burdick recalled, "I didn't know if she would read those sentences to herself, out loud to me, or at all."[82] Occasional prompts enabled Burdick's mother to read every word—the bibliographic equivalent of call-ing for a line.

The second approach to aging readers pushes back against the provision of children's literature as infantilizing, calling for adult literature instead: Shakespeare over Dr. Seuss.[83] A report issued by the Reader, a charity based in Liverpool, explicitly warns against seeking to protect people with de-mentia from the full range of human experiences represented in literature.[84] Other groups have likewise contended that the classics need not be aban-doned since the appreciation of complex language may be preserved until late in the disease's course. This does not necessarily mean that everyone needs to read the original narrative, however. As the editors of Dovetale Press note, "It can be challenging to understand a story if sentences are very long."[85] Their report identifies ways of making books "dementia-friendly" instead through aides-mémoire such as cast lists, large fonts, illustrations, and abridgement, for not everyone capable of understanding pages from classic literature will be able to remember them.[86]

Dovetale Press "adaptations" (a term favored over "abridgements") present one model for how to refashion classic titles to accommodate dementia. Although detective fiction might seem especially ill suited to people affected by memory loss—a group for whom the climactic reveal may not be all that revealing—the editors have tried reconfiguring *The Adventures of Sherlock Holmes* to hold the reader's attention long after the original crime has been forgotten. Opening with a cast list introducing Holmes as a "renowned detective," Dovetale reprints just one of the collection's original twelve stories, cutting "The Adventure of the Blue Carbuncle" in half, from roughly 8,000 to 4,000 words, and omitting potential clues inserted to leave readers guessing.[87] By removing aliases, digressions, and uncommon phrases ("disjecta membra"), Dovetale aims to make the narrative more accessible, as does dividing the seamless original into multiple sections, each accompanied by plot summaries labeled "In the previous chapter . . ." to refresh the memories of forgetful readers. Whereas Doyle's original narrative ends with a pun yoking together a roast goose and a "gaol-bird," the adaptation finishes with a blunt recap of events ("Sherlock Holmes realises that James Ryder is the thief"), ensuring closure for anyone who missed it the first time around.[88] Narrowing the gap between *fabula* and *sujet*, or between events and their presentation, the streamlined narrative effectively strips away the mind games inviting audiences to match wits against the world's most famous detective. To that end, Dovetale's excision of the lens and forceps used by Holmes to inspect evidence, which are mentioned in the original story's opening paragraph, points to the press's broader mission to minimize the cognitive burdens of forensic analysis. The tale no longer characterizes a man's billycock as "an intellectual problem," nor does Holmes invite the story's readers—via the surrogate figure of Dr. Watson— to test their own skills of deduction. The revised script caters instead to an audience for whom the slightest misdirection or false lead will generate confusion instead of intellectual pleasure.

There is some evidence that "dementia-friendly" adaptations do indeed make a difference. Book groups centered on Dickens's *A Christmas Carol* have expressed appreciation for minor alterations such as appending plot summaries to each chapter, substituting proper names for pronouns (swapping "Scrooge" for "He"), or even removing ambiguity (the opening paragraph of the Dovetale text clarifies that the deceased Marley was Scrooge's business partner).[89] Reducing cognitive load can help make texts accessible to those reading not for the plot but despite it.[90] Closure, or what Peter Brooks calls "the anticipation of retrospection," will hold little appeal for readers who are unable to retrospect.[91]

What the two approaches agree on is that conventional narratives may be too challenging for people with cognitive impairments. Once-avid readers might now be found leafing through books or ignoring them altogether. The speech language pathologists who founded Reading2Connect therefore advocate making literature accessible by adapting its formal attributes, including layout, length, and syntax (especially cognitively demanding stylistic features such as passive voice, negations, and clauses—in short, no Henry James). Fidelity to the original text is a minor concern here; the overriding one is finding ways for people to continue engaging with books. As Reading2Connect's directors have said of their readers, "Whether they are comprehending the text in its entirety, dwelling on a few pages, contemplating a phrase, or just enjoying the images, they are interacting with print material."[92] Making this material accessible enables people with cognitive deficits to continue engaging with books—what I've been insisting should be called reading—even if their methods of doing so only faintly resemble the way they used to read.

READING IN THE DARK

Memoirs about dementia began appearing in the 1990s.[93] Many of them were written by relatives (usually daughters) or caregivers since the people affected by memory loss were no longer capable of telling their own stories—less a long goodbye than a long hello. Figuratively, the genre counteracts a loved one's cognitive decline by recording that individual's memories for posterity and memorializing lives in danger of being seen as no longer fully human.[94] These memoirs capture the experience of cognitive decline from the perspective of both insiders and outsiders. As one woman described the experience of living with dementia: "It's as if you're reading a book and someone has torn the pages out."[95]

The genre's best-known example may be *Elegy for Iris*, John Bayley's 1999 account of the toll taken by Alzheimer's on his wife, the novelist Iris Murdoch. The memoir moves from the couple's bookish courtship at Oxford in the 1950s to the novelist's cognitive decline in the 1990s—what she memorably called "sailing into the darkness."[96] Being at a loss for words proved to be particularly stressful for a couple who had organized their lives around letters and viewed the world largely through the prism of books. Near the end of Murdoch's life, one of the twentieth century's most celebrated novelists could not even remember that she wrote novels.

Bayley's efforts to read aloud to his wife did little more than expose the gulf between the novelist's mind before and after the diagnosis. Reading Murdoch's favorite stories, from *The Tale of Genji* to *The Lord of the Rings*, somehow felt "unnatural" now that she no longer found it easy to engage with those imaginary worlds. "For someone who had been accustomed not so much to read books as to slip into their world as effortlessly as she slipped into a river or the sea," Bayley speculates, "this laborious procession of words clumping into her consciousness must have seemed a tedious irrelevance."[97] Nor was Murdoch the only member of the household whose reading was brought to a halt by the neurodegenerative disease: Bayley stopped reading for pleasure, too. This pair of intellectuals who used to read together over lunch now spent their afternoons watching *Teletubbies*.

Watching a loved one lose interest in books can drive caregivers to seek refuge in them. Although the poet Rachel Hadas and her husband had bonded over a mutual love of Proust, there came a point when he could scarcely make sense of the newspaper. His behavior changed the way Hadas read, too, provoking her to see familiar books from a new angle. She found herself increasingly drawn to Dickens's eccentric, obsessive, paranoid, traumatized, and outright psychotic characters. "Had Dickens seen people with dementia?" she wondered after noticing the resemblance between her husband and the eccentric Mr. Dick from *David Copperfield*.[98]

A more revealing comparison would have been to George Eliot's *Romola*, in which a character named Baldassarre Calvo expresses the anguish caused by dementia. This scholar, once renowned for his knowledge of Greek, comes to find the language unintelligible (an incident mentioned briefly in Chapter 3). Letters that had once been "magic signs that conjure up a world" revert to ordinary black marks.[99] As Baldassarre laments of his forgotten knowledge, "It is gone!—it is all gone!"[100] A century before Murdoch spoke of "sailing into the darkness," Eliot used a similar metaphor to represent the void opened by dementia. An aging Baldassarre spends most days encumbered by "a new darkness within him," though not without experiencing tantalizing flashes of lucidity before "the darkness closing in again seemed the more horrible."[101] He finds the uncertainty of not knowing whether his literacy will return to be particularly distressing, as in the meantime all he sees on the page are "mocking symbols of his utter helplessness."[102] Books that were once a source of comfort now humiliate him.

Incidents of reader's block alerted other spouses that something had gone awry. In *The Diminished Mind*, Jean Tyler recounts watching her husband's transition from an inspirational teacher with a passion for reading history books into someone who stares at the photographs in *National Geographic*. "He can't read anymore," she realized before bursting into tears. "His intellectuality had been the most interesting part of his life. That was gone now."[103] Steph Booth first noticed her husband's cognitive problems when he began talking about the characters from a novel as if they were real people. Formerly a voracious reader, Tony Booth could no longer remember the last chapter, paragraph, or even sentence that he read. Yet he continued to take comfort from books after he could no longer read them, visiting bookshops and buying new ones, and even quoting excerpts from Shakespeare remembered from his acting days. Steph satisfied her husband's craving for "holding on to words" by reading poetry to him.[104]

Stacks of unread books and newspapers were another warning sign that a person might be letting go of words. Pam Faulkner retired from reading because her form of Alzheimer's (the same as Terry Pratchett's) made it too easy to lose her place on the page. "Where do I go next?" she would ask in confusion at the end of each line in a newspaper column.[105] She no longer touches her personal library of over three thousand books.

People who were once at home in libraries might no longer know what to do with print. Marie Marley fell in love with a man with a doctorate in Romance languages and literature whom she affectionally referred to as "a walking library."[106] Yet this same scholar who wrote his dissertation on the eighteenth-century Swiss aesthetician Johann Georg Sulzer now struggled to get through the front page of the *New York Times*. "Kitty, I can't understand the newspaper," complained this walking library. "There are too many stories. There's so much information here. It confuses me."[107] Newspapers provided other people, though, with a reassuring sense of continuity. For example, Jonathan Kozol renewed his father's subscription to the *Boston Globe* long after he had stopped reading it.[108] People in the advanced stages of Alzheimer's have been known to spend the entire day holding a newspaper. When asked what they were doing, one of them replied "reading."[109]

Filial memoirs record the mortifying details of what it feels like to swap roles with your parents. For Vicki Tapia, hearing her mother read the newspaper felt "like listening to a first grader learning to read by sounding out words"—a second childhood obligating a second parenthood.[110] Similarly, an elementary school teacher found it peculiar watching kids learn how to read by day and her mother forget how to read by night.[111] In such cases, the adult brain's regression seemed to happen in parallel to a child's development: children learning to read as adults unlearned it. One man's granddaughter interrupted his garbled bedtime story to ask, "Grandpa, did you forget how to read?"[112]

Other faltering readers committed sins of omission rather than commission. Sarah Leavitt's graphic memoir *Tangles* juxtaposes reminiscences of being read to as a child with a panel of her aging mother skipping entire paragraphs from childhood favorites.[113] At least those misreadings took place in the privacy of the home rather than in front of an audience. Not everyone was so fortunate. A funeral address given by the Scottish journalist Mamie Baird held the audience spellbound until she began reading the exact same script a second time without realizing it.[114] In an attempt to pass as readers, people with dementia may camouflage themselves by continuing to visit bookstores, surrounding themselves with books, and even holding onto them as a kind of totem. Still, children notice when parents stop reading. A few clues: following the words with an index finger, never turning the page, holding a book upside down. A memoir titled *Did I Ever Have Children?* features a mother who starts Dickens's *A Tale of Two Cities* from the first page every time she picks up the novel.[115] Contrary to Frank Kermode's contention that "it is one of the great charms of books that they have to end," for readers with dementia, books never have to end.[116]

The authors of filial memoirs invariably begin by reminiscing about being read to in their childhoods before disclosing that they now read to their parents. Sophie's children began reading to her after she found herself forgetting the beginnings of novels.[117] A father whose impressions of Eeyore once brought his children to the brink of tears before bedtime eventually found himself listening to his daughter read the Bible.[118] One daughter read so many stories to a parent that she began referring to herself as Scheherazade.[119] A parent's declining literacy may force children to confront what therapists call the "ambiguous loss" that occurs when a loved one is physically present but psychologically absent.[120] Alex Witchel recognized her mother's cognitive decline after watching her struggle to get through an issue of *Time* magazine—another case of Struldbrugg-itis. "I start reading something," her mother explained, "but by the time I get to the end of a paragraph, I can't remember how it started."[121] Similarly, Faith Marshall accepted her mother's diagnosis only after watching her read a book without realizing that it was the wrong one. As the grieving daughter lamented, "My mother, the avid reader, was gone."[122]

Andrea Gillies takes a less sentimental perspective, depicting in unflinching detail the cognitive decline of her parents-in-law. But Gillies's memoir similarly equates loss of brain function with loss of self. The question underpinning Gillies's diary entries charting the degeneration of "Nancy" (a pseudonym) from doting grandmother into foul-mouthed, aggressive paranoiac: At what stage does a person with dementia cease to be themselves? Thus, Nancy's inability to recognize letters is taken to be the sign of a more profound loss of identity. "Your mother can't read; she can't read anymore," Gillies tells her husband after watching Nancy run her finger over the brass letters outside the house. "It's stunning because it's so absolute, so concrete a loss."[123] It is tempting to find metaphorical significance in the way Nancy surreptitiously dumps her supper into the bookcase—an entire row of books obliterated by sausages and vegetables as the vinaigrette bleeds into the pages of an Edith Wharton novel. As we saw happen to John Bayley, reader's block within the family tends to be contagious: Gillies, a novelist, finds herself unable to read novels now that the demands of caretaking thwart any attempt to escape to imaginary worlds.

STILL READING

The dementia memoir might strike you as an oxymoron. The very term "memoir" points toward the remembrance of things past as the genre's defining trait. How can people who struggle to recall events, to know what they have written, or even to use language fluently be expected to tell their own stories? At least one memoir begins with a note excusing its repetitiveness or, to put it politely, "dementia-friendly" qualities by an author who could not remember what she had written—a case of memoir lapsing into re-memoir.[124]

Dementia poses a unique challenge to narrative representation since the speakers have lost what many people consider to be essential to the conception of selfhood.[125] As Anne Davis Basting asks, "Is a 'self' possible when the ability to construct narrative through memory is broken?"[126] Dementia is an inevitable touchstone among bioethical debates over what constitutes personhood.[127] Philosophers have long insisted that memory is essential to the constitution of identity and to maintaining psychological continuity: no memory, no self. Memories shape the narratives we tell in an attempt to make sense of our lives as part of what Charles Taylor calls "an unfolding story."[128]

Memory loss is what distinguishes dementia narratives from those about other terminal illnesses. The authors of dementia narratives know all too well that they risk losing their very standing as persons in what Stephen Post calls a "hypercognitive culture" that values rationality over other attributes.[129] Writing a memoir about dementia thus represents a refusal to be dismissed as a nonperson. Instead, these narratives propose alternative ways of conceptualizing identity that are not defined by memory. If memoirs about aging typically celebrate the pleasures of rereading books, the dementia memoir shares the lessons learned from failing to reread them.[130] Losing the ability to read print may seem like no big deal. After all, it is a mechanical skill that can easily be replaced by surrogate activities such as listening to audiobooks or text-to-speech software. But, as this book has repeatedly demonstrated, print reading is rarely thought of as a mechanical skill by readers themselves. Instead, many former readers continue to think of it as a crucial attribute of their identity. As Thomas DeBaggio asks in *Losing My Mind*, "Am I anything without my memory and the simple skills of reading and writing I learned in childhood?"[131]

Adults who have read for their entire life may struggle to accept their new identity as a nonreader. The journalist Kate Swaffer, for one, found reading increasingly pointless. As she laments in her memoir *What the Hell*

Happened to My Brain?, "I read then I forget; I read, I take notes, and then I forget; I read, I highlight and take notes, and I still forget."[132] In fact, that very line may have been forgotten since she repeats it a few chapters later. Notetaking made little difference, for Swaffer resembles no one so much as the character in Lydia Davis's *Almost No Memory* who has a shelf lined with notebooks commenting on "what she had read but did not remember reading."[133] As a formerly avid reader, Swaffer finds the condition of postliteracy awkward, demeaning, and even threatening. Reading about her condition, the only form of therapy that she finds soothing, is the one option closed off to her. Her memoir is as much about the negative feelings generated by dementia as the symptoms themselves. Throughout the mourning period, she writes, her sole consolation is that she usually forgets why she's been crying in the first place: The book is less a memoir than an anti-memoir.

The prospect of losing the ability to read may be worse than actually losing it. For Christine Bryden, the most distressing part of being diagnosed with dementia at the age of forty-six was not knowing exactly how long her memory would hold out. Reading became increasingly difficult for Bryden as she struggled to follow lines, remember names, and keep track of stories. "Have I read this before?" was inevitably Bryden's first question about a book, though it was a moot one since she would not remember the plot either way. A silver lining: Memory loss made reading a book for the second time feel like reading it for the first. Bryden resisted the slow decline of her memory through speed reading. "Mostly I skim read, as otherwise I can't grasp the thread of the story," Bryden explained.

> If I go too slow, I forget what has just gone before, so I need to go fast to make the story somehow hang together. It seems as if there are just too many words to put together and make sense, and not enough space inside my head to sort the words into a story and to hang onto it long enough to follow the plot.[134]

Just as the publishers mentioned earlier in this chapter sought to reduce the number of words on the page, skimming enables readers to reduce the number of words that reach the eye. Such compensatory techniques can be effective but also exhausting. The manual labor of taking notes, for instance, drove Bryden to seek her own way out from Aleksandr Solzhenitsyn's *Gulag Archipelago*. For readers with dementia, escapism usually means shutting the book.

Few are in a better position to preserve memories than a professional historian. Diagnosed with Alzheimer's at fifty-five, Cary Smith Henderson continued teaching history for two years before waning literacy forced him into early retirement. He found himself sitting for hours trying to read a single page. Yet Henderson, a historian to the end, could still use a pocket tape recorder to capture the phenomenological experience of reader's block. According to Henderson's testimony, words wouldn't stand still, wavering and moving around the page, just out of his grasp: "[T]hey can be over yonder and over yonder and I can't catch them."[135] Words began to serve less as a means of communication than as an obstacle to it. As Henderson explained,

> I couldn't read a book if I had to. I tried very many times to actually read a book, even a small book. But the printed word is something that I find very puzzling. I can see the letters and I can halfway understand what they're all about, but if I try to put the letters in a logical sequence, I'll probably not be able to read.[136]

Dementia effectively turned Henderson into a historian who was shut out from the historical record.

Frustration drove other retirees to give up reading altogether. A man named Bill edited a magazine for the Foreign Service Division of the United States Information Agency before an Alzheimer's diagnosis brought his career to an end. Despite a lifetime spent working with words, he began losing his place or forgetting what was on the page unless he read at an exasperatingly slow pace. Instead of adapting, though, he preferred avoiding books altogether since they only highlighted the extent of his cognitive decline. Or as he put it, "Trying to read just tells me how bad I am."[137] For readers with dementia, the hermeneutic circle can feel more like a square.

A common response to being diagnosed with a terminal illness is to read everything available on the subject. Dementia patients seldom have this option, of course. Despite holding a PhD, Richard Taylor began forgetting information as fast as he could read it. Nor were handwritten notes helpful since he couldn't make sense of them afterward. After Taylor attended an Alzheimer's support group at which nearly half the attendees admitted that they could no longer read, he initially thought to himself, "How can you forget to read? What must life be like if you can't read? Why aren't they more upset that they can't read?"[138] He found out soon enough that postliteracy was even more complicated than illiteracy, though, and Taylor would go on to distinguish between knowing *how* to read and *being able* to read. In his case, he understood words, grammar, and the protocols of reading, after all, and could still make sense of street signs, instructions, and the like. What he could not do was understand an entire newspaper article, even after multiple attempts. As he explains in his memoir *Alzheimer's from the Inside Out*, "I know how to read! I just can't."[139]

Similarly conflicted responses suggest that dementia may have less to do with stopping reading altogether than adapting to new ways of doing it. Wendy Mitchell used to avoid looking at the dog-eared book on her bedside table ("the characters stuck in a storyline that hasn't moved on") because it reminded her of how she used to spend evenings.[140] The notion of a "page-turner" means little to someone who cannot remember what was on the previous page. As Mitchell explained, "I've found myself reading and re-reading the same few pages, the plot never quite sticking in my head until I've given up altogether."[141] Getting lost in a book takes on an entirely new meaning for readers affected by memory loss. Yet Mitchell found middle ground between the stark alternatives of literacy and illiteracy by switching from novels to short stories, a genre whose brevity was better suited to her shrinking attention span. Memory loss might even have made her a more attentive reader by getting her to notice formal elements that had previously been subordinated to the thrust of the story; she found herself "delighting in the words on the page instead of the plot itself."[142] Reading for the page rather than the plot allowed Mitchell to carry on reading by revising her ideas about what she thought reading should be.

Fictional narratives have similarly tracked changes to the way people with dementia read.[143] The neuroscientist-turned-novelist Lisa Genova traces dementia's impact with forensic precision in *Still Alice*, a fictional narrative about a Harvard psychology professor who is slowly losing her memory.[144] Dr. Alice Howland's diagnosis of early onset Alzheimer's at the age of fifty follows disquieting episodes of forgetfulness that go beyond memory lapses. The novel moves from an opening paragraph in which Howland reads the same sentence three times without understanding it to the final pages in which she fails to recognize a book that she herself has written.[145] The pages in between these scenes of reader's block log the down-ward trajectory from the patient's point of view—an increasingly limited third-person perspective. Expertise in psycholinguistics makes Howland's gradual loss of language all the more distressing; she cannot even understand her own suicide note.

Written by a neuroscientist in prose best described as clinical, Genova's novel might be thought of as the fictional equivalent of a diagnostic chart. The novel records Howland's cognitive decline symptom by symptom in a way that could apply to anyone with Alzheimer's. Shortly after Howland completes a questionnaire with categories like "Has given up reading," we witness the symptom's impact over her life:

> Reading was fast becoming a heartbreaking chore. She had to reread pages over and over to retain the continuity of the thesis or narrative, and if she put the book down for any length of time, she had to go back sometimes a full chapter to find the thread again.[146]

Diminishing literacy steadily undermines Howland's ambition to read the classics while there is still time. She lasts only a few pages into Shakespeare's *King Lear*, an aging king beset by his own memory problems, and accidentally leaves *Moby Dick* in the microwave, leaving her little choice but to settle for watching the film adaptions instead. Reader's block interferes with Howland's ability to make sense of her own prose, too. When giving a plenary speech at the Dementia Care Conference, this once-commanding speaker avoids looking up from the words on the script since she will inevitably lose her place. The film adaption of *Still Alice* shows Howland marking off each line with a highlighter to keep track of which ones have already been read (Figure 11).

Yet the novel's popularity among people with dementia points toward a more complicated story of decline. Reading *Still Alice* (or at least watching the film adaptation) was for a time a common reference point among people diagnosed with dementia. For instance, Genova's novel became the first work of fiction added to the UK's Reading Well Books on Prescription list of titles intended to support people with dementia.[147] Anecdotal evidence suggests that *Still Alice* met a demand for personal stories reflecting the lived experience of cognitive decline. Greg O'Brien, for one, compared reading the novel to looking into a mirror: "I was Alice, *sans* the dress."[148] And Wendy Mitchell read the novel three times (even if each of those times felt like the first time).[149]

FIGURE 11. Alice Howland (played by Julianne Moore in the film adaptation of *Still Alice*) using a highlighter while speaking at a conference to avoid losing her place on the page.

Still Alice (Sony Pictures Classics, 2014).

They are among the many people with dementia who can still read novels portraying how they will one day no longer be capable of reading novels—or of remembering that they had ever read the novel *Still Alice* in the first place. But, until that day arrives, and possibly after, these readers with dementia—or any of the other memory disorders covered by this chapter—will keep turning to narratives as a source of pleasure, just like other readers do. For whatever else these individuals may be doing, they are still reading.

Epilogue

THIS BOOK SET OUT TO CHANGE the way we think about reading. Whereas reading is often taken to be a straightforward activity, closer inspection reveals the term to cover an array of disparate activities that have no single defining feature in common. *Reader's Block* has marshaled together atypical styles of reading to show it to be a more varied phenomenon than is usually acknowledged. These instances call for an expansive definition of reading that would extend to the diverse ways people interact with texts beyond a restrictive understanding of the process exclusively in terms of the decoding, comprehension, and interpretation of verbal symbols. Building on a key insight of the neurodiversity movement, which recognizes the value of different forms of cognition, I propose that we have much to gain from paying attention to methods of interacting with print that have been dismissed as pathological, aberrant, or "nonreading." The six types of reader's block singled out here—dyslexia, hyperlexia, alexia, synesthesia, hallucinations, and dementia—bring into view aspects of reading that tend to go unnoticed when that process functions smoothly. Thinking about reading in terms of a spectrum capable of accommodating the full range of behaviors documented throughout this book can therefore help all of us achieve a richer understanding of what it means to read.

My alternative history of reading has sought to recover the testimonies of those "unideal" or neurodivergent readers whose stories have been left out of the prevailing histories of reading. Accounts of this sort take on the formidable task of trying to communicate the phenomenological experience of what it feels like to read in unconventional ways. As the philosopher Gillian Rose observed of growing up with dyslexia, "Reading was never just reading."[1] In contrast to fluent readers, for whom brains and bodies work in harmony to make sense of the page, the readers featured here confront the page with brains and bodies in tension or outright conflict—an outcome that will be unsurprising to anyone who has paused to consider the intricacy of the neurological foundation to reading and, consequently, how many opportunities there are for something to go wrong. Cases of reader's block demonstrate the ways the brain, for better or worse, can influence, interfere with, or interrupt the reading process—what I've called "reading against the brain." Yet this book also cautions against viewing reading differences in overly negative terms since these alternative reading processes can have advantages as well. As we have seen, reading continues to feature prominently in the life of many people affected by reader's block, even if they must resort to alternative ways of doing it—a situation better expressed by the phrase "reading along with the brain."

A goal of this book has been to challenge the widespread assumption that there is a standard approach to reading. This epilogue is no exception. Those of you reading this section of the book last should know better than to presume that other readers will necessarily be working their way through it sequentially, too. For all I know, you might be reading my book backwards. While it is a good thing that people who find literacy challenging are no longer referred to as "backwards" readers, there are individuals who literally do read backwards. Medical journals from the turn of the twentieth century reported numerous cases of people reading in reverse (apprehending "God" as "dog," for example), inadvertently moving from right to left or from the end of a sentence to the beginning.[2] One woman who was asked to read looked down at the lower righthand corner of the page and then began pronouncing the words backwards.[3] While most of you have been reading *Reader's Block*, some of you may be reading *kcolB s'redaeR*.

My history of reading and neurodiversity has made the case for an inclusive understanding of the term "reading." The introduction conveniently deferred the challenge of defining the term in favor of accumulating examples demonstrating just how many ways there are of doing it: a bottom-up rather than top-down approach to understanding the nature of reading.

My aim has been less to offer a new definition of reading than to encourage people to recognize the full range of activities that might be covered by the term. To that end, the phrase "reader's block" applies not only to the episodes of neurodivergent reading documented throughout this book but also to people's reluctance to recognize alternative ways of doing it as forms of reading.

Tellingly, the people who know the most about reading will usually be the first to acknowledge the term's elasticity. As literacy researcher James Maxwell observed nearly half a century ago, "It seems easier to write a book about reading than to define it."[4] Maxwell's essay presciently identified the terminological confusion characteristic of many discussions about reading today: the fact that we use the same term with different and even conflicting meanings. Schoolchildren sounding out the words in *The Very Hungry Caterpillar* and literary critics wending their way through *Moby Dick* are performing very different cognitive activities even though the same term will be used in both cases. Disputes over what counts as reading should begin by acknowledging the fluidity of the term itself.

There is no need to propose a new definition of reading since we already have plenty of serviceable ones. These range from elaborate, if unwieldy, formulations that attempt to cover every permutation to concise, if strategically vague, ones that would seem to cover a whole lot more than just reading. Maxwell himself tried to formulate a comprehensive definition, breaking down the term into the three distinct categories of "Reading C" (content), "Reading R" (reader), and "Reading P" (process). More succinct formulations range from Rudolf Flesch's classic definition of reading as "getting meaning from certain combinations of letters" to recent accounts of it as a form of "thinking guided by print."[5] Each of these definitions has benefits and limitations depending on the situation. Their usefulness will depend on whether the goal is to delimit what qualifies as reading or, conversely, to recognize the multifarious ways people engage with print. I am calling for existing definitions to be used not only to figure out what types of behavior to exclude but also to accommodate alternative ways of doing it. We don't need more definitions of reading. We need to use the definitions we already have with greater generosity.

For me, the most useful accounts of reading leave space for various ways of doing it. Maryanne Wolf's definition of reading as "the multiple perceptual, cognitive, linguistic, affective, and physiological processes involved in the act of decoding and comprehending written language," for example, comes close to capturing the full assortment of activities brought into play when someone opens a book.[6] Yet this is true only if we interpret the wording loosely. A strict interpretation (decoding *and* comprehending) leaves out all sorts of activities covered by my book, whereas an accommodating one (decoding *and/or* comprehending) would admit a far greater range of bookish behaviors that may fall short of total understanding. Treating reading as a spectrum does not mean that a line can never be drawn between reading and nonreading. An elementary school teacher may be entirely justified in wanting to use a narrow definition to determine whether a child would benefit from additional support. But we should be equally mindful about using definitions in less restrictive ways to shift the focus from what sets various acts apart toward what they share. This book has presented one model for an inclusive understanding of reading that would accommodate the full panoply of reading or reading-like behaviors that historically have been denied recognition—you might even say blocked.

Expanding the term "reading" to cover unusual ways of doing it is not merely a matter of social justice. Everyone stands to benefit from the inclusive definition of reading promoted by this book, which confirms a fundamental principle of disability studies: Making people with disabilities part of the conversation can transform the way we think about a topic. The value of these voices is a point on which disability studies and the medical humanities (two fields that intersect under the more capacious banner of the health humanities) have come to agree. Many practitioners who once privileged clinical perspectives over the patient's viewpoint would no longer find contentious Oliver Sacks's cardinal rule that "one must always *listen* to the patient."[7] This advice applies to humanists, too. As we have seen from numerous examples of patients speaking back to medical authorities, the experiential knowledge of reader's block challenges many of our most basic assumptions about reading. The perspectives of people affected by cognitive differences effectively draw attention to aspects of the reading process that are rarely addressed by studies governed by a more limited understanding of the term. Above all, these testimonies convey the value reading might hold for people even when what they are doing does not look like reading.

Reader's Block is more than a history of people who can't read. It's also a history of people who read differently than other people do. My findings are meant to encourage book historians to revisit the historical record with an eye toward neurodiversity. Although an internal history of reading based on the cognitive processes of past readers may remain out of reach, as the field's founders predicted, this book has shown how forms of textual evidence such as anecdotes, personal testimonies, and scientific case studies can nevertheless impart a sense of the phenomenological experiences of neurodivergent readers or those for whom differences in competence may conceal differences in cognition. Spanning the earliest medical diagnoses of reading difficulties to modern-day memoirs written by patients themselves, my book supplies a historical framework in which to situate the testimonies of people affected by evolving attitudes toward literacy, intelligence, and disability. The recent surge in memoirs written from the perspective of people with disabilities has been described by G. Thomas Couser as one of the most significant developments in life writing; memoirs focused specifically on dyslexia, autism, dementia, and other neurological conditions offer an invaluable archive for anyone who wants to understand the impact of neurodiversity alongside other kinds of socioeconomic diversity.[8]

The arc of my study brings us up to the present moment in which digital media offer unprecedented access to the subjective experiences of people whose lives have been affected by cognitive differences (digital media have been especially beneficial to those autistic individuals who prefer online communication over face-to-face interactions). It will be the job of future historians to track these conversations proliferating across the internet, where the evidential challenge will be one of abundance rather than scarcity. Fortunately, they will have access to tools that did not exist before the digital era. Tomorrow's researchers will not have to settle for reading about neurological conditions since they will be able to experience those differences in perspective for themselves—or at least simulations that attempt to recreate the sensory experiences of reading from the viewpoint of someone with dyslexia, synesthesia, or other conditions.[9]

Neurodiversity should likewise be taken into account by disciplines oriented toward the present. The cognitive sciences have made enormous progress in helping us to move beyond a mystical conception of reading, as what the philosopher Henri Bergson once referred to as a form of "divination."[10] The analytical tools of neuroscience have proven particularly adept at making visible the hidden mental operations at work when someone opens a book. Yet literary cognitive theorists need to recognize how differ-ent cognitive profiles can influence the reading process if they want to avoid reductive models that fail to account for the full range of human experi-ence. For instance, the basic presupposition that verbal narratives generate imagery in the reader's mind should be qualified by the fact that some indi-viduals won't see any mental imagery at all whereas others will see images that bear little relation to the words on the page. In contrast to neurotypical readers for whom reading is associated with converting graphic symbols into meaning, atypical readers tend to get from them either too much or too little meaning. Such discrepancies reflect the complex nature of read-ing itself, which may be experienced differently by individual readers while simultaneously relying on a set of mental processes broadly shared among all readers. Factoring in both the continuities and discontinuities across dif-ferent reading styles should result in more accurate, robust, and potentially illuminating models than those predicated on the misguided notion of a universal reader.

Even expert readers have something to learn from those who do it in unfamiliar ways. If routine use makes the act of reading seem "deceptively knowable," in Leah Price's words, the examples featured throughout this book offer reminders of how much we still don't know about the process.[11] The tendency of literary critics to equate "reading" with interpretation ne-glects all the preceding steps that make interpretation possible in the first place. That process starts with perception itself. As one of the dyslexic read-ers featured in Chapter 1 invited us to consider: What would be the effect of skipping over everything in a novel but the dialogue? Unconventional ways of engaging with books direct attention to dimensions of the reading process that are usually taken for granted even though they can dramati-cally shape how people respond to texts. Specifically, attention, emotion, memory, perception, physiology, sensations, and mental imagery all influ-ence textual reception in ways that may vary from one individual to the next. Thinking about aspects of decoding and comprehension that usually go unnoticed, or at least unmentioned, can help literary critics recognize how these preliminary components of the interpretive process might con-tribute to their own aesthetic judgments.

The typical reader should leave this book knowing that there is no such thing as a "typical" reader. There are only lots of different ones who read in distinctive and highly specific ways. In this sense, every reader is atypical. The preceding examples of neurodivergent readers have sought to raise awareness about the full spectrum of reading methods while at the same time encouraging people to reflect on where their own preferences match up with or deviate from those of other readers—as I have found myself doing while writing this book. This knowledge may help people appreciate aspects of the reading process that tend to be kept private. Although one motive for writing this book was the sense that my own peculiar reading habits set me apart from other people, subsequent conversations have left me with the impression that almost no one seems to think that their reading is entirely "normal." Anyone who feels this way should take comfort from knowing that you are not alone.

Acknowledgments

THIS HISTORY OF READING COULD not have been written without the help of other readers. My thanks first of all to everyone who shared with me their personal experiences of reader's block. My next debt of gratitude is to Garrett Stewart, Helen Small, Jay Clayton, Herbert Tucker, and Francis O'Gorman for generously supporting funding applications to complete this book. I'm grateful to other colleagues for advice on sections of the manuscript: Joni Adamson, Paul Armstrong, Brian Boyd, Eleanor Courtemanche, Paul Fyfe, Christopher Krentz, Scott McCracken, Emily Silk, Jane Thrailkill, and Tom Wright. Ralph Savarese kindly took the time to meet with me and critique an early draft of Chapter 2. I would like to thank Heather Tilley and Terra Vance for sensitivity readings.

My thinking benefited from conversations and correspondences with Weihong Bao, Andrea Brady, Christopher Cannon, Steven Connor, Louise Creechan, Stephen Donovan, Robert Douglas-Fairhurst, Simonetta Falasca-Zamponi, Mary Favret, Anna Fenton-Hathaway, Matt ffytche, Melissa Shields Jenkins, Ling Hon Lam, Christina Lupton, Deidre Lynch, Bonnie Mak, John McGowan, Leah Price, Sophie Ratcliffe, Cate Reilly, Elaine Scarry, Sally Shuttleworth, Gillian Silverman, Matthew J. Smith, Priscilla Wald, and Susan Zieger. My gratitude extends to those who shared expertise: Ben Alderson-Day, Ric Burns, Luke Dittrich, Dominic ffytche,

Alison Hale, Alex Leff, Evelyne Mercure, Brenda Rapp, Julia Simner, and the Synesthesia and SHARP email lists. For ongoing support, I wish to thank my colleagues in the School of English and Drama at QMUL. Finally, a big thank you to my editor Erica Wetter and her team at Stanford University Press (especially Caroline McKusick, Emily Smith, Jennifer Gordon, and Meg Wallace) along with the anonymous reviewers who offered helpful advice on the manuscript.

This book also profited from the chance to present my work at the "Sensorium of Reading" seminar at Johns Hopkins University; "Touch This Page! A Symposium on Ability, Access, and the Archive" at Harvard University; the Franklin Humanities Institute's Health Humanities Lab at Duke University; the Victorian Graduate Seminar at the University of Oxford; and at the University of North Carolina, the University of Virginia, and Wake Forest University. The chapter on alexia was enriched by conversations at the "Literature, Education, and the Sciences of the Mind in Britain and America, 1850–1950" conference at the University of Kent and the North American Victorian Studies Association (NAVSA) conference in Florence.

A sabbatical at the National Humanities Center gave me the chance to do much of the research for this book. I'm grateful to the staff and fellows of 2018–19 for their comradery. The NHC librarians deserve a special mention for helping me to track down all sorts of unusual requests: Thank you Brooke Andrade, Sarah Harris, and Joe Milillo. I'm grateful as well for resources supplied by the British Library, Wellcome Library, Senate House Library, Queen Mary University of London Library, Chapel Hill Public Library, Royal Greenwich Libraries, and UCL Library Special Collections. Versions of Chapters 3 and 4 appeared in *Literature and Medicine* 37.2 (2019): 251–277 and *Configurations* 28.3 (2020): 333–358 and have been reprinted here with permission from Johns Hopkins University Press.

My final thanks go to friends and family for their love and support. Victoria, Joseph, and Coco, you were wonderful company throughout the lockdowns here in London.

Notes

INTRODUCTION

1. Charles Dickens, *Great Expectations*, ed. Margaret Cardwell (Oxford: Oxford University Press, 2008), 42.

2. Fran Peek, *The Real Rain Man: Kim Peek*, ed. Stevens W. Anderson (Salt Lake City: Harkness, 1996), 16.

3. Fran Peek and Lisa Hanson, *The Life and Message of the Real Rain Man: The Journey of a Mega-Savant* (Port Chester, NY: Dude Publishing, 2008), 53.

4. The term "neurodiversity" has a complex genealogy in blogs, journalism, memoirs, websites, and scholarship. One of the most accessible introductions to the concept is Thomas Armstrong, *The Power of Neurodiversity: Unleashing the Advantages of Your Differently Wired Brain* (Cambridge, MA: Da Capo, 2010).

5. Laura Otis, *Rethinking Thought: Inside the Minds of Creative Scientists and Artists* (Oxford: Oxford University Press, 2015), 3.

6. See, for example, V. S. Ramachandran, *The Tell-Tale Brain: A Neuroscientist's Quest for What Makes Us Human* (New York: W. W. Norton, 2011), 46.

7. Richard E. Cytowic and David M. Eagleman, *Wednesday Is Indigo Blue: Discovering the Brain of Synesthesia* (Cambridge, MA: MIT Press, 2011), 37.

8. Jonathan Swift, *Gulliver's Travels*, ed. Robert DeMaria Jr. (New York: Penguin, 2001), 197.

9. Ludwig Wittgenstein, *Philosophical Investigations*, trans. G. E. M. Anscombe, 2nd ed. (Oxford: Blackwell, 1958), 32 / §67.

10. The neurological forms of reader's block discussed by this book should be distinguished from previous uses of the term to describe, for instance: psychological obstacles in Eve Kosofsky Sedgwick and Adam Frank, "Shame in the Cybernetic

Fold: Reading Silvan Tomkins," in *Shame and Its Sisters: A Silvan Tomkins Reader*, ed. Sedgwick and Frank (Durham: Duke University Press, 1995), 1–28; the accumulation of anecdotes collated by David Markson, *Reader's Block* (Normal, IL: Dalkey Archive, 1996); the antisocial uses of books in Leah Price, "Reader's Block," *Victorian Studies* 46.2 (2004): 231–242; or the diminished motivation associated with age in Geoff Dyer, "Reader's Block," in *Working the Room: Essays and Reviews, 1999–2010* (Edinburgh: Canongate, 2010), 343–347.

11. Alberto Manguel, *A History of Reading* (New York: Penguin, 1996), 39.

12. Daniel C. Dennett, *From Bacteria to Bach and Back: The Evolution of Minds* (London: Allen Lane, 2017), 75.

13. Mark Seidenberg, *Language at the Speed of Sight: How We Read, Why So Many Can't, and What Can Be Done About It* (New York: Basic Books, 2017), 3. See also Daniel T. Willingham, *The Reading Mind: A Cognitive Approach to Understanding How the Mind Reads* (San Francisco: Jossey-Bass, 2017).

14. Stanislas Dehaene, *Reading in the Brain: The New Science of How We Read* (London: Penguin, 2009), 219.

15. Steven Roger Fischer, *A History of Reading* (London: Reaktion, 2005), 11.

16. Fischer, *A History of Reading*, 343.

17. William Morris, *News from Nowhere*, ed. David Leopold (Oxford: Oxford University Press, 2003), 25.

18. Philip B. Gough and Michael L. Hillinger, "Learning to Read: An Unnatural Act," *Bulletin of the Orton Society* 30.1 (1980): 179–195.

19. Maryanne Wolf, *Proust and the Squid: The Story and Science of the Reading Brain* (New York: HarperCollins, 2007), 3. On the brain's repurposing of neuronal networks for reading, see Dehaene, *Reading in the Brain.*

20. Sigmund Freud, *On Aphasia: A Critical Study* (New York: International Universities Press, 1953), 75–76.

21. Frank Smith, *Reading Without Nonsense*, 2nd ed. (New York: Teachers College Press, 1985), 93.

22. Anne Castles, Kathleen Rastle, and Kate Nation, "Ending the Reading Wars: Reading Acquisition from Novice to Expert," *Psychological Science in the Public Interest* 19.1 (2018): 5–51, at 6; Keith Rayner et al., "How Psychological Science Informs the Teaching of Reading," *Psychological Science in the Public Interest* 2.2 (2001): 31–74, at 34.

23. Sally Andrews, "Individual Differences in Skilled Visual Word Recognition and Reading: The Role of Lexical Quality," in *Visual Word Recognition, Volume 2: Meaning and Context, Individuals and Development*, ed. James S. Adelman (Hove, UK: Psychology Press, 2012), 151.

24. On the move away from hermeneutics among literary studies, see Rachel Sagner Buurma and Matthew K. Gold, "Contemporary Proposals About Reading in the Digital Age," in *A Companion to Literary Theory*, ed. David H. Richter (Chichester: Wiley Blackwell, 2018), 139–150; Deidre Shauna Lynch and Evelyne Ender, "Introduction—Time for Reading," *PMLA* 133.5 (2018): 1073–1082; and "Introduction:

Reading Spaces," *PMLA* 134.1 (2019): 9–17; and Matthew Rubery and Leah Price, eds., *Further Reading* (Oxford: Oxford University Press, 2020).

25. N. Katherine Hayles, *How We Think: Digital Media and Contemporary Technogenesis* (Chicago: University of Chicago Press, 2012), 79; Mara Mills, "What Should We Call Reading?" *Flow* (December 3, 2012): https://www.flowjournal.org/2012/12/what-should-we-call-reading/

26. McLuhan describes his elective hemineglect in "My Reading Habits (1967)," YouTube (August 29, 2012): https://www.youtube.com/watch?v=Xi8ULoGh8DY

27. Jenni A. Ogden, *Trouble in Mind: Stories from a Neuropsychologist's Casebook* (New York: Oxford University Press, 2012), 90.

28. Ludwig Wittgenstein, *The Blue and Brown Books* (New York: Harper & Row, 1958), 19–20.

29. Sarah McNicol and Liz Brewster, eds., *Bibliotherapy* (London: Facet, 2018).

30. John Stuart Mill, *Autobiography*, ed. John M. Robson (New York: Penguin, 1989).

31. Robert Burton, *The Anatomy of Melancholy*, ed. Holbrook Jackson (London: J. M. Dent, 1932), 38.

32. James Boswell, *Life of Johnson*, ed. R. W. Chapman (Oxford: Oxford University Press, 2008), 690.

33. Andrew Solomon, *The Noonday Demon: An Atlas of Depression* (New York: Scribner, 2001), 99.

34. Quoted in Siegfried Wenzel, *The Sin of Sloth: Acedia in Medieval Thought and Literature* (Chapel Hill: University of North Carolina Press, 1967), 28.

35. Raymond Klibansky, Erwin Panofsky, and Fritz Saxl, *Saturn and Melancholy* (London: Nelson, 1964), 85; Stanley W. Jackson, *Melancholia and Depression: From Hippocratic Times to Modern Times* (New Haven: Yale University Press, 1986), 191.

36. N. S. Sutherland, *Breakdown: A Personal Crisis and a Medical Dilemma*, 2nd ed. (Oxford: Oxford University Press, 1998), 3.

37. Sutherland, *Breakdown*, 3.

38. Matt Haig, *Reasons to Stay Alive* (Edinburgh: Canongate, 2016), 130. Emphasis in original.

39. Daniel Smith, *Monkey Mind: A Memoir of Anxiety* (New York: Simon & Schuster, 2013), 136.

40. Kay R. Jamison, *An Unquiet Mind: A Memoir of Moods and Madness* (London: Picador, 2015), 37.

41. Jamison, *Unquiet Mind*, 95.

42. Jamison, *Unquiet Mind*, 98.

43. Susanne Antonetta, *A Mind Apart: Travels in a Neurodiverse World* (New York: Jeremy P. Tarcher, 2007), 2.

44. R. G. Bickford et al., "Reading Epilepsy: Clinical and Electroencephalographic Studies of a New Syndrome," *Transactions of the American Neurological Association* 81 (1956): 100–102.

45. Herbert Spencer, *An Autobiography*, 2 vols. (London: Williams and Norgate, 1904), 1:467.

46. Spencer, *An Autobiography*, 1:474. For a fuller account of Spencer's symptoms, see Martin N. Raitiere, "Did Herbert Spencer Have Reading Epilepsy?" *Journal of the History of the Neurosciences* 20.4 (2011): 357–367.

47. Abena D. Osei-Lah et al., "Focal Reading Epilepsy—A Rare Variant of Reading Epilepsy: A Case Report," *Epilepsia* 51.11 (2010): 2352–2356.

48. M. Koutroumanidis et al., "The Variants of Reading Epilepsy. A Clinical and Video-EEG Study of 17 Patients with Reading-Induced Seizures," *Brain* 121.8 (1998): 1409–1427, at 1416.

49. Donald F. Weaver, "Font Specific Reading-Induced Seizures," *Clinical Neurology and Neurosurgery* 125 (2014): 210–211, at 210.

50. Quoted in Oliver Sacks, *An Anthropologist on Mars: Seven Paradoxical Tales* (London: Picador, 1995), 81.

51. John Wiltshire, *Samuel Johnson in the Medical World: The Doctor and the Patient* (Cambridge: Cambridge University Press, 1991), 29–34.

52. Samuel Johnson, *Johnsonian Miscellanies*, ed. George Birkbeck Hill, 2 vols. (Oxford: Clarendon, 1897), 2:297. Robert DeMaria Jr. discusses additional accounts in *Samuel Johnson and the Life of Reading* (Baltimore: Johns Hopkins University Press, 1997).

53. Quoted in Margaret Cheney, *Tesla: Man Out of Time* (New York: Simon & Schuster, 1981), 39.

54. See, for example, statement 42 in Ezio Sanavio, "Obsessions and Compulsions: The Padua Inventory," *Behaviour Research and Therapy* 26.2 (1988): 169–177.

55. Marc Summers, *Everything in Its Place: My Trials and Triumphs with Obsessive Compulsive Disorder* (New York: Penguin Putnam, 1999), 72–73.

56. Amy Wilensky, *Passing for Normal: Tourette's, OCD and Growing Up Crazy* (London: Simon & Schuster, 2006), 151.

57. Summers, *Everything in Its Place*, 42.

58. Catherine Malabou, *The New Wounded: From Neurosis to Brain Damage* (New York: Fordham University Press, 2012), 9.

59. Tracy Kidder, *Old Friends* (London: Granta, 1994), 30.

60. Manguel, *A History of Reading*, 293.

61. Robert McCrum, *My Year Off* (London: Picador, 1998), 75.

62. See, for example, John T. MacCurdy, *War Neuroses* (Cambridge: Cambridge University Press, 1918), 52.

63. Adhémar Gelb and Kurt Goldstein, "Analysis of a Case of Figural Blindness," in *A Source Book of Gestalt Psychology*, ed. Willis D. Ellis (New York: Harcourt, Brace, 1938), 317.

64. "Minerva," *British Medical Journal* 318 (1999): 1018.

65. According to one study, a group tasked with reading novels upside down three times per week achieved dramatic gains in fluency. Elsa Ahlén et al., "Learning to Read Upside-Down: A Study of Perceptual Expertise and Its Acquisition," *Experimental Brain Research* 232.3 (2014): 1025–1036.

66. Quoted in Darold A. Treffert, *Islands of Genius: The Bountiful Mind of the Autistic, Acquired, and Sudden Savant* (London: Jessica Kingsley, 2010), 200.

67. Kara L. Swanson, *I'll Carry the Fork! Recovering a Life After Brain Injury* (Los Altos, CA: Rising Star, 1999), 18. More firsthand accounts are available in the Routledge series *After Brain Injury: Survivor Stories*: https://www.routledge.com/After-Brain-Injury-Survivor-Stories/book-series/ABI

68. Barbara K. Lipska and Elaine McArdle, *The Neuroscientist Who Lost Her Mind: My Tale of Madness and Recovery* (Boston: Houghton Mifflin Harcourt, 2018), 139.

69. Tom Lubbock, *Until Further Notice, I Am Alive* (London: Granta, 2012), 22.

70. Lubbock, *Until Further Notice*, 134.

71. Lubbock, *Until Further Notice*, 129.

72. Marion Coutts, *The Iceberg: A Memoir* (London: Atlantic, 2015), 107.

73. Quoted in Oliver W. Sacks, *Awakenings*, rev. ed (London: Picador, 2012), 88.

74. Sacks, *Awakenings*, 120.

75. Sacks, *Awakenings*, 132 fn 77.

76. Sacks, *Awakenings*, 212.

77. Ogden, *Trouble in Mind*, 227–249.

78. On the potential benefits of having a disability, see H-Dirksen L. Bauman and Joseph J. Murray, eds., *Deaf Gain: Raising the Stakes for Human Diversity* (Minneapolis: University of Minnesota Press, 2014).

79. Quoted in Barbara A. Wilson, *Case Studies in Neuropsychological Rehabilitation* (New York: Oxford University Press, 1999), 206.

80. Roger Chartier and Guglielmo Cavallo, "Introduction," in *A History of Reading in the West*, ed. Guglielmo Cavallo and Roger Chartier (Cambridge: Polity Press, 1999), 4.

81. Karin Littau, *Theories of Reading: Books, Bodies, and Bibliomania* (Cambridge: Polity Press, 2006), 10.

82. *Reading Sites: Social Difference and Reader Response*, edited by Patrocinio Schweickart and Elizabeth A. Flynn (New York: MLA, 2004) exemplifies the field's reorientation toward cultural variations. For overviews to the field, see Shafquat Towheed, Rosalind Crone, and Katie Halsey, eds., *The History of Reading: A Reader* (London: Routledge, 2011); and Mary Hammond and Jonathan Rose, eds., *The Edinburgh History of Reading*, 4 vols. (Edinburgh: Edinburgh University Press, 2020).

83. Chartier and Cavallo, "Introduction," 3.

84. Robert Darnton, "First Steps Toward a History of Reading," *Australian Journal of French Studies* 23.1 (1986): 5–30, at 15.

85. Darnton, "First Steps Toward a History of Reading," 7.

86. Representative approaches can be found in Lisa Zunshine, ed., *The Oxford Handbook of Cognitive Literary Studies* (New York: Oxford University Press, 2015). Useful discussions of reading through the lens of the cognitive sciences include Paul B. Armstrong, *Stories and the Brain: The Neuroscience of Narrative* (Baltimore: Johns Hopkins University Press, 2020); Elaine Auyoung, "What We Mean by Reading," *New Literary History* 51.1 (2020): 93–114; and Andrew Elfenbein, *The Gist of*

Reading (Stanford: Stanford University Press, 2018). These studies, valuable as they are, show minimal interest in neurodiversity (with the notable exception of Zunshine and Ralph Savarese's work on autism) and largely embrace universal cognitive models that do not vary from one reader to the next.

87. The phrase is used in Wolfgang Iser, *The Act of Reading: A Theory of Aesthetic Response* (London: Routledge & Kegan Paul, 1978), 29; and Jonathan Culler, *Structuralist Poetics: Structuralism, Linguistics and the Study of Literature* (London: Routledge & Kegan Paul, 1975), 124. Further discussion of this rhetorical figure can be found in Elizabeth Freund, *The Return of the Reader: Reader-Response Criticism* (London: Methuen, 1987).

88. See, for example, Gillian Silverman, "Neurodiversity and the Revision of Book History," *PMLA* 131.2 (2016): 307–323.

89. Oliver Sacks, *The Man Who Mistook His Wife for a Hat* (London: Picador, 1986), x.

90. Oliver Sacks, *On the Move: A Life* (New York: Alfred A. Knopf, 2016), 14.

91. Oliver Sacks, *The Mind's Eye* (London: Picador, 2010), 165. Sacks describes having suicidal thoughts in *On the Move*, 379.

92. Walter Benjamin, *Selected Writings, Volume 2: 1927–1934*, ed. Michael W. Jennings, Howard Eiland, and Gary Smith, trans. Rodney Livingstone and others (Cambridge, MA: Belknap, 1999), 123.

93. The most forceful critique can be found in Tom Shakespeare's review of Oliver Sacks's *An Anthropologist on Mars* in *Disability and Society* 11.1 (1996): 137–142. More measured appraisals include Leonard Cassuto, "Oliver Sacks and the Medical Case Narrative," in *Disability Studies: Enabling the Humanities*, eds. Sharon L. Snyder, Brenda Jo Brueggemann, and Rosemarie Garland-Thomson (New York: MLA, 2002): 118–130; and G. Thomas Couser, *Vulnerable Subjects: Ethics and Life Writing* (Ithaca: Cornell University Press, 2004), 74–122.

94. The importance of self-advocacy to the disability rights movement is captured by the title of James I. Charlton's *Nothing About Us Without Us: Disability Oppression and Empowerment* (Berkeley: University of California Press, 1998). On the value of personal testimony, see Arthur W. Frank, *The Wounded Storyteller: Body, Illness and Ethics* (Chicago: University of Chicago Press, 1995); and Anne Hudson Jones, "Reading Patients—Cautions and Concerns," *Literature and Medicine* 13.2 (1994): 190–200.

95. Brian Hurwitz discusses the critical role played by mediation among medical case studies in "Narrative Constructs in Modern Clinical Case Reporting," *Studies in History and Philosophy of Science* 62 (2017): 65–73.

96. Sacks, *Awakenings*, xxxi.

97. Robin Nunn, "Mere Anecdote: Evidence and Stories in Medicine," *Journal of Evaluation in Clinical Practice* 17.5 (2011): 920–926.

98. William St. Clair, *The Reading Nation in the Romantic Period* (Cambridge: Cambridge University Press, 2004), 5–6.

99. A formidable defense of the anecdote's utility can be found in Catherine Gallagher and Stephen Greenblatt, *Practicing New Historicism* (Chicago: University

of Chicago Press, 2000), 49–74. See also Daniel Allington, "On the Use of Anecdotal Evidence in Reception Study and the History of Reading," in *Reading in History: New Methodologies from the Anglo-American Tradition*, ed. Bonnie Gunzenhauser (London: Pickering and Chatto, 2010), 11–28.

100. Kathryn Montgomery Hunter, *Doctors' Stories: The Narrative Structure of Medical Knowledge* (Princeton: Princeton University Press, 1991), 75.

101. Aldous Huxley, *Point Counter Point* (New York: Modern Library, 1928), 465. On the relation between neurological speech disorders and literature, see Laura Salisbury, "Aphasic Modernism: Languages for Illness from a Confusion of Tongues," in *The Edinburgh Companion to the Critical Medical Humanities*, ed. Anne Whitehead and Angela Woods (Edinburgh: Edinburgh University Press, 2016), 444–462.

102. Huxley, *Point Counter Point*, 465.

103. Diane Price Herndl, "Disease Versus Disability: The Medical Humanities and Disability Studies," *PMLA* 120.2 (2005): 593–598. On the move toward the more encompassing label of "health humanities," which widens the scope beyond medical frameworks to the social, cultural, and historical dimensions affecting well-being, see Therese Jones et al., "The Almost Right Word: The Move from *Medical* to *Health* Humanities," *Academic Medicine* 92.7 (2017): 932–935.

104. For insightful reflections on the competing models of disability, see Tobin Siebers, *Disability Theory* (Ann Arbor: University of Michigan Press, 2008).

105. A brief note about the book's terminology: I have sought to use language respectful of people with disabilities and evolving standards of judgment while at the same time considering stylistic constraints. Concision motivates the use of identity-first terms like "dyslexic" or "dyslexic person" when the risk of offense is minimal, whereas person-first formulations have been used for phrases such as "person with dementia" for which there is no acceptable shorthand. Where possible, my choices have largely been guided by the precedents of and preferences expressed by people personally affected by these disabilities.

106. See especially Michael Bérubé, *The Secret Life of Stories: From Don Quixote to Harry Potter, How Understanding Intellectual Disability Transforms the Way We Read* (New York: NYU Press, 2016); G. Thomas Couser, *Vulnerable Subjects: Ethics and Life Writing* (Ithaca: Cornell University Press, 2004); Eva Feder Kittay, *Learning from My Daughter: The Value and Care of Disabled Minds* (New York: Oxford University Press, 2019); Ralph James Savarese, *See It Feelingly: Classic Novels, Autistic Readers, and the Schooling of a No-Good English Professor* (Durham: Duke University Press, 2018); and Siebers, *Disability Theory*.

107. Kate Brousseau and H. G Brainerd, *Mongolism: A Study of the Physical and Mental Characteristics of Mongolian Imbeciles* (Baltimore: Williams & Wilkins, 1928), 172.

108. Nigel Hunt, *The World of Nigel Hunt: The Diary of a Mongoloid Youth* (New York: Garrett, 1976), 23.

109. Bérubé, *The Secret Life of Stories*, 6–12.

110. Georgina Kleege, *Sight Unseen* (New Haven: Yale University Press, 1999), 167.

111. Siebers calls for disability studies to recognize both the negative and the positive aspects of disability in *Disability Theory*, 5; Susan Wendell and Tom Shakespeare criticize the field's neglect of the negative aspects of impairment in Wendell, "Unhealthy Disabled: Treating Chronic Illnesses as Disabilities," *Hypatia* 16.4 (2001): 17–33; and Shakespeare, "The Social Model of Disability," in *The Disability Studies Reader*, 4th ed., ed. Lennard J. Davis (New York: Routledge, 2013), 217–218. Christina Crosby writes explicitly, and movingly, about the experience of loss in *A Body, Undone: Living on After Great Pain* (New York: NYU Press, 2016); and Michael Davidson explores loss's critical potential in "Cleavings: Critical Losses in the Politics of Gain," *Disability Studies Quarterly* 36.2 (2016): https://dsq-sds.org/article/view/4287

112. Claudia L. Osborn, *Over My Head: A Doctor's Own Story of Head Injury from the Inside Looking Out* (Kansas City, MO: Andrews McMeel, 1998), 91.

113. William Empson, *Seven Types of Ambiguity*, 2nd ed. (Harmondsworth: Penguin, 1973), 32.

114. William James, *The Writings of William James: A Comprehensive Edition*, ed. John J. McDermott (Chicago: University of Chicago Press, 1977), 630.

115. Marcel Proust, *In the Shadow of Young Girls in Flower: In Search of Lost Time, Volume 2*, trans. James Grieve (London: Penguin, 2003), 378.

116. Vladimir Nabokov, *Pale Fire* (New York: Vintage, 1989), 289.

117. Quoted in William James, *The Principles of Psychology* (Cambridge, MA: Harvard University Press, 1983), 741. James is quoting from Moritz Lazarus, *Das Leben der Seele* (1857), 2:31.

118. Jeanne L. Lee, *Just Love Me: My Life Turned Upside-Down by Alzheimer's* (West Lafayette, IN: Purdue University Press, 2003), 26.

119. Barb Rentenbach and Lois Prislovsky, *Neurodiversity: A Humorous and Practical Guide to Living with ADHD, Anxiety, Autism, Dyslexia, the Gays, and Everyone Else* (Knoxville: Mule and Muse Productions, 2016).

CHAPTER 1

1. Macdonald Critchley, *The Dyslexic Child*, 2nd ed. (London: Heinemann Medical, 1970), 112.

2. A more comprehensive definition can be found in Jim Rose, *Identifying and Teaching Children and Young People with Dyslexia and Literacy Difficulties* (London: Department for Children, Schools and Families [DCSF], 2009), 28–34: https://webarchive.nationalarchives.gov.uk/20130321060616/https://www.education.gov.uk/publications/eOrderingDownload/00659-2009DOM-EN.pdf

3. Mark Seidenberg speaks of "the dyslexia spectrum" in *Language at the Speed of Sight: How We Read, Why So Many Can't, and What Can Be Done About It* (New York: Basic Books, 2017), 178.

4. See, for example, Thomas G. West, *In the Mind's Eye: Visual Thinkers, Gifted People with Dyslexia and Other Learning Difficulties, Computer Images, and the Ironies of Creativity* (Amherst, NY: Prometheus, 1997).

5. Sally E. Shaywitz, *Overcoming Dyslexia: A New and Complete Science-Based Program for Reading Problems at Any Level* (New York: Alfred A. Knopf, 2004), 116.

6. Maryanne Wolf with Stephanie Gottwald, *Tales of Literacy for the 21st Century* (Oxford: Oxford University Press, 2016), 3.

7. Rudolf Flesch, *Why Johnny Can't Read—And What You Can Do About It* (New York: Harper & Brothers, 1955), 130.

8. Isaac Asimov, *In Memory Yet Green: The Autobiography of Isaac Asimov, 1920–1954* (New York: Doubleday, 1979), 48.

9. Charles Dickens, *Great Expectations*, ed. Margaret Cardwell (Oxford: Oxford University Press, 2008), 40.

10. Jean-Paul Sartre, *The Family Idiot: Gustave Flaubert, 1821–1857*, vol. 1 (Chicago: University of Chicago Press, 1981), 8.

11. Critchley, *The Dyslexic Child*, 97.

12. Janice Edwards, *The Scars of Dyslexia: Eight Case Studies in Emotional Reactions* (New York: Cassell, 1994); John Osmond, *The Reality of Dyslexia* (Cambridge, MA: Brookline, 1995); Shirley Kurnoff, ed., *The Human Side of Dyslexia: 142 Interviews with Real People Telling Real Stories* (Monterey, CA: Universal, 2001).

13. Many of these narratives belong in the category of "autobiographical collaborations" since they involve multiple authors. For more on this category, see Philippe Lejeune, *On Autobiography*, ed. Paul John Eakin, trans. Katherine Leary (Minneapolis: University of Minnesota Press, 1989), 186.

14. Eileen B. Simpson, *Reversals: A Personal Account of Victory over Dyslexia* (Boston: Houghton Mifflin, 1979), viii.

15. Peter A. Harrower, *The World Through My Dyslexic Eyes: Battling Learning Disabilities Depression and Finding Purpose* (self-pub., CreateSpace, 2018).

16. Quoted in Paul J. Gerber and Marshall H. Raskind, *Leaders, Visionaries, and Dreamers: Extraordinary People with Dyslexia and Other Learning Disabilities* (New York: Novinka, 2014), 26.

17. Jan van Gijn, "A Patient with Word Blindness in the Seventeenth Century," *Journal of the History of the Neurosciences* 24.4 (2015): 352–360. Other historical cases can be found in Arthur L. Benton and Robert J. Joynt, "Early Descriptions of Aphasia," *Archives of Neurology* 3.2 (1960): 205–222.

18. Rudolf Berlin, *Eine besondere Art der Wortblindheit (Dyslexie)* (Wiesbaden: J. F. Bergmann, 1887).

19. Sylvia O. Richardson, "Historical Perspectives on Dyslexia," *Journal of Learning Disabilities* 25.1 (1992): 40–47.

20. James Kerr, "School Hygiene, in Its Mental, Moral, and Physical Aspects," *Journal of the Royal Statistical Society* 60.3 (1897): 613–680, at 668.

21. W. Pringle Morgan, "A Case of Congenital Word Blindness," *British Medical Journal* 2 (1896): 1378.

22. Hinshelwood would later publish his findings in *Letter-, Word-, and Mind-Blindness* (London: H. K. Lewis, 1900), a seminal work on reading disabilities.

23. Quoted in James Hinshelwood, "Congenital Word-Blindness," *Lancet* 155.4004 (1900): 1506–1508, at 1508.

24. James Hinshelwood, "A Case of Congenital Word-Blindness," *British Medical Journal* 2.2289 (1904): 1303–1304, at 1303; Charles Dickens, *The Personal History of David Copperfield*, ed. Trevor Blount (London: Penguin, 1966), 103.

25. On the establishment of dyslexia as a diagnostic category, see Tom Campbell, *Dyslexia: The Government of Reading* (New York: Palgrave Macmillan, 2013).

26. Hinshelwood, "Congenital Word-Blindness," 1508.

27. Peggy L. Anderson and Regine Meier-Hedde, "Early Case Reports of Dyslexia in the United States and Europe," *Journal of Learning Disabilities* 34.1 (2001): 9–21, at 17.

28. Josephine Horton Bowden, "Learning to Read," *Elementary School Teacher* 12.1 (1911): 21–33, at 21.

29. For more on attitudes toward learning disability, see Scot Danforth, *The Incomplete Child: An Intellectual History of Learning Disabilities* (New York: Peter Lang, 2009).

30. Marion Monroe, *Children Who Cannot Read: The Analysis of Reading Disabilities and the Use of Diagnostic Tests in the Instruction of Retarded Readers* (Chicago: University of Chicago Press, 1932), 1.

31. Samuel T. Orton, "'Word-Blindness' in School Children," *Archives of Neurology and Psychiatry* 14.5 (1925): 581–615, at 611. See also Samuel Torrey Orton, *Reading, Writing and Speech Problems in Children: A Presentation of Certain Types of Disorders in the Development of the Language Faculty* (New York: W. W. Norton 1937).

32. Orton, "'Word-Blindness' in School Children," 581.

33. Quoted in Orton, "'Word-Blindness' in School Children," 593.

34. On efforts to raise dyslexia's profile, see Philip Kirby, "Literacy, Advocacy and Agency: The Campaign for Political Recognition of Dyslexia in Britain (1962–1997)," *Social History of Medicine* 33.4 (2020): 1306–1326.

35. On the dyslexia movement, see Philip Kirby, "Worried Mothers? Gender, Class and the Origins of the 'Dyslexia Myth,'" *Oral History* 47.1 (2019): 92–104.

36. Macdonald Critchley, *Developmental Dyslexia* (London: Heinemann Medical, 1964), vii.

37. Quoted in Clara Schmitt, "Congenital Word-Blindness, or Inability to Learn to Read," *Elementary School Journal* 18.9 (1918): 680–700, at 682.

38. On recent disputes over terminology, see Julian G. Elliott and Elena L. Grigorenko, *The Dyslexia Debate* (Cambridge: Cambridge University Press, 2014).

39. Frank R. Vellutino, *Dyslexia: Theory and Research* (Cambridge, MA: MIT Press, 1979).

40. Stanislas Dehaene, *Reading in the Brain: The New Science of How We Read* (London: Penguin, 2009), 236–261.

41. Quoted in Saskia van der Stoel, ed., *Parents on Dyslexia* (Clevedon, UK: Multilingual Matters, 1990), 169.

42. Girard J. Sagmiller and Gigi Lane, *Dyslexia, My Life: One Man's Story of His Life with a Learning Disability: An Autobiography* (Waverly, IA: G & R Publishing, 1995), 116.

43. Naomi Folb, "Introduction," in *Forgotten Letters: An Anthology of Literature by Dyslexic Writers*, ed. Naomi Folb (London: RASP, 2011), 7. Further reflections on the complex relationship between dyslexia and authorship can be found in Naomi Folb, "Dyslexic Writers and the Idea of Authorship," *Journal of Writing in Creative Practice* 5.1 (2012): 125–139.

44. Robert Tate, *Former NFL Veteran Robert Tate Reveals How He Made It from Little League to the NFL: Overcoming His Secret Battle with Dyslexia* (self-pub., 2010).

45. John D. Rodrigues, *High School Dropout to Harvard* (self-pub., 2013).

46. Jeff Nichols, *Trainwreck: My Life as an Idoit* (New York: Simon & Schuster, 2009); Sky Rota, *Look Mom, I'm the Dumest One in My Clas!: One Boy's Dyslexic Journey* (Centennial, CO: Wavecloud Corporation, 2017).

47. Argie Ella Hoskins, *Please Don't Call Me Dumb!: Memoirs of Unique Cognitive Processing: Dyslexia, Sequencing, or What?* (Provo, UT: Argies, 2018); Abraham Schmitt and Mary Lou Hartzler Clemens, *Brilliant Idiot: An Autobiography of a Dyslexic* (Intercourse, PA: Good Books, 1994).

48. Nelson C. Lauver, *Most Unlikely to Succeed: The Trials, Travels, and Ultimate Triumphs of a "Throwaway Kid": A Memoir* (New York: Five City Media, 2011).

49. Margaret Rooke, ed., *Dyslexia Is My Superpower (Most of the Time)* (London: Jessica Kingsley, 2018).

50. Richard W. Kraemer, *Dyslexic Dick: True Adventures of My World* (self-pub., CreateSpace, 2012), back cover.

51. Jo Rees, *Don't Forget to . . . Smile: A Memoir Uncovering the Hidden Difficulties of Dyslexia* (self-pub., Another Way Round, 2017), 4.

52. See, for example, Barbara Maughan, "Annotation: Long-Term Outcomes of Developmental Reading Problems," *Journal of Child Psychology and Psychiatry* 36.3 (1995): 357–371.

53. "Will, 13, Victoria, Australia," in Rooke, *Dyslexia Is My Superpower*, 96.

54. "Louise Baker" and Margaret B. Rawson, "I Am Me!" *Bulletin of the Orton Society* 25 (1975): 192–193.

55. Schmitt and Clemens, *Brilliant Idiot*, 19.

56. Christopher M. Lee and Rosemary F. Jackson, *Faking It: A Look into the Mind of a Creative Learner* (Portsmouth, NH: Boynton/Cook, 1992), 11–12.

57. Quoted in Osmond, *Reality of Dyslexia*, 37.

58. Nichols, *Trainwreck*, 13.

59. Nichols, *Trainwreck*, 82.

60. Osmond, *Reality of Dyslexia*, 24.

61. Ruth Fuller Lature, *Dyslexia: A Teacher's Journey: A Memoir* (Louisville: Darby, 2013), xii.

62. "X," "Experiences of a Sufferer from Word-Blindness," *British Journal of Ophthalmology* 20.2 (1936): 73–76, at 74; Victor Villaseñor, *Burro Genius: A Memoir* (New York: Rayo, 2004), 13.

63. Villaseñor, *Burro Genius*, 198.

64. Schmitt and Clemens, *Brilliant Idiot*, 24.

65. Dayle A. Upham and Virginia H. Trumbull, *Making the Grade: Reflections on Being Learning Disabled* (Portsmouth, NH: Heinemann, 1997), 12.

66. Erving Goffman, *Stigma: Notes on the Management of Spoiled Identity* (Englewood Cliffs, NJ: Prentice-Hall, 1963), 5.

67. John Young Stewart, "Sir Jackie Stewart OBE," in *Creative, Successful, Dyslexic: 23 High Achievers Share Their Stories*, ed. Margaret Rooke (London: Jessica Kingsley, 2016), 183.

68. W. Somerset Maugham, *Trio: Original Stories* (Garden City, NY: Doubleday, 1950), 8.

69. Sally E. Shaywitz, "Dyslexia," *Scientific American* 275.5 (1996): 98–104, at 98.

70. Lissa Weinstein and David Siever, *Reading David: A Mother and Son's Journey Through the Labyrinth of Dyslexia* (New York: Berkley, 2003), 214.

71. Quoted in Lature, *Dyslexia*, xi.

72. Quoted in Osmond, *Reality of Dyslexia*, 10.

73. Lee and Jackson, *Faking It*, 48.

74. Esme Fuller-Thomson and Stephen R. Hooper, "The Association Between Childhood Physical Abuse and Dyslexia: Findings from a Population-Based Study," *Journal of Interpersonal Violence* 30.9 (2015): 1583–1592.

75. Kenny Logan, "Kenny Logan," in Rooke, *Creative, Successful, Dyslexic*, 120.

76. Quoted in Lature, *Dyslexia*, 50.

77. Edwards, *Scars of Dyslexia*, 26.

78. Quoted in Barbara Riddick, *Living with Dyslexia: The Social and Emotional Consequences of Specific Learning Difficulties* (London: Routledge, 1996), 193.

79. W. B. Yeats, *The Autobiography of William Butler Yeats* (New York: Macmillan, 1938), 23. On the evidence of Yeats's dyslexia, see Marylou Miner and Linda S. Siegel, "William Butler Yeats: Dyslexic?" *Journal of Learning Disabilities* 25.6 (1992): 372–375.

80. Lauver, *Most Unlikely to Succeed*, 72.

81. Quoted in Shaywitz, *Overcoming Dyslexia*, 359.

82. Tobin Siebers, *Disability Theory* (Ann Arbor: University of Michigan Press, 2008), 96–119.

83. Simpson, *Reversals*, ix.

84. "X," "Experiences of a Sufferer from Word-Blindness," 75.

85. Howard D. Rome, "The Psychiatric Aspects of Dyslexia," *Bulletin of the Orton Society* 21 (1971): 64–70, at 68.

86. Lee and Jackson, *Faking It*, 11.

87. Archie Willard, with Colleen Wiemerslage, *Last Reader Standing: The Story of Archie Willard* (Solana Beach, CA: Bettie Youngs, 2013), 55.

88. Lature, *Dyslexia*, xi.

89. Rees, *Don't Forget to . . . Smile*, 38.

90. Jennifer Smith, *Dyslexia Wonders: Understanding the Daily Life of a Dyslexic from a Child's Point of View* (New York: Morgan James, 2010), 4.

91. Catherine A. Hirschman and R. Christine Melton, *Backwords Forword: My Journey Through Dyslexia* (self-pub., Hirschman Publishing, 2011), 16.

92. Alby Lee Lewis, *Life with No Words* (self-pub., Lulu, 2016), 53.

93. Simpson, *Reversals*, 8.

94. Osmond, *Reality of Dyslexia*, 14.

95. Recent examples include Alberto Manguel's *Packing My Library: An Elegy and Ten Digressions* (New Haven: Yale University Press, 2018) and Rebecca Mead's *My Life in Middlemarch* (New York: Crown, 2014).

96. ̈X," "Experiences of a Sufferer from Word-Blindness," 74.

97. Quoted in Gerber and Raskind, *Leaders, Visionaries, and Dreamers*, 26.

98. Quoted in Anne Boyd Rioux, *Meg, Jo, Beth, Amy: The Story of Little Women and Why It Still Matters* (New York: W. W. Norton, 2018), 125.

99. Simpson, *Reversals*, 78, 79.

100. Louisa May Alcott, *Little Women*, ed. Valerie Alderson (Oxford: Oxford University Press, 2008), 39.

101. Simpson, *Reversals*, 79; Alcott, *Little Women*, 167.

102. Elizabeth L. Eisenstein, *The Printing Press as an Agent of Change: Communications and Cultural Transformations in Early Modern Europe* (Cambridge: Cambridge University Press, 1979), 113.

103. Simpson, *Reversals*, 42.

104. Lois Letchford, *Reversed: A Memoir* (Acorn, 2018); Robert Chilcoate, *My Backward Life with Dyslexia* (Baltimore: PublishAmerica, 2006).

105. Nancy Lelewer, *Something's Not Right: One Family's Struggle with Learning Disabilities: An Autobiography* (Acton, MA: VanderWyk and Burnham, 1994).

106. A six-year-old who "mixed the letters up" is mentioned in J. Herbert Fisher, "Case of Congenital Word-Blindness (Inability to Learn to Read)," *Ophthalmic Review* 24 (1905): 315–318, at 315.

107. Orton, *Reading, Writing and Speech Problems in Children*, 71.

108. Dehaene, *Reading in the Brain*, 239.

109. Gregg T. Lueder et al., "Learning Disabilities, Dyslexia, and Vision," *Pediatrics* 124.2 (2009): 837–44.

110. Quoted in Knud Hermann, *Reading Disability: A Medical Study of Word-Blindness and Related Handicaps*, trans. P. G. Aungle (Copenhagen: Munksgaard, 1959), 33.

111. Simpson, *Reversals*, 42. See, for example, Sam Barclay's print simulation *I Wonder What It's Like to Be Dyslexic* (self-pub., 2013) and Victor Widell's digital simulation at http://geon.github.io/programming/2016/03/03/dsxyliea

112. Susan Hampshire, *Susan's Story: An Autobiographical Account of My Struggle with Dyslexia* (New York: St. Martin's, 1982), 137, 12.

113. Hampshire, *Susan's Story*, 26–27.

114. Arthur Sweeney, "Mirror-Writing, Inverted Vision, and Allied Ocular Defects," *St. Paul Medical Journal* 2 (1900): 374–391, at 378.

115. See, for example, Orton, "'Word-Blindness' in School Children," 592; and Samuel T. Orton, "Specific Reading Disability—Strephosymbolia," *Journal of*

the *American Medical Association* 90.14 (1928): 1095–1099, at 1096; Critchley, *The Dyslexic Child*, 31. Brain injury survivors might even find reverse scripts easier to read than ordinary writing. See the case of an Australian woman who read mirror scripts twice as fast as other ones, as reported in Matthew A. Lambon-Ralph, Carrie Jarvis, and Andrew W. Ellis, "Life in a Mirrored World: Report of a Case Showing Mirror Reversal in Reading and Writing and for Non-Verbal Materials," *Neurocase* 3.4 (1997): 249–258.

116. Giorgio Vasari, *The Lives of the Most Excellent Painters, Sculptors, and Architects*, ed. Philip Jacks, trans. Gaston du C. de Vere (New York: Modern Library, 2006), 237.

117. Maryanne Wolf provides a detailed analysis of da Vinci's reading differences in "Dyslexia: Through the Eyes of da Vinci," in *Further Reading*, eds. Matthew Rubery and Leah Price (Oxford: Oxford University Press, 2020), 294–308.

118. Macdonald Critchley, *Mirror-Writing* (London: Kegan Paul, Trench, Trubner, 1928), 8.

119. G. D. Schott, "Mirror Writing: Allen's Self Observations, Lewis Carroll's 'Looking-Glass' Letters, and Leonardo da Vinci's Maps," *Lancet* 354.9196 (1999): 2158–2161, at 2159.

120. Kraemer, *Dyslexic Dick*.

121. Upham and Trumbull, *Making the Grade*, 1.

122. Quoted in Phyllis Steingard and "Gail," "The Unheard Cry—Help Me! A Plea to Teachers of Dyslexic Children," *Bulletin of the Orton Society* 25 (1975): 178–184, at 181.

123. Riddick, *Living with Dyslexia*, 73; Upham and Trumbull, *Making the Grade*, 11.

124. O. Frank [Overton Frank Turner], *O. Turtle's Journal: The Captivating Life of an Autistic/Dyslexic* (self-pub., O. Turtle Publishing, 2018), 115.

125. Lee and Jackson, *Faking It*, 107.

126. Lee and Jackson, *Faking It*, 42.

127. Hampshire, *Susan's Story*, 34.

128. Randymary de Rosier, *Dyslexia: I Live with It* (Bloomington, IN: Balboa, 2018), xii–xvii.

129. Simpson, *Reversals*, 14.

130. Quoted in Rooke, *Creative, Successful, Dyslexic*, 84; John Corcoran, *The Teacher Who Couldn't Read: One Man's Triumph Over Illiteracy* (self-pub., Amazon Digital Services, 2018), Kindle edition, 494.

131. Stephen Sutton, *Life in a Jar: Living with Dyslexia* (Bloomington, IN: AuthorHouse, 2005), 2.

132. Phyllis Dunakin Snyder, *Nothin Keep You Movin Like the Trooth* (self-pub., Amazon Digital Services, 2014), Kindle edition, 82.

133. Osmond, *The Reality of Dyslexia*, 29; Evelyne, "Evelyne, 17, County Whitlow, Ireland," in Rooke, *Dyslexia Is My Superpower*, 200; Jane Austen, *Emma* (New York: Bantam, 1981), 3.

134. Sutton, *Life in a Jar*, 23.

135. Lee and Jackson, *Faking It*, 24.

136. Schmitt and Clemens, *Brilliant Idiot*, 138.

137. Smith, *Dyslexia Wonders*, 20.

138. Osmond, *The Reality of Dyslexia*, 20.

139. Lee and Jackson, *Faking It*, 43.

140. Simpson, *Reversals*, 58.

141. Eva Germanò, Antonella Gagliano, and Paolo Curatolo, "Comorbidity of ADHD and Dyslexia," *Developmental Neuropsychology* 35.5 (2010): 475–493.

142. Schmitt and Clemens, *Brilliant Idiot*, 146.

143. Schmitt and Clemens, *Brilliant Idiot*, 16.

144. Frank Smith, *Reading Without Nonsense*, 2nd ed. (New York: Teachers College Press, 1985), 140.

145. Kate Kelly and Peggy Ramundo, *You Mean I'm Not Lazy, Stupid or Crazy?! The Classic Self-Help Book for Adults with Attention Deficit Disorder* (New York: Scribner, 2006), 4. For more on the reading difficulties associated with hyperactivity, see Mark Selikowitz, *ADHD: The Facts*, 2nd ed. (Oxford: Oxford University Press, 2009), 34.

146. Gail Saltz, *The Power of Different: The Link Between Disorder and Genius* (New York: Flatiron, 2017), 57.

147. Tom Nardone, *Chasing Kites: A Memoir About Growing up with ADHD* (self-pub., CreateSpace, 2015), 89.

148. These characters can be found in Heinrich Hoffmann, *Struwwelpeter, or, Merry Rhymes and Funny Pictures* (London: Blackie & Son, 1903). On the history of ADHD, see Matthew Smith, *Hyperactive: The Controversial History of ADHD* (London: Reaktion, 2012).

149. Robert Reinhold, "Drugs That Help Control the Unruly Child," *New York Times* (July 5, 1970): 96.

150. Robert Reinhold, "Rx for Child's Learning Malady," *New York Times* (July 3, 1970): 27.

151. Nichols, *Trainwreck*, 187.

152. Olive Meares, "Figure/Ground, Brightness Contrast, and Reading Disabilities," *Visible Language* 14.1 (1980): 13–29, at 24.

153. Hirschman and Melton, *Backwords Forword*, 12.

154. Quoted in Hermann, *Reading Disability*, 154.

155. Paul Nixon, "Paul Nixon," in Rooke, *Creative, Successful, Dyslexic*, 152.

156. Quoted in Rooke, *Dyslexia Is My Superpower*, 210.

157. Simpson, *Reversals*, 80.

158. Gavin Newsom, who is currently the governor of California, once said of his reading habits, "I will be daydreaming and still reading." Quoted in Gerber and Raskind, *Leaders, Visionaries, and Dreamers*, 22.

159. Hoskins, *Please Don't Call Me Dumb!*, 14.

160. Quoted in Orton, "'Word-Blindness' in School Children," 587.

161. Rees, *Don't Forget to . . . Smile*, 8.

162. Philip Schultz, *My Dyslexia* (New York: W. W. Norton, 2012), 26. The chapter opening epigraph is also from this page.

163. Schultz, *My Dyslexia*, 68.

164. Steingard and Gail, "The Unheard Cry," 184.

165. Natalie Nielson, "Natalie Nielson, Recent Graduate, Brigham Young University," in Kurnoff, *Human Side of Dyslexia*, 297.

166. Lauver, *Most Unlikely to Succeed*, 233.

167. Peter M. Allen, Bruce J. W. Evans, and Arnold J. Wilkins, *Vision and Reading Difficulties* (London: Ten Alps Creative, 2010), 4–7.

168. Arnold J. Wilkins, *Reading Through Colour: How Coloured Filters Can Reduce Reading Difficulty, Eye Strain, and Headaches* (Chichester, UK: John Wiley, 2003), 16.

169. Jeannette Jefferson Jansky, "A Case of Severe Dyslexia with Aphasic-like Symptoms," *Bulletin of the Orton Society* 8 (1958): 8–11, at 10. This case is cited in Critchley, *Developmental Dyslexia*, 62.

170. Quoted in Meares, "Figure/Ground, Brightness Contrast, and Reading Disabilities," 16.

171. After seeing reports of Irlen's methods in the press, a Cambridge psychologist designed the Intuitive Colorimeter to assess the effectiveness of various tints. Arnold J. Wilkins, *Visual Stress* (Oxford: Oxford University Press, 1995), xvi.

172. Helen Irlen, *Reading by the Colors: Overcoming Dyslexia and Other Reading Disabilities Through the Irlen Method* (New York: Avery, 1991), 19.

173. Quoted in Irlen, *Reading by the Colors*, 33.

174. Quoted in Irlen, *Reading by the Colors*, 35.

175. Quoted in Irlen, *Reading by the Colors*, 39.

176. Quoted in Irlen, *Reading by the Colors*, 39.

177. Quoted in Irlen, *Reading by the Colors*, 41.

178. Quoted in Irlen, *Reading by the Colors*, 43.

179. Irlen, *Reading by the Colors*, 50.

180. Quoted in Irlen, *Reading by the Colors*, 43.

181. Lauver, *Most Unlikely to Succeed*, 249.

182. Lauver, *Most Unlikely to Succeed*, 249.

183. Quoted in David Grant, *That's the Way I Think: Dyslexia, Dyspraxia, ADHD and Dyscalculia Explained*, 3rd ed. (New York: Routledge, 2017), 118.

184. Alison Hale, *My World Is Not Your World*, 2nd ed. (self-pub., CreateSpace, 2017), 22.

185. Hale, *My World Is Not Your World*, 80. An animated reconstruction of Hale's view of the page can be found at http://www.hale.ndo.co.uk/scotopic/index.htm

186. On the effectiveness of colored lenses, see Philip G. Griffiths et al., "The Effect of Coloured Overlays and Lenses on Reading: A Systematic Review of the Literature," *Ophthalmic & Physiological Optics: The Journal of the British College of Ophthalmic Opticians (Optometrists)* 36.5 (2016): 519–544.

187. Lee and Jackson, *Faking It*, 57.

188. T. A. McMullin, *Gathering Courage: A Life-Changing Journey Through Adoption, Adversity, and a Reading Disability* (self-pub., Gathering Courage Media, 2016), 185.

189. Simpson, *Reversals*, 158.

CHAPTER 2

1. Fran Peek and Lisa Hanson, *The Life and Message of the Real Rain Man: The Journey of a Mega-Savant* (Port Chester, NY: Dude Publishing, 2008), 53. Uta Frith refers to Peek as the "Human Google" in *Autism: A Very Short Introduction* (Oxford: Oxford University Press, 2008), 28.

2. Fran Peek, *The Real Rain Man, Kim Peek*, ed. Stevens W. Anderson (Salt Lake City, UT: Harkness, 1996), 6.

3. Peek and Hanson, *Life and Message of the Real Rain Man*, 131.

4. Peek, *The Real Rain Man*, 27.

5. Peek, *The Real Rain Man*, 47.

6. Darold A. Treffert, *Islands of Genius: The Bountiful Mind of the Autistic, Acquired, and Sudden Savant* (London: Jessica Kingsley, 2010), xiv.

7. William James, *The Principles of Psychology*, eds. Frederick Burkhardt, Fredson Bowers, and Ignas K. Skrupskelis (Cambridge, MA: Harvard University Press, 1981), 621 fn 19.

8. Approximately half of all savants show signs of autism, and as many as one in ten people with autism qualify as savants. Darold A. Treffert, "The Savant Syndrome: An Extraordinary Condition. A Synopsis: Past, Present, Future," *Philosophical Transactions of the Royal Society B: Biological Sciences* 364.1522 (2009): 1351–1357, at 1352. See also Francesca Happé and Uta Frith, eds., *Autism and Talent* (Oxford: Oxford University Press, 2010).

9. For concision, this book will use the phrase "autism" as shorthand to refer to autism spectrum condition (ASC) or what medical resources refer to as autism spectrum disorder (ASD). Recent histories of autism include Bonnie Evans, *The Metamorphosis of Autism: A History of Child Development in Britain* (Manchester: Manchester University Press, 2017); John Donvan and Caren Zucker, *In a Different Key: The Story of Autism* (New York: Crown, 2016); Steve Silberman, *Neurotribes: The Legacy of Autism and the Future of Neurodiversity* (New York: Avery, 2015); Mitzi Waltz, *Autism: A Social History and Medical History* (Basingstoke, UK: Palgrave Macmillan, 2013); and Adam Feinstein, *A History of Autism: Conversations with the Pioneers* (Chichester, UK: Wiley-Blackwell, 2010).

10. See, for example, the *Diagnostic and Statistical Manual of Mental Disorders: DSM-5*, 5th ed. (Washington, DC: American Psychiatric Association, 2013).

11. A note about terminology: This book uses the phrases "autistic," "autistic person," and "person with autism" in accordance with the precedents set by writers who either identify as autistic or are parents of children with autism. Thoughtful reflections on the advantages and disadvantages of various terms can be found in

Stuart Murray, *Autism* (New York: Routledge, 2012), xiv; Jim Sinclair, "Why I Dislike 'Person First' Language," in *Loud Hands: Autistic People, Speaking*, ed. Julia Bascom (Washington, DC: Autistic Press, 2012), 223–224; and Terra Vance, "On Autism and Intelligence: Language and Advocacy," *NeuroClastic* (April 12, 2020): https://neuroclastic.com/2020/04/12/on-autism-and-intelligence-language-and -advocacy/

12. See, for example, Steven K. Kapp et al., "Deficit, Difference, or Both? Autism and Neurodiversity," *Developmental Psychology* 49.1 (2013): 59–71.

13. On the potential strengths of neurodiversity, see Laurent Mottron, "The Power of Autism," *Nature* 479.3 (2011): 33–35; and Simon Baron-Cohen, "Neuro-diversity—A Revolutionary Concept for Autism and Psychiatry," *Journal of Child Psychology and Psychiatry* 58.6 (2017): 744–747.

14. Douglas Biklen, "Framing Autism," in *Autism and the Myth of the Person Alone*, ed. Douglas Biklen (New York: NYU Press, 2005), 57.

15. Mark Osteen discusses the challenges of representing people with cognitive differences in "Autism and Representation: A Comprehensive Introduction," in *Autism and Representation*, ed. Mark Osteen (New York: Routledge, 2007), 6–9. On the challenges presented by using autism case studies, see Mitzi Waltz, "Reading Case Studies of People with Autistic Spectrum Disorders: A Cultural Studies Approach to Issues of Disability Representation," *Disability & Society* 20.4 (2005): 421–435. See also Julia Miele Rodas on the potential hazards of relying on autistic life writing as source material, in *Autistic Disturbances: Theorizing Autism Poetics from the* DSM *to* Robinson Crusoe (Ann Arbor: University of Michigan Press, 2018), 19–24.

16. See Melania Yergeau's moving personal response to theories of mindblindness in "Clinically Significant Disturbance: On Theorists Who Theorize Theory of Mind," *Disability Studies Quarterly* 33.4 (2013): http://dsq-sds.org/article/view/3876/ 3405. On the theory's disputed use within cognitive literary studies, see Michael Bérubé, *The Secret Life of Stories: From Don Quixote to Harry Potter, How Understanding Intellectual Disability Transforms the Way We Read* (New York: NYU Press, 2016), 22–25, 167–171. Additional misunderstandings have been recounted in publications by the Autistic Self Advocacy Network such as *Loud Hands: Autistic People, Speaking* (Washington, DC: Autistic Press, 2012).

17. Kamran Nazeer, *Send in the Idiots: Stories from the Other Side of Autism* (London: Bloomsbury, 2007), 38–39.

18. Mel Baggs, "In My Language," YouTube (January 14, 2007): https://www .youtube.com/watch?v=JnylM1hI2jc; Gillian Silverman, "Neurodiversity and the Revision of Book History," *PMLA* 131.2 (2016): 307–323, at 321 fn 19.

19. Silverman, "Neurodiversity and the Revision of Book History"; Ralph James Savarese, *See It Feelingly: Classic Novels, Autistic Readers, and the Schooling of a No-Good English Professor* (Durham, NC: Duke University Press, 2018), 197–198.

20. See, for example, Ian Hacking, "Humans, Aliens & Autism," *Daedalus* 138.3 (2009): 44–59.

21. Joseph Spence, *A Parallel; in the Manner of Plutarch: Between a Most Celebrated Man of Florence; and One, Scarce Ever Heard of, in England* (London: William Robinson, 1758), 39.

22. See Theodore W. Koch, "Some Old-Time Old-World Librarians," *North American Review* 200.705 (1914): 244–259, at 245.

23. Spence, *A Parallel*, 15.

24. Spence, *A Parallel*, 28.

25. On the shifting terminology used for cognitive disabilities, see Patrick McDonagh, *Idiocy: A Cultural History* (Liverpool: Liverpool University Press, 2008). For a critique of that terminology, see Joseph Straus, "Idiots Savants, Retarded Savants, Talented Aments, Mono-Savants, Autistic Savants, Just Plain Savants, People with Savant Syndrome, and Autistic People Who Are Good at Things: A View from Disability Studies," *Disability Studies Quarterly* 34.3 (2014): https://doi.org/10.18061/dsq.v34i3.3407

26. Edward Seguin [Édouard Séguin], *New Facts and Remarks Concerning Idiocy, Being a Lecture Delivered Before the New York Medical Journal Association, October 15, 1869* (New York: William Wood, 1870), 17.

27. John Langdon Down, *Mental Affectations of Childhood and Youth* (London: MacKeith, 1990), 58.

28. Down, *Mental Affectations of Childhood*, 58.

29. "The Life of Jedediah Buxton," *Gentleman's Magazine* (1754): 251–252. For more on calculating prodigies, see Steven B. Smith, *The Great Mental Calculators: The Psychology, Methods, and Lives of Calculating Prodigies, Past and Present* (New York: Columbia University Press, 1983).

30. Edward Seguin [Édouard Séguin], *Idiocy: And Its Treatment by the Physiological Method* (New York: William Wood, 1866), 444.

31. Down, *Mental Affectations of Childhood*, 59.

32. Down, *Mental Affectations of Childhood*, 59.

33. A. F. Tredgold, *Mental Deficiency*, 2nd ed. (London: Baillière, Tindall and Cox, 1914), 306.

34. Quoted in A. A. Brill, "Some Peculiar Manifestations of Memory with Special Reference to Lightning Calculators," *Journal of Nervous and Mental Disease* 90.6 (1940): 709–726, at 720–721. The source is Eugen Bleuler, *Die Mneme als Grundlage des Lebens und der Psyche* (Berlin: Julius Springer, 1933), 14.

35. Quoted in Sarah Warfield Parker, "A Pseudo-Talent for Words," *Psychological Clinic* 11.1 (1917): 1–17, at 6.

36. By way of comparison, see Ron Suskind's account of how his son communicated using dialogue from Disney films. *Life, Animated: A Story of Sidekicks, Heroes, and Autism* (New York: Kingswell, 2014).

37. Hans Asperger, "'Autistic Psychopathy' in Childhood," in *Autism and Asperger Syndrome*, ed. Uta Frith (Cambridge: Cambridge University Press, 1991), 75.

38. Hiram Byrd, "A Case of Phenomenal Memorizing by a Feeble-Minded Negro," *Journal of Applied Psychology* 4.2–3 (1920): 202–206, at 205. For further details

about Hoskins's life, see Jesse Bering, "Eugene Hoskins Is His Name," *Slate* (February 15, 2012): https://slate.com/technology/2012/02/eugene-hoskins-the-black-autistic-man-who-crossed-paths-with-william-faulkner.html

39. "Remarkable Powers of Memory Manifested in an Idiot," *Lancet* 173.4475 (1909): 1641.

40. Harold Ellis Jones, "Phenomenal Memorizing as a 'Special Ability,'" *Journal of Applied Psychology* 10.3 (1926): 367–377, at 375.

41. Jones, "Phenomenal Memorizing," 371.

42. Jones, "Phenomenal Memorizing," 376.

43. Michael J. A. Howe, *Fragments of Genius: The Strange Feats of Idiots Savants* (New York: Routledge, 1989), 46.

44. Martin Scheerer, Eva Rothmann, and Kurt Goldstein, "A Case of 'Idiot Savant': An Experimental Study of Personality Organization," *Psychological Monographs* 58.4 (1945): 1–63, at 14.

45. Quoted in Scheerer, Rothmann, and Goldstein, "A Case of 'Idiot Savant,'" 9.

46. This concept is usually traced back to Rosemarie Garland-Thomson, "What We Have to Gain from Disability," Disabling Normalcy Symposium (July 29, 2014), University of Virginia.

47. See Stuart Murray, *Representing Autism: Culture, Narrative, Fascination* (Liverpool: Liverpool University Press, 2008), 65–103.

48. On the links between savant syndrome and autism, see Pamela Heaton and Gregory L. Wallace, "Annotation: The Savant Syndrome," *Journal of Child Psychology and Psychiatry, and Allied Disciplines* 45.5 (2004): 899–911.

49. Straus, "Idiots Savants."

50. Asperger, "'Autistic Psychopathy' in Childhood," 56.

51. Leo Kanner, "Autistic Disturbances of Affective Contact," *Nervous Child* 2 (1943): 217–250, at 243.

52. Warren Burton, *The District School as It Was: By One Who Went to It* (Boston: Carter, Hendee, 1833), 59.

53. Quoted in Burton, *The District School*, 62.

54. Burton, *The District School*, 62.

55. Parker, "A Pseudo-Talent for Words," 12.

56. Leta Stetter Hollingworth, *Special Talents and Defects: Their Significance for Education* (New York: Macmillan, 1923), 52.

57. Marion Monroe, *Children Who Cannot Read; the Analysis of Reading Disabilities and the Use of Diagnostic Tests in the Instruction of Retarded Readers* (Chicago: University of Chicago Press, 1932), 1.

58. Norman E. Silberberg and Margaret C. Silberberg, "Hyperlexia—Specific Word Recognition Skills in Young Children," *Exceptional Children* 34.1 (1967): 41–42, at 41.

59. N. E. Silberberg and M. C. Silberberg, "Case Histories in Hyperlexia," *Journal of School Psychology* 7 (1968): 3–7, at 4; C. C. Mehegan and F. E. Dreifuss, "Hyperlexia. Exceptional Reading Ability in Brain-Damaged Children," *Neurology* 22.11 (1972): 1105–1111, at 1106.

60. Yvan Lebrun, Claudie Van Endert, and Henri Szliwowski, "Trilingual Hyperlexia," in *The Exceptional Brain: Neuropsychology of Talent and Special Abilities*, eds. Loraine K. Obler and Deborah Fein (New York: Guilford, 1988), 253–264.

61. Mehegan and Dreifuss, "Hyperlexia," 1106.

62. Mehegan and Dreifuss, "Hyperlexia," 1106.

63. Audra Jensen, *When Babies Read: A Practical Guide to Help Young Children with Hyperlexia, Asperger Syndrome and High-Functioning Autism* (London: Jessica Kingsley, 2005), 15.

64. Alexia Ostrolenk et al., "Hyperlexia: Systematic Review, Neurocognitive Modelling, and Outcome," *Neuroscience & Biobehavioral Reviews* 79 (2017): 134–139, at 139.

65. Darold A. Treffert, "Hyperlexia III: Separating 'Autistic-like' Behaviors from Autistic Disorder; Assessing Children Who Read Early or Speak Late," *WMJ: Official Publication of the State Medical Society of Wisconsin* 110.6 (2011): 281–286, at 281.

66. P. R. Huttenlocher and J. Huttenlocher, "A Study of Children with Hyperlexia," *Neurology* 23.10 (1973): 1107–1116, at 1108.

67. Quoted in Luke Jackson, *Freaks, Geeks and Asperger Syndrome: A User Guide to Adolescence* (London: Jessica Kingsley, 2003), 117.

68. See Nancy Ewald Jackson, "Precocious Reading of English: Origins, Structure, and Predictive Significance," in *To Be Young and Gifted*, ed. Pnina S. Klein and Abraham J. Tannenbaum (Norwood, NJ: Ablex, 1992), 171–203.

69. Francis Galton to Adèle Galton, February 15, 1827. Quoted in Karl Pearson, *The Life, Letters and Labours of Francis Galton*, 4 vols. (Cambridge: Cambridge University Press, 1914), 1:66.

70. Amy Wallace, *The Prodigy* (New York: E. P. Dutton, 1986), 23.

71. John Stuart Mill, *Autobiography*, ed. John M. Robson (New York: Penguin, 1989), 39.

72. Jean-Henri-Samuel Formey, *The Life of John Philip Baratier* (London: Golden Lion, 1745), 245–248. Further examples of precocious reading can be found in *Genetic Studies of Genius, Volume 2, The Early Mental Traits of Three Hundred Geniuses*, ed. Catharine Morris Cox (Stanford: Stanford University Press, 1926).

73. Richard Holmes, *Coleridge: Early Visions* (New York: Viking, 1990), 130.

74. John Matteson, *The Lives of Margaret Fuller: A Biography* (New York: W. W. Norton, 2012), 1; Joan Von Mehren, *Minerva and the Muse: A Life of Margaret Fuller* (Amherst: University of Massachusetts Press, 1994), 12.

75. Harriet Martineau, *Autobiography*, ed. Linda Peterson (Peterborough: Broadview, 2007), 62.

76. Lewis M. Terman, "An Experiment in Infant Education," *Journal of Applied Psychology* 2.3 (1918): 219–228, at 219.

77. Terman, "An Experiment in Infant Education," 219.

78. Jane M. Healy, "The Enigma of Hyperlexia," *Reading Research Quarterly* 17.3 (1982): 319–338, at 333.

79. Stephanie Allen Crist, *Discovering Autism, Discovering Neurodiversity: A Memoir* (self-pub., CreateSpace, 2015), 107; Silberberg and Silberberg, "Case Histories in Hyperlexia," 5.

80. Healy, "The Enigma of Hyperlexia," 324.

81. Michael Lewis, "Gifted or Dysfunctional: The Child Savant," *Pediatric Annals* 14.10 (1985): 733–742, at 737.

82. Joan Goodman, "A Case Study of an 'Autistic-Savant': Mental Function in the Psychotic Child with Markedly Discrepant Abilities," *Journal of Child Psychology and Psychiatry* 13.4 (1972): 267–278, at 270.

83. Mehegan and Dreifuss, "Hyperlexia," 1107.

84. Huttenlocher and Huttenlocher, "A Study of Children with Hyperlexia," 1109.

85. Stephen Best and Sharon Marcus, "Surface Reading: An Introduction," *Representations* 108.1 (2009): 1–21.

86. Savarese, *See It Feelingly*, 54.

87. Alison Hale, *My World Is Not Your World*, 2nd ed. (self-pub., CreateSpace, 2017), 5.

88. David Miedzianik, *My Autobiography* (Nottingham: University of Nottingham, Child Development Research Unit, 1986), 36.

89. Crist, *Discovering Autism*, 132.

90. Barry Neil Kaufman, *Son-Rise: The Miracle Continues* (Tiburon, CA: H. J. Kramer, 1994), 325.

91. Donna Williams, *Nobody Nowhere: The Extraordinary Autobiography of an Autistic* (New York: Times Books, 1992), 25. The chapter opening epigraph is from p. 126.

92. Clara Claiborne Park, *The Siege: The First Eight Years of an Autistic Child: With an Epilogue, Fifteen Years Later* (Boston: Little, Brown, 1982), 264.

93. Tito Rajarshi Mukhopadhyay, *The Mind Tree: A Miraculous Child Breaks the Silence of Autism* (New York: Arcade, 2003), 120.

94. Lucy Blackman, *Lucy's Story: Autism and Other Adventures* (London: Jessica Kingsley, 2001), 121, 173, 145.

95. Jim Sinclair, "Bridging the Gaps: An Inside-Out View of Autism (Or, Do You Know What I Don't Know?)," in *High-Functioning Individuals with Autism*, eds. Eric Schopler and Gary B. Mesibov (New York: Plenum, 1992), 298.

96. Barry Nurcombe and Neville Parker, "The Idiot Savant," *Journal of the American Academy of Child Psychiatry* 3.3 (July 1964): 469–487, at 473.

97. Sparrow Rose Jones, *No You Don't: Essays from an Unstrange Mind* (self-pub., Unstrange Publications, 2013), 31.

98. Mary-Ann Tirone Smith, *Girls of Tender Age: A Memoir* (New York: Free Press, 2006), 52.

99. Trevor Clark, *Exploring Giftedness and Autism: A Study of a Differentiated Educational Program for Autistic Savants* (New York: Routledge, 2016), 14.

100. Catherine Maurice, *Let Me Hear Your Voice: A Family's Triumph over Autism* (New York: Alfred A. Knopf, 1993), 50.

101. Quoted in Bruno Bettelheim, *The Empty Fortress: Infantile Autism and the Birth of the Self* (New York: Collier Macmillan, 1972), 235.

102. Bettelheim, *The Empty Fortress*, 252.

103. Bettelheim, *The Empty Fortress*, 252.

104. Stephen M. Shore, *Beyond the Wall: Personal Experiences with Autism and Asperger Syndrome*, 2nd ed. (Shawnee Mission, KS: Autism Asperger Publishing, 2003), 55.

105. Ralph James Savarese, *Reasonable People: A Memoir of Autism & Adoption: On the Meaning of Family and the Politics of Neurological Difference* (New York: Other Press, 2007), 33. It is worth repeating here that many autistic readers engage with books in conventional ways, too. See also David James Savarese's account of reading classic fiction such as *The Adventures of Huckleberry Finn* in "Coming to My Senses," *Autism in Adulthood* 1.2 (2019): 90–92.

106. Tito Rajarshi Mukhopadhyay, *How Can I Talk If My Lips Don't Move? Inside My Autistic Mind* (New York: Arcade, 2008), 202.

107. Jen Birch, *Congratulations! It's Asperger's Syndrome* (London: Jessica Kingsley, 2003), 98.

108. Macdonald Critchley, *The Divine Banquet of the Brain and Other Essays* (New York: Raven, 1979), 173.

109. Gustave Flaubert, *Bibliomania: A Tale*, trans. Theodore Wesley Koch (Evanston: Northwestern University Library, 1929), 10. On the history of bibliomania, see Nicholas A. Basbanes, *A Gentle Madness: Bibliophiles, Bibliomanes, and the Eternal Passion for Books* (New York: Henry Holt, 1995).

110. Baggs, "In My Language."

111. Kenneth Hall, *Asperger Syndrome, the Universe and Everything* (London: Jessica Kingsley, 2001), 36.

112. Frith, *Autism*, 93; Shore, *Beyond the Wall*, 58.

113. Charlotte Moore, *George and Sam: Autism in the Family* (London: Viking, 2004), 39.

114. Therese Jolliffe, Richard Lansdown, and Clive Robinson, "Autism: A Personal Account," *Communication* 26.3 (1992): 12–13.

115. Elena L. Grigorenko, Ami Klin, and Fred Volkmar, "Annotation: Hyperlexia: Disability or Superability?," *Journal of Child Psychology and Psychiatry, and Allied Disciplines* 44.8 (2003): 1079–1091, at 1079.

116. Grigorenko, Klin, and Volkmar, "Annotation," 1084; Ostrolenk et al., "Hyperlexia," 146.

117. Dawn Prince-Hughes, *Songs of the Gorilla Nation: My Journey Through Autism* (New York: Harmony, 2004), 26.

118. Asperger, "'Autistic Psychopathy' in Childhood," 56.

119. Tito Rajarshi Mukhopadhyay and Douglas Biklen, "II. Questions and Answers," in *Autism and the Myth of the Person Alone*, ed. Douglas Biklen (New York: NYU Press, 2005), 142.

120. Jean Bryant, *The Opening Door* (self-pub., 1993), 151.

121. Autistics stretch the limits of slow reading, too. Page-turners made Lois Prislovsky self-conscious in airports and other public spaces where people could see how infrequently she moved from one page to the next. Barb Rentenbach and Lois Prislovsky, *Neurodiversity: A Humorous and Practical Guide to Living with ADHD, Anxiety, Autism, Dyslexia, the Gays, and Everyone Else* (Knoxville: Mule and Muse Productions, 2016), 162.

122. Margaret Eastham and Anne Grice, *Silent Words: The Story of David Eastham* (Ottawa: Oliver-Pate, 1992), 58.

123. Quoted in Blackman, *Lucy's Story*, 137–138.

124. Bernard Rimland and Deborah Fein, "Special Talents of Autistic Savants," in *The Exceptional Brain: Neuropsychology of Talent and Special Abilities*, eds. Loraine K. Obler and Deborah Fein (New York: Guilford, 1988), 480; Jeanne Simons and Sabbine Oishi, *The Hidden Child: The Linwood Method for Reaching the Autistic Child* (Rockville: Woodbine House, 1997), 226.

125. Rentenbach and Prislovsky, *Neurodiversity*, 195.

126. Arthur Fleischmann and Carly Fleischmann, *Carly's Voice: Breaking Through Autism* (New York: Touchstone, 2012), 181.

127. *Temple Grandin*, dir. Mick Jackson ([New York]: HBO Home Entertainment, 2010), DVD.

128. Temple Grandin, *Thinking in Pictures: And Other Reports from My Life with Autism* (New York: Vintage, 1996), 31.

129. Grandin, *Thinking in Pictures*, 38.

130. Gunilla Gerland, *A Real Person: Life on the Outside*, trans. Joan Tate (London: Souvenir, 2003), 52.

131. Gerland, *A Real Person*, 52.

132. Gerland, *A Real Person*, 228.

133. Gerland, *A Real Person*, 150.

134. Priscilla Gilman, *The Anti-Romantic Child: A Memoir of Unexpected Joy* (New York: Harper Perennial, 2012), 45.

135. Nazeer, *Send in the Idiots*, 80.

136. Birch, *Congratulations! It's Asperger's Syndrome*, 93.

137. Tom Cutler, *Keep Clear: My Adventures with Asperger's* (London: Scribe, 2019), 304.

138. Shore, *Beyond the Wall*, 51.

139. Shore, *Beyond the Wall*, 57.

140. Savarese, *See It Feelingly*, 43.

141. Park, *The Siege*, 281.

142. Blackman, *Lucy's Story*, 69.

143. Alberto Frugone, "II. Salient Moments in the Life of Alberto as a Child, a Youth, a Young Man," in *Autism and the Myth of the Person Alone*, ed. Douglas Biklen (New York: NYU Press, 2005), 186.

144. Gerland, *A Real Person*, 125.

145. Quoted in Biklen, "Framing Autism," 68.

146. On the complex relationship between speech and autism, see Melanie Yergeau, *Authoring Autism: On Rhetoric and Neurological Queerness* (Durham: Duke University Press, 2018).

147. Quoted in Silberman, *Neurotribes*, 96.

148. John Elder Robison, *Look Me in the Eye: My Life with Asperger's* (New York: Crown, 2007), 267.

149. See, for example, Francesca G. E. Happé, "The Autobiographical Writings of Three Asperger Syndrome Adults: Problems of Interpretation and Implications for Theory," in *Autism and Asperger Syndrome*, ed. Uta Frith (Cambridge: Cambridge University Press, 1991), 223.

150. Simon Baron-Cohen et al., "The Autism-Spectrum Quotient (AQ): Evidence from Asperger Syndrome/High-Functioning Autism, Males and Females, Scientists and Mathematicians," *Journal of Autism and Developmental Disorders* 31.1 (2001): 5–17, at 15.

151. Judy Barron and Sean Barron, *There's a Boy in Here* (New York: Simon & Schuster, 1992), 256.

152. Frith, *Autism*, 8.

153. N. V. Smith and Ianthi-Maria Tsimpli, *The Mind of a Savant: Language Learning and Modularity* (Oxford: Blackwell, 1995), 1–2.

154. "Jim," in *Aquamarine Blue 5: Personal Stories of College Students with Autism*, ed. Dawn Prince-Hughes (Athens: Swallow Press/Ohio University Press, 2002), 67.

155. Gerland, *A Real Person*, 126.

156. Peek and Hanson, *The Life and Message of the Real Rain Man*, 47.

157. Sue Rubin, "II. A Conversation with Leo Kanner," in *Autism and the Myth of the Person Alone*, ed. Douglas Biklen (New York: NYU Press, 2005), 87.

158. Shore, *Beyond the Wall*, 87.

159. Shore, *Beyond the Wall*, 87.

160. Daniel Tammet, *Every Word Is a Bird We Teach to Sing: Encounters with the Mysteries and Meanings of Language* (New York: Little, Brown, 2017), 6.

161. Gerland, *A Real Person*, 145.

162. Williams, *Nobody Nowhere*, 43.

163. Williams, *Nobody Nowhere*, 116.

164. Williams, *Nobody Nowhere*, 43.

165. Oliver Sacks, "Foreword," in Grandin, *Thinking in Pictures,* 14. For a counterpoint to Sacks's account, see the discussion of Grandin's sensitivity to literature in Savarese, *See It Feelingly*, 155–190.

166. Tammet, *Every Word Is a Bird We Teach to Sing*, 10; Daniel Tammet, *Born on a Blue Day: Inside the Extraordinary Mind of an Autistic Savant: A Memoir* (New York: Free Press, 2007), 130.

167. Tammet, *Every Word Is a Bird We Teach to Sing*, 11.

168. Tim Page, *Parallel Play* (New York: Anchor, 2010), 74.

169. Liane Holliday Willey, *Pretending to Be Normal: Living with Asperger's Syndrome* (London: Jessica Kingsley, 1999), 20.

CHAPTER 3

1. Sam Martin and June Martin, *A Stroke of Luck: Learning How to Read After a Stroke* (self-pub., 2013), 5. The chapter opening epigraph is from George Gissing, *The Private Papers of Henry Ryecroft* (Westminster: Archibald Constable, [1903]), 165.

2. Martin and Martin, *A Stroke of Luck*, 9.

3. For a comprehensive review, see Alexander Leff and Randi Starrfelt, *Alexia: Diagnosis, Treatment and Theory* (London: Springer-Verlag, 2014).

4. David F. Mitch, *The Rise of Popular Literacy in Victorian England: The Influence of Private Choice and Public Policy* (Philadelphia: University of Pennsylvania Press, 1992), xvi.

5. Carl F. Kaestle, "Preface," in *Literacy in the United States: Readers and Reading Since 1880*, ed. Carl F. Kaestle et al. (New Haven: Yale University Press, 1991), xix.

6. Samuel Smiles, *Self-Help, with Illustrations of Character, Conduct, and Perseverance*, ed. Peter W. Sinnema (Oxford: Oxford University Press, 2002), 274.

7. Francis Bacon, *The Essayes or Counsels, Civill and Morall*, ed. Michael Kiernan (Oxford: Clarendon, 1985), 153.

8. C. S. Moss, "Notes from an Aphasic Psychologist, or Different Strokes for Different Folks," in *Injured Brains of Medical Minds: Views from Within*, ed. Narinder Kapur (Oxford: Oxford University Press, 1997), 79.

9. Gustave Flaubert to Mademoiselle Leroyer de Chantepie, June 1857, in Gustave Flaubert, *Correspondance: Nouvelle Édition Augmentée: Quatrième Série (1854–1861)*, 9 vols. (Paris: Louis Conard, 1927), 4:197. Emphasis in original.

10. Various perspectives on reading's benefits can be found in Shafquat Towheed, Rosalind Crone, and Katie Halsey, eds., *The History of Reading: A Reader* (London: Routledge, 2011). See also Frank Furedi, *The Power of Reading: From Socrates to Twitter* (London: Bloomsbury, 2015).

11. Helen Keller, *The Story of My Life* (London: Doubleday, Page, 1903), 117.

12. Samuel Johnson, "Illiterate," in *Johnson's Dictionary Online, A Dictionary of the English Language* (1755, 1773), eds. Beth Rapp Young et al. (2021): http://johnsonsdictionaryonline.com/?p=14863

13. Robert Darnton, "First Steps Toward a History of Reading," *Australian Journal of French Studies* 23 (1986): 5–30, at 15.

14. See Pliny, *Natural History*, 5 vols., trans. H[arris] Rackham (London: Folio Society, 2012), 1:346. This and other historical cases of alexia are documented in Arthur L. Benton and Robert J. Joynt, "Early Descriptions of Aphasia," *Archives of Neurology* 3.2 (1960): 205–222.

15. Jan van Gijn, "A Patient with Word Blindness in the Seventeenth Century," *Journal of the History of the Neurosciences* 24.4 (2015): 352–360.

16. Benton and Joynt, "Early Descriptions of Aphasia," 209.

17. Quoted in Walther Riese, "Auto-Observation of Aphasia: Reported by an Eminent Nineteenth-Century Medical Scientist," *Bulletin of the History of Medicine* 28 (1954): 237–242, at 238. A survey of self-reports of aphasics can be found in Claude

Scott Moss, *Recovery with Aphasia: The Aftermath of My Stroke* (Urbana: University of Illinois Press, 1972), 185–199. Moss describes his own struggles with reading as "an unholy, tortuous business" (7).

18. Quoted in Riese, "Auto-Observation," 238.

19. Quoted in Riese, "Auto-Observation," 238

20. Joseph Arnould, *Memoir of Thomas, First Lord Denman Formerly Lord Chief Justice of England*, 2 vols. (London: Longmans, Green, 1873), 2:343.

21. Alberto Manguel, "Some Thoughts About Thinking," *Cognitive and Behavioral Neurology* 28.2 (2015): 43–45.

22. On early efforts at brain localization, see Edwin Clarke and L. S. Jacyna, *Nineteenth-Century Origins of Neuroscientific Concepts* (Berkeley: University of California Press, 1987), 212–307.

23. On the emergence of aphasiology in the nineteenth century, see L. S. Jacyna, *Lost Words: Narratives of Language and the Brain, 1825–1926* (Princeton: Princeton University Press, 2000).

24. H. Charlton Bastian, "On the Various Forms of Loss of Speech in Cerebral Disease," *British and Foreign Medico-Chirurgical Review* 43 (1869): 209–236, 470–492, at 484. Emphasis in original.

25. James J. Adams, "On the Amaurosis and Painful Affections Which Attend Strabismus," *Provincial Medical and Surgical Journal* 2.30 (1841): 66–68, at 66.

26. Thomas Inman, "Remarks upon the Treatment of Threatened Apoplexy and Hemiplegia," *British Medical Journal* (November 14, 1857): 944–947.

27. John Buckley Bradbury, "A Discussion on Headaches and Their Treatment," *British Medical Journal* (November 4, 1899): 1241–1243, at 1242.

28. J. Crichton Browne, "Clinical Lectures on Mental and Cerebral Diseases," *British Medical Journal* (May 6, 1871): 467–468, at 467.

29. J[ohn] Hughlings Jackson, "On a Case of Loss of Power Expression; Inability to Talk, to Write, and to Read Correctly After Convulsive Attacks," *British Medical Journal* (July 28, 1866): 92–94, at 93.

30. William Henry Broadbent, "On the Cerebral Mechanism of Speech and Thought," *Medico-Chirurgical Transactions* 55 (1872): 145–194, at 166.

31. Quoted in Broadbent, "On the Cerebral," 163.

32. Quoted in Broadbent, "On the Cerebral," 164.

33. Quoted in Broadbent, "On the Cerebral," 164.

34. Broadbent, "On the Cerebral," 151.

35. J[ohn] T[homas] Banks, "On the Loss of Language in Cerebral Disease," *Dublin Quarterly Journal of Medical Science* 39.77 (1865): 62–80, at 78.

36. George Eliot, *Romola*, ed. Dorothea Barrett (London: Penguin, 1996), 273.

37. Sally Shuttleworth, *George Eliot and Nineteenth-Century Science: The Make-Believe of a Beginning* (Cambridge: Cambridge University Press, 1984), 111.

38. Eliot, *Romola*, 352.

39. Jack Goody and Ian Watt, "The Consequences of Literacy," *Comparative Studies in Society and History* 5.3 (1963): 304–345, at 335.

40. See, for example, Georges Poulet, "Phenomenology of Reading," *New Literary History* 1.1 (1969): 53–68.

41. Armand Trousseau, *Lectures on Clinical Medicine, Delivered at the Hôtel-Dieu, Paris,* 5 vols., trans. P. Victor Bazire (London: Robert Hardwicke, 1866), 1:238.

42. Alfred Mantle, "Motor and Sensory Aphasia," *British Medical Journal* (February 6, 1897): 325–328, at 325.

43. Quoted in Mantle, "Motor," 326.

44. Quoted in Mantle, "Motor," 326.

45. "Phases of Aphasia," *Saint Paul Globe* (Minn.) (September 10, 1899): 22, *Chronicling America: Historic American Newspapers*: http://chroniclingamerica.loc.gov/

46. Quoted in Banks, "On the Loss," 75.

47. Banks, "On the Loss," 75.

48. Trousseau, *Lectures,* 224. Emphasis in original.

49. Freud discusses the concept of magical thinking in Sigmund Freud, *The Origins of Religion: Totem and Taboo, Moses and Monotheism and Other Works,* The Pelican Freud Library, trans. James Strachey, vol. 13 (London: Penguin, 1985), 143–145.

50. Trousseau, *Lectures,* 260.

51. J. S. Bristowe, "The Lumleian Lectures on the Pathological Relations of the Voice and Speech," *British Medical Journal* (May 17, 1879): 731–734, at 732.

52. Bristowe, "The Lumleian Lectures," 731.

53. Trousseau, *Lectures,* 260–61.

54. Trousseau, *Lectures,* 258.

55. A[dolph] Kussmaul, "Disturbances of Speech," in *Cyclopaedia of the Practice of Medicine,* ed. Dr. H[ugo] von Ziemssen, trans. E. Buchanan Baxter et al. (New York: William Wood, 1877), 14:770, 14:775. Kussmaul's monograph was published simultaneously in German as *Die Störungen der Sprache* (Leipzig: Verlag von F. C. W. Vogel, 1877).

56. Quoted in Willy O. Renier, "Jules Dejerine," in *Reader in the History of Aphasia: From Franz Gall to Norman Geschwind,* ed. Paul Eling (Amsterdam: John Benjamins, 1994), 207. The case study reprinted by this volume is translated from "Contribution à l'étude anatomique et cliniques des différentes variétés de cêcité verbale," *Mémoires de la Société de Biologie* 4 (1892): 61–65.

57. Quoted in Daniel N. Bub, Martin Arguin, and André Roch Lecours, "Jules Dejerine and His Interpretation of Pure Alexia," *Brain and Language* 45.4 (1993): 531–559, at 542.

58. Quoted in Israel Rosenfeld, *The Invention of Memory: A New View of the Brain* (New York: Basic Books, 1988), 34. The translation is Rosenfeld's own.

59. Quoted in Rosenfeld, *Invention,* 36.

60. J. M. Charcot, *Clinical Lectures on Diseases of the Nervous System,* ed. Ruth Harris (London: Tavistock/Routledge, 1991), 133.

61. Quoted in Charcot, *Clinical Lectures,* 136.

62. James Hinshelwood, "The Treatment of Word-Blindness, Acquired and Congenital," *British Medical Journal* 2.2703 (1912): 1033–1035, at 1033.

63. James Hinshelwood, *Letter-, Word-, and Mind-Blindness* (London: H. K. Lewis, 1900), 12.

64. Hinshelwood, *Letter-*, 14.

65. Hinshelwood, *Letter-*, 38.

66. Hinshelwood, *Letter-*, 44.

67. Henry R. Swanzy, "The Bowman Lecture on the Value of Eye Symptoms in the Localisation of Cerebral Disease," *British Medical Journal* (November 17, 1888): 1089–1096, at 1095.

68. Poulet, "Phenomenology of Reading," 54.

69. William Ogle, "Aphasia and Agraphia," in *St. George's Hospital Reports*, 10 vols., eds. John W. Ogle and Timothy Holmes (London: John Churchill and Sons, 1867), 2:83–122.

70. H. Charlton Bastian, "The Lumleian Lectures on Some Problems in Connection with Aphasia and Other Speech Defects," *British Medical Journal* (May 1, 1897): 1076–1080, at 1077.

71. Charcot, *Clinical Lectures*, 139. Emphasis in original.

72. Bub et al., "Jules Dejerine," 547.

73. Oliver Sacks, *The Mind's Eye* (London: Picador, 2010), 78. See also Oliver Sacks, "Afterword," in Howard Engel, *The Man Who Forgot How to Read* (New York: Thomas Dunne Books/St. Martin's Press, 2007), 149–157.

74. This case is described in Adhémar Gelb and Kurt Goldstein, "Analysis of a Case of Figural Blindness," in *A Source Book of Gestalt Psychology*, ed. Willis D. Ellis (London: Kegan Paul, Trench, Trubner, [1938]), 315–325.

75. Oliver Sacks, "Afterword," in Howard Engel, *Memory Book* (New York: Carroll & Graf, 2006), 245.

76. Kurt Goldstein, *The Organism: A Holistic Approach to Biology Derived from Pathological Data in Man* (New York: Zone, 1995), 196.

77. J. Richard Hanley and Janice Kay, "Monsieur C: Dejerine's Case of Alexia Without Agraphia," in *Classic Cases in Neuropsychology*, 2 vols., eds. Chris Code et al. (Hove, UK: Psychology Press, 2002), 2:64.

78. A. Hughes Bennett, "Clinical Lectures on Diseases of the Nervous System," *British Medical Journal* (February 18, 1888): 339–342, at 340.

79. Hinshelwood, *Letter-*, 70.

80. Kurt Goldstein, *Language and Language Disturbances: Aphasic Symptom Complexes and Their Significance for Medicine and Theory of Language* (New York: Grune & Stratton, 1948), 124.

81. On the limited benefits of therapeutic treatment, see Randi Starrfelt, Rannveig Rós Ólafsdóttir, and Ida-Marie Arendt, "Rehabilitation of Pure Alexia: A Review," *Neuropsychological Rehabilitation* 23.5 (2013): 755–779.

82. Marlene Behrmann, "Pure Alexia: Underlying Mechanisms and Remediation," in *Converging Methods for Understanding Reading and Dyslexia*, eds. Raymond M. Klein and Patricia McMullen (Cambridge, MA: MIT Press, 1999), 156.

83. Quoted in Barbara A. Wilson, *Case Studies in Neuropsychological Rehabilitation* (Oxford: Oxford University Press, 1999), 217.

84. Quoted in Wilson, *Case Studies*, 221.

85. Victor W. Henderson explains the twentieth century's contrasting approaches in "Alexia and Agraphia," in *History of Neurology*, eds. Stanley Finger, Francois Boller, and Kenneth L. Tyler (Edinburgh: Elsevier, 2010), 583–601, esp. 596–599.

86. Goldstein, *The Organism*, 203.

87. Norman Geschwind, "Disconnexion Syndromes in Animals and Man (Part I)," *Brain* 88.2 (1965): 237–294, at 239. The term "diagram makers" was originally used in Henry Head, *Aphasia and Kindred Disorders of Speech*, 2 vols. (Cambridge: Cambridge University Press, 1926), 1:54.

88. Quoted in A. R. Luria, *The Man with a Shattered World: The History of a Brain Wound*, trans. Lynn Solotaroff (Cambridge, MA: Harvard University Press, 1972), 64.

89. Quoted in Luria, *The Man*, 62, 63.

90. Quoted in Luria, *The Man*, 64.

91. Quoted in Luria, *The Man*, 99.

92. Quoted in Luria, *The Man*, 75.

93. Quoted in Luria, *The Man*, 35.

94. Luria, *The Man*, xxi.

95. Philippe F. Paquier et al, "Acquired Alexia with Agraphia Syndrome in Childhood," *Journal of Child Neurology* 21.4 (2006): 324–330; C. A. H. Fisher and A. J. Larner, "Jean Langlais (1907–91): An Historical Case of a Blind Organist with Stroke-Induced Aphasia and Braille Alexia but Without Amusia," *Journal of Medical Biography* 16.4 (2008): 232–234; Ian McDonald, "Musical Alexia with Recovery: A Personal Account," *Brain* 129 (2006): 2554–2561; Jordan S. Robinson, Robert L. Collins, and Shalini V. Mukhi, "Alexia Without Agraphia in a Right-Handed Individual Following Right Occipital Stroke," *Applied Neuropsychology: Adult* 23.1 (2016): 65–69.

96. See, for example, the essays in Rachel Ablow, ed., *The Feeling of Reading: Affective Experience and Victorian Literature* (Ann Arbor: University of Michigan Press, 2010). Mary A. Favret considers the experiences of those who find reading difficult in "The Pathos of Reading," *PMLA* 130.5 (2015): 1318–1331, esp. 1320–1321.

97. Hinshelwood, *Letter-*, 2.

98. Engel, *The Man Who Forgot How to Read*, xiv.

99. Engel, *The Man Who Forgot How to Read*, xiii, 7. Engel's case is described at length in Sacks, *The Mind's Eye*, 53–81.

100. Engel, *The Man Who Forgot How to Read*, 28.

101. Banks, "On the Loss," 78.

102. Engel, *The Man Who Forgot How to Read*, 43, 29.

103. Engel, *The Man Who Forgot How to Read*, 37.

104. Engel, *The Man Who Forgot How to Read.* 73.

105. Engel, *The Man Who Forgot How to Read*, 41.

106. Engel, *The Man Who Forgot How to Read*, 99.

107. Engel, *The Man Who Forgot How to Read*, 133.

108. Engel, *The Man Who Forgot How to Read*, 134.

109. Engel, *The Man Who Forgot How to Read*, 129.

110. Engel, *Memory Book*, 13.

111. Engel, *Memory Book*, 226.

112. See, for example, the prophetic remarks about a "post-literate time" made in Marshall McLuhan, *The Gutenberg Galaxy: The Making of Typographic Man* (London: Routledge & Kegan Paul, 1967), 2.

113. Quoted in Jason Cuomo, Murray Flaster, and José Biller, "Right Brain: A Reading Specialist with Alexia Without Agraphia: Teacher Interrupted," *Neurology* 82.1 (January 7, 2014): e5–e7, at e5.

114. Quoted in Cuomo et al., "Right Brain," e7.

CHAPTER 4

1. Gladys A. Reichard, Roman Jakobson, and Elizabeth Werth, "Language and Synesthesia," *Word* 5.2 (1949): 224–233, at 224.

2. Ludwig Wittgenstein, *Zettel*, eds. G. E. M. Anscombe and G. H. von Wright, trans. G. E. M. Anscombe (Oxford: Basil Blackwell, 1967), 32e.

3. A detailed overview of this multivariant condition is available in Julia Simner and Edward M. Hubbard, eds., *The Oxford Handbook of Synesthesia* (Oxford: Oxford University Press, 2013). Another good starting point is Richard E. Cytowic, *Synesthesia* (Cambridge, MA: MIT Press, 2018).

4. Julia Simner et al., "Synaesthesia: The Prevalence of Atypical Cross-Modal Experiences," *Perception* 35.8 (2006): 1024–1033.

5. Julia Simner identifies synesthesia's key features in "Defining Synaesthesia," *British Journal of Psychology* 103.1 (2012): 1–15. See also Jamie Ward and Julia Simner, "Synesthesia: The Current State of the Field," in *Multisensory Perception: From Laboratory to Clinic*, eds. Krishnankutty Sathian and V. S. Ramachandran (Amsterdam: Academic, 2019), 283–300.

6. Jacques Lusseyran, *And There Was Light: The Autobiography of a Blind Hero in the French Resistance* (Edinburgh: Floris, 1985), 76. Numerous accounts of colored hearing can be found in Oliver W. Sacks, *Musicophilia: Tales of Music and the Brain* (London: Picador, 2007), 165–183.

7. Isador H. Coriat, "An Unusual Type of Synesthesia," *Journal of Abnormal Psychology* 8.2 (1913): 109–112; Janina Nielsen et al., "Synaesthesia and Sexuality: The Influence of Synaesthetic Perceptions on Sexual Experience," *Frontiers in Psychology* 4 (2013): https://doi.org/10.3389/fpsyg.2013.00751. Sean Day maintains a comprehensive list of the different forms of synesthesia: http://www.daysyn.com/Types-of -Syn.html

8. Vladimir Nabokov, *Strong Opinions* (London: Penguin, 2012), 34.

9. Vladimir Nabokov, *Speak, Memory: An Autobiography Revisited* (London: Penguin, 2012), 17. For an artist's rendition of Nabokov's letters, see Jean Holabird, Vladimir Nabokov, and Brian Boyd, *Vladimir Nabokov: AlphaBet in Color* (Corte Madera, CA: Gingko, 2005).

242 Notes to Chapter 4

10. The emerging field of neuroaesthetics seeks to understand the neural under pinnings of artistic encounters. A good entry point is G. Gabrielle Starr, *Feeling Beauty: The Neuroscience of Aesthetic Experience* (Cambridge, MA: MIT Press, 2015).

11. Francis Galton, "Visualised Numerals," *Journal of the Anthropological Institute of Great Britain and Ireland* 10 (1881): 85–102, at 85.

12. Sean A. Day, "Some Demographic and Socio-Cultural Aspects of Synesthesia," in *Synesthesia: Perspectives from Cognitive Neuroscience*, eds. Lynn C. Robertson and Noam Sagiv (Oxford: Oxford University Press, 2005), 27.

13. Jerome J. McGann, *The Textual Condition* (Princeton: Princeton University Press, 1991), 57.

14. Maurice Merleau-Ponty, *Phenomenology of Perception*, trans. Colin Smith (London: Routledge, 2005); see also André J. Abath, "Merleau-Ponty and the Problem of Synaesthesia," in *Sensory Blending: On Synaesthesia and Related Phenomena*, ed. Ophelia Deroy (New York: Oxford University Press, 2017), 151–165.

15. Stanislas Dehaene, *Reading in the Brain: The New Science of How We Read* (New York: Penguin, 2009), 225.

16. Michael Tye, "Qualia," in *The Stanford Encyclopedia of Philosophy*, ed. Edward N. Zalta (Stanford: Stanford University, 2017): https://plato.stanford.edu/archives/win2017/entries/qualia/

17. Max Velmans, *Understanding Consciousness*, 2nd ed. (New York: Routledge, 2009), 121–148.

18. Robert Darnton, "First Steps Toward a History of Reading," *Australian Journal of French Studies* 23.1 (1986): 5–30, at 7.

19. Richard P. Feynman, *"What Do You Care What Other People Think?": Further Adventures of a Curious Character* (New York: W. W. Norton, 1988), 59.

20. Sach's dissertation was written in Latin and subsequently translated into German. There is no English translation. See Jörg Jewanski, Sean A. Day, and Jamie Ward, "A Colorful Albino: The First Documented Case of Synaesthesia, by Georg Tobias Ludwig Sachs in 1812," *Journal of the History of the Neurosciences* 18.3 (2009): 293–303.

21. Jörg Jewanski et al., "The Development of a Scientific Understanding of Synesthesia from Early Case Studies (1849–1873)," *Journal of the History of the Neurosciences* 20.4 (2011): 284–305.

22. Quoted in Francis Galton, *Inquiries into Human Faculty and Its Development* (London: Macmillan, 1883), 110. See also David Burbridge, "Galton's 100: An Exploration of Francis Galton's Imagery Studies," *British Journal for the History of Science* 27.4 (1994): 443–463, at 443.

23. Alfred Binet, "The Problem of Colored Hearing," *Popular Science Monthly* 43 (1893): 812–823, at 815; translated from "Le problème de l'audition colorèe," *La revue de deux mondes* 113 (1892): 586–614.

24. John E. Harrison, *Synaesthesia: The Strangest Thing* (Oxford: Oxford University Press, 2001).

25. Lynn C. Robertson and Noam Sagiv, eds., *Synesthesia: Perspectives from Cognitive Neuroscience* (Oxford: Oxford University Press, 2005).

26. On the history of artistic experimentation with synesthesia, see Crétien van Campen, *The Hidden Sense: Synesthesia in Art and Science* (Cambridge, MA: MIT Press, 2008).

27. Charles Baudelaire, "Correspondences" ("Correspondances"), in *The Flowers of Evil*, trans. James McGowan (Oxford: Oxford University Press, 1993), 19.

28. Arthur Rimbaud, "Voyelles," in *Selected Poems and Letters*, trans. Jeremy Harding and John Sturrock (London: Penguin, 2004), 211–212.

29. Joris-Karl Huysmans, *Against Nature* (Harmondsworth: Penguin, 1973), 58. On synesthesia's persistence as a Romantic ideal among the arts, see Kevin T. Dann, *Bright Colors Falsely Seen: Synaesthesia and the Search for Transcendental Knowledge* (New Haven: Yale University Press, 1998).

30. Arthur Rimbaud, *Collected Poems*, trans. Oliver Bernard (Harmondsworth: Penguin, 1997), 327. Quoted in Lawrence E. Marks, *The Unity of the Senses: Interrelations Among the Modalities* (New York: Academic, 1978), 235.

31. Simon Baron-Cohen and John Harrison, "Synaesthesia," in *Encyclopedia of Cognitive Science*, ed. Lynn Nadel, 4 vols. (London: Nature Publishing, 2003), 4:296.

32. Max Nordau, *Degeneration* (London: William Heinemann, 1896), 142.

33. William Empson, *Seven Types of Ambiguity*, 2nd ed. (Harmondsworth: Penguin, 1973), 33; Irving Babbitt, *The New Laokoon: An Essay on the Confusion of the Arts* (New York: Houghton Mifflin, 1929), 175.

34. Rudyard Kipling, *Rudyard Kipling's Verse* (London: Hodder and Stoughton, 1940), 418; Edith Sitwell, *Façade* (London: Duckworth, 1987), 33; F. Scott Fitzgerald, *The Great Gatsby*, ed. Matthew Joseph Bruccoli (New York: Scribner, 2003), 44.

35. Glenn O'Malley, *Shelley and Synesthesia* (Evanston: Northwestern University Press, 1968), 178.

36. Vladimir Nabokov, *Bend Sinister* (London: Penguin Classics, 2012), 104; Patricia Lynne Duffy provides a useful survey of fictional representations in "Synesthesia in Literature," in *The Oxford Handbook of Synesthesia*, eds. Julia Simner and Edward M. Hubbard (Oxford: Oxford University Press, 2013), 647–670.

37. June E. Downey, "Literary Synesthesia," *Journal of Philosophy, Psychology and Scientific Methods* 9.18 (1912): 490–498, at 490.

38. See Harrison, *Synaesthesia*, 115–140.

39. D. F. McKenzie, *Bibliography and the Sociology of Texts* (London: British Library, 1986), 8.

40. Quoted in Galton, *Inquiries into Human Faculty*, 150.

41. Théodore Flournoy, *Des Phénomènes de Synopsie (Audition Colorée): Photismes, Schèmes Visuels, Personnifications* (Paris: Félic Alcan, 1893), 79.

42. V. S. Ramachandran and Edward M. Hubbard, "Synaesthesia—A Window into Perception, Thought and Language," *Journal of Consciousness Studies* 8.12 (2001): 3–34, at 26.

43. Quoted in Patricia Lynne Duffy, *Blue Cats and Chartreuse Kittens: How Synesthetes Color Their Worlds* (New York: Times Books, 2001), 55.

44. Galton, *Inquiries into Human Faculty*, 47.

45. Richard E. Cytowic and David M. Eagleman, *Wednesday Is Indigo Blue: Discovering the Brain of Synesthesia* (Cambridge, MA: MIT Press, 2009), 2.

46. Galton, "Visualised Numerals," 99.

47. Nathan Witthoft and Jonathan Winawer, "Learning, Memory, and Synesthesia," *Psychological Science* 24.3 (2013): 258–265. See also Peter Hancock, "Synesthesia, Alphabet Books, and Fridge Magnets," in Simner and Hubbard, *Oxford Handbook of Synesthesia*, 83–99.

48. Nicolas Rothen and Beat Meier, "Acquiring Synaesthesia: Insights from Training Studies," *Frontiers in Human Neuroscience* 8 (2014): https://doi.org/10.3389/fnhum.2014.00109

49. Nabokov, *Speak, Memory*, 18.

50. Alexandra Dittmar, *Synaesthesia: A "Golden Thread" Through Life?* (Essen: Verl Die Blaue Eule, 2009), 43.

51. Richard E. Cytowic, *Synesthesia: A Union of the Senses* (Cambridge, MA: MIT Press, 2002), 34.

52. Daniel Tammet, *Born on a Blue Day: Inside the Extraordinary Mind of an Autistic Savant: A Memoir* (New York: Free Press, 2007), 11. This chapter's opening epigraph is from p. 160.

53. Quoted in Sean A. Day, *Synesthetes: A Handbook* (Granada: International Foundation Artecittà Publishing, 2016), 31.

54. Joanna Atkinson et al., "Synesthesia for Manual Alphabet Letters and Numeral Signs in Second-Language Users of Signed Languages," *Neurocase* 22.4 (2016): 379–386.

55. Simner, "Defining Synaesthesia," 4.

56. Email correspondence with Marie Harris (November 1, 2017).

57. Carol Bergfeld Mills et al., "The Color of Two Alphabets for a Multilingual Synesthete," *Perception* 31.11 (2002): 1371–1394, at 1375.

58. Quoted in Mills et al., "The Color of Two Alphabets," 1374.

59. Quoted in Mills et al., "The Color of Two Alphabets," 1375.

60. Quoted in Dittmar, *Synaesthesia*, 143.

61. Cytowic, *Synesthesia*, 34.

62. Mary Whiton Calkins, "A Statistical Study of Pseudo-Chromesthesia and of Mental-Forms," *American Journal of Psychology* 5.4 (1893): 439–464, at 459.

63. Quoted in Mary Whiton Calkins, "Synæsthesia," *American Journal of Psychology* 7.1 (1895): 90–107, at 98.

64. Mary Collins, "A Case of Synaesthesia," *Journal of General Psychology* 2.1 (1929): 12–27, at 13.

65. Quoted in Thomas D. Cutsforth, "The Role of Emotion in a Synaesthetic Subject," *American Journal of Psychology* 36.4 (1925): 527–543, at 539: https://doi.org/10.2307/1413908

66. Raymond H. Wheeler, "The Synaesthesia of a Blind Subject," *University of Oregon Publications* I (1920): 3–61, at 49.

67. Quoted in Dittmar, *Synaesthesia*, 127.

68. Quoted in Megan S. Steven and Colin Blakemore, "Visual Synaesthesia in the Blind," *Perception* 33.7 (2004): 855–868, at 859.

69. Quoted in Steven and Blakemore, "Visual Synaesthesia in the Blind," 864.

70. Quoted in Cytowic, *Synesthesia: A Union of the Senses*, 27.

71. See Christine Mohr, "Synesthesia in Space Versus the 'Mind's Eye': How to Ask the Right Questions," in Simner and Hubbard, *Oxford Handbook of Synesthesia*, 440–458.

72. Mills et al., "The Color of Two Alphabets for a Multilingual Synesthete," 1374.

73. Quoted in Jamie Ward, *The Frog Who Croaked Blue: Synesthesia and the Mixing of the Senses* (New York: Routledge, 2008), 5.

74. Collins, "A Case of Synaesthesia," 16.

75. On the mental imagery generated by fictional narratives, see Elaine Scarry, *Dreaming by the Book* (Princeton: Princeton University Press, 2001).

76. Quoted in Cytowic, *Synesthesia: A Union of the Senses*, 36.

77. Cytowic, *Synesthesia: A Union of the Senses*, 29.

78. Cytowic and Eagleman, *Wednesday Is Indigo Blue*, 74.

79. Maureen Seaberg, *Tasting the Universe: People Who See Colors in Words and Rainbows in Symphonies* (Pompton Plains, NJ: Career Press/New Page Books, 2011), 21.

80. Cytowic, *Synesthesia: A Union of the Senses*, 34.

81. Duffy, *Blue Cats and Chartreuse Kittens*, 25.

82. Ward, *The Frog Who Croaked Blue*, 83.

83. Clare N. Jonas et al., "Visuo-Spatial Representations of the Alphabet in Synaesthetes and Non-Synaesthetes," *Journal of Neuropsychology* 5.2 (2011): 302–322.

84. Cytowic, *Synesthesia: A Union of the Senses*, 199.

85. Duffy, *Blue Cats and Chartreuse Kittens*, 18.

86. Tammet, *Born on a Blue Day*, 9.

87. Galton, *Inquiries into Human Faculty*, 96.

88. Quoted in David Grant, *That's the Way I Think: Dyslexia, Dyspraxia, ADHD and Dyscalculia Explained* (New York: Routledge, 2017), 102.

89. Noam Sagiv and Chris D. Frith, "Synesthesia and Consciousness," in Simner and Hubbard, *Oxford Handbook of Synesthesia*, 934.

90. Quoted in Cytowic and Eagleman, *Wednesday Is Indigo Blue*, 74.

91. Quoted in Cytowic, *Synesthesia: A Union of the Senses*, 35.

92. Charlotte A. Chun and Jean-Michel Hupé, "Mirror-Touch and Ticker Tape Experiences in Synesthesia," *Frontiers in Psychology* 4 (2013): https://doi.org/10.3389/fpsyg.2013.00776

93. Alison Motluk, "Two Synaesthetes Talking Colour," in *Synaesthesia: Classic and Contemporary Readings*, eds. Simon Baron-Cohen and John E. Harrison (Oxford: Blackwell, 1997), 271.

94. Seaberg, *Tasting the Universe*, 69.

95. Quoted in Cytowic, *Synesthesia: A Union of the Senses*, 1.

96. Ward, *The Frog Who Croaked Blue*, 84.

97. Quoted in Dittmar, *Synaesthesia*, 224.

98. Quoted in Dittmar, *Synaesthesia*, 224.

99. Quoted in William O. Krohn, "Pseudo-Chromesthesia, or the Association of Colors with Words, Letters and Sounds," *American Journal of Psychology* 5.1 (1892): 20–41, at 29.

100. Mills et al., "The Color of Two Alphabets for a Multilingual Synesthete," 1376.

101. Cytowic and Eagleman, *Wednesday Is Indigo Blue*, 175.

102. Nabokov, *Speak, Memory*, 18.

103. Mills et al., "The Color of Two Alphabets for a Multilingual Synesthete," 1376.

104. Quoted in Ward, *The Frog Who Croaked Blue*, 5–6.

105. Quoted in Alison Motluk, "Living with Coloured Names," *New Scientist* 143.1938 (1994): 36; Mills et al., "The Color of Two Alphabets for a Multilingual Synesthete," 1376.

106. Quoted in Cytowic, *Synesthesia: A Union of the Senses*, 45.

107. Quoted in Sacks, *Musicophilia*, 175 fn 8.

108. Richard E. Cytowic, "Synaesthesia: Phenomenology and Neuropsychology," in *Synaesthesia: Classic and Contemporary Readings*, eds. Simon Baron-Cohen and John E. Harrison (Oxford: Blackwell, 1997), 19.

109. Tito Rajarshi Mukhopadhyay, *How Can I Talk If My Lips Don't Move? Inside My Autistic Mind* (New York: Arcade, 2008), 200–201. This passage is discussed in Ralph James Savarese, "What Some Autistics Can Teach Us About Poetry: A Neurocosmopolitan Approach," in *The Oxford Handbook of Cognitive Literary Studies*, ed. Lisa Zunshine (Oxford: Oxford University Press, 2015), 406.

110. A. R. Luria, *The Mind of a Mnemonist: A Little Book About a Vast Memory*, trans. Lynn Solotaroff (Cambridge, MA: Harvard University Press, 1987), 113.

111. Quoted in Mathew H. Gendle, "Word-Gustatory Synesthesia: A Case Study," *Perception* 36.4 (2007): 495–507, at 502.

112. Quoted in Cytowic and Eagleman, *Wednesday Is Indigo Blue*, 145.

113. Ward, *The Frog Who Croaked Blue*, 55–56.

114. Jamie Ward and Julia Simner, "Lexical-Gustatory Synaesthesia: Linguistic and Conceptual Factors," *Cognition* 89.3 (2003): 237–261, at 240.

115. Ward, *The Frog Who Croaked Blue*, 43.

116. Olympia Colizoli, Jaap M. J. Murre, and Romke Rouw, "A Taste for Words and Sounds: A Case of Lexical-Gustatory and Sound-Gustatory Synesthesia," *Frontiers in Psychology* 4 (2013): https://doi.org/10.3389/fpsyg.2013.00775; Gendle, "Word-Gustatory Synesthesia," 497.

117. Calkins, "Synæsthesia," 107.

118. Quoted in Calkins, "Synæsthesia," 107.

119. Quoted in Calkins, "A Statistical Study of Pseudo-Chromesthesia and of Mental-Forms," 454.

120. Quoted in Calkins, "A Statistical Study of Pseudo-Chromesthesia and of Mental-Forms," 454.

121. Calkins, "Synæsthesia," 100.

122. Noam Sagiv, Monika Sobcak-Edmans, and Adrian L. Williams, "Personification, Synaesthesia, and Social Cognition," in *Sensory Blending: On Synaesthesia and Related Phenomena*, ed. Ophelia Deroy (Oxford: Oxford University Press, 2017), 304.

123. Quoted in Maina Amin et al., "Understanding Grapheme Personification: A Social Synaesthesia?" *Journal of Neuropsychology* 5.2 (2011): 255–282, at 261.

124. Daniel Smilek et al., "When '3' Is a Jerk and 'E' Is a King: Personifying Inanimate Objects in Synesthesia," *Journal of Cognitive Neuroscience* 19.6 (2007): 981–992, at 986.

125. Quoted in Sagiv, Sobcak-Edmans, and Williams, "Personification, Synaesthesia, and Social Cognition," 298.

126. Quoted in Smilek et al., "When '3' Is a Jerk and 'E' Is a King," 987.

127. Théodore Flournoy, "Strange Personifications," *Popular Science Monthly* 51 (1897): 112–116, at 113; translated from "Un cas de personnification," *L'Année Psychologique* 1 (1894): 191–197.

128. G. Devereux, "An Unusual Audio-Motor Synesthesia in an Adolescent. Significance of This Phenomenon in Psychoanalytic Therapy," *Psychiatric Quarterly* 40.3 (1966): 459–471, at 463.

129. Henry Laures, *Les synesthésies* (Paris: Bloud, 1908), 44.

130. Tammet, *Born on a Blue Day*, 161.

CHAPTER 5

1. The original questionnaire is reprinted in Table 1 of David Burbridge, "Galton's 100: An Exploration of Francis Galton's Imagery Studies," *British Journal for the History of Science* 27.4 (1994): 443–463, at 448. The final version can be found in an appendix to Francis Galton, *Inquiries into Human Faculty and Its Development* (New York: Macmillan, 1883), 378–380.

2. Quoted in Francis Galton, "The Visions of Sane Persons," *Fortnightly Review* 29 (1881): 731–732.

3. For personal accounts of reading without mental imagery, see Alan Kendle, *Aphantasia: Experiences, Perceptions, and Insights* (Oakamoor, UK: Dark River, 2017). The chapter opening epigraph is from Siri Hustvedt, "Lifting, Lights, and Little People," Migraine blog, *New York Times* (February 17, 2008): https://migraine.blogs.nytimes.com/2008/02/17/lifting-lights-and-little-people/

4. William James, *The Principles of Psychology*, 2 vols. (Cambridge, MA: Harvard University Press, 1981), 2:759.

5. Johanna C. Badcock, Hedwige Dehon, and Frank Larøi, "Hallucinations in Healthy Older Adults: An Overview of the Literature and Perspectives for Future

Research," *Frontiers in Psychology* 8 (2017): https://www.frontiersin.org/articles/10
.3389/fpsyg.2017.01134/full

6. Northrop Frye, *The Great Code: The Bible and Literature* (Toronto: Academic, 1981), 218.

7. See, for example, Elaine Scarry, *Dreaming by the Book* (New York: Farrar, Straus and Giroux, 1999).

8. Fiona Macpherson, "The Philosophy and Psychology of Hallucination: An Introduction," in *Hallucination: Philosophy and Psychology*, eds. Fiona Macpherson and Dimitris Platchias (Cambridge, MA: MIT Press, 2013), 1.

9. Pamela Spiro Wagner and Carolyn S. Spiro, *Divided Minds: Twin Sisters and Their Journey Through Schizophrenia* (New York: St. Martin's Press, 2005), 218.

10. Roland Barthes, *The Rustle of Language*, trans. Richard Howard (Berkeley: University of California Press, 1989), 42.

11. Galton, "The Visions of Sane Persons," *Fortnightly Review*, 740.

12. "D.," "Faces in the Dark," *St. James's Gazette* (February 15, 1882): 6.

13. On the development of psychiatric approaches to mental illness, see Andrew Scull, *Madness in Civilization: A Cultural History of Insanity from the Bible to Freud, from the Madhouse to Modern Medicine* (Princeton: Princeton University Press, 2015). German E. Barrios and Ivana S. Marková discuss the shifting lexicon used to classify mental illness in "The Epistemology and Classification of 'Madness' since the Eighteenth Century," in *The Routledge History of Madness and Mental Health*, ed. Greg Eghigian (New York: Routledge, 2017), 115–134.

14. Jean-Étienne Dominique Esquirol, "Rapport statistique sur la Maison Royale de Charenton, pendant les années 1826, 1827 et 1828," *Annales D'Hygiène Publique et de Médecine Légale* 1 (1829): 101–151, at 122.

15. Jean-Étienne Dominique Esquirol, *Mental Maladies: A Treatise on Insanity*, trans. E. K. Hunt (Philadelphia: Lea and Blanchard, 1845), 109.

16. Tony James traces these debates over the status of hallucinations in *Dream, Creativity, and Madness in Nineteenth-Century France* (Oxford: Clarendon, 1995).

17. See, for example, Louis A. Sass, *Madness and Modernism: Insanity in the Light of Modern Art, Literature and Thought* (Cambridge, MA: Harvard University Press, 1994); and Allen Thiher, *Revels in Madness: Insanity in Medicine and Literature* (Ann Arbor: University of Michigan Press, 1999).

18. A. Brierre de Boismont, *Hallucinations: Or, the Rational History of Apparitions, Visions, Dreams, Ecstasy, Magnetism, and Somnambulism* (Philadelphia: Lindsay and Blakiston, 1853), 369–370.

19. De Boismont, *Hallucinations*, 306.

20. Forbes Winslow, *Obscure Diseases of the Brain and Mind*, 3rd ed. (London: Robert Hardwicke, 1863), 61.

21. Philip J. Weimerskirch, "Benjamin Rush and John Minson Galt, II: Pioneers of Bibliotherapy in America," *Bulletin of the Medical Library Association* 53.4 (1965): 510–526.

22. Benjamin Rush, *Medical Inquiries and Observations upon the Diseases of the Mind*, 5th ed. (Philadelphia: Grigg and Elliot, 1835), 123, 239.

23. *Report of the Metropolitan Commissioners in Lunacy* (London: Bradbury and Evans, 1844), 130.

24. John Conolly, "The Physiognomy of Insanity: No. 9.—Religious Mania," *Medical Times and Gazette* 38.982 (1858): 81–83, at 83.

25. John M. Galt, "On the Reading, Recreation, and Amusements of the Insane," *Journal of Psychological Medicine and Mental Pathology* 6.24 (1853): 581–589, at 584.

26. [James Frame], *The Philosophy of Insanity* (Edinburgh: MacLachlan and Stewart, 1860), 64.

27. [Frame], *The Philosophy of Insanity*, 64.

28. [Frame], *The Philosophy of Insanity*, 24. Nor was Frame's the only account of reading with the gut. James Cowles Prichard's *A Treatise on Insanity and Other Disorders Affecting the Mind* (Philadelphia: E. L. Carey & A. Hart, 1837) cites an alleged case of a woman who read by pressing text against her stomach (300).

29. W. A. F. Browne, "II. Cases of Disease of the Organs of Perception," *Phrenological Journal* 14 (1841): 77–79, at 77.

30. Quoted in William W. Ireland, *The Blot upon the Brain: Studies in History and Psychology* (Edinburgh: Bell and Bradfute, 1885), 11.

31. See Janet Oppenheim, *The Other World: Spiritualism and Psychical Research in England, 1850–1914* (Cambridge: Cambridge University Press, 1985).

32. Quoted in Edmund Gurney, Frederic W. H. Myers, and Frank Podmore, *Phantasms of the Living*, 2 vols. (London: Society for Psychical Research, 1886), 1:542.

33. Quoted in Henry Sidgwick et al., "Report on the Census of Hallucinations," in *Proceedings of the Society for Psychical Research*, vol. 10 (London: Kegan Paul, Trench, Trübner, 1894), 152.

34. Quoted in Sidgwick et al., "Report on the Census of Hallucinations," 87.

35. Quoted in Gurney, Myers, and Podmore, *Phantasms of the Living*, 1:490.

36. Daniel 5:1–31.

37. Jonathan Swift, "The Run upon the Bankers," in *Jonathan Swift: Major Works*, eds. Angus Ross and David Woolley (Oxford: Oxford University Press, 2003), 409. Emphasis in original.

38. Saint Augustine, *Confessions,* trans. Henry Chadwick (Oxford: Oxford University Press, 2008), 152.

39. Barbara Newman, "What Did It Mean to Say 'I Saw'? The Clash Between Theory and Practice in Medieval Visionary Culture," *Speculum* 80.1 (2005): 1–43.

40. Saint Teresa of Ávila, *The Life of St. Teresa of Avila, Including the Relations of Her Spiritual State, Written by Herself,* trans. David Lewis (London: Burns and Oates, 1962), 123.

41. Quoted in T. M. Luhrmann, *When God Talks Back: Understanding the American Evangelical Relationship with God* (New York: Alfred A. Knopf, 2012), 69.

42. Luhrmann, *When God Talks Back*, 138. Emphasis in original.

43. Luhrmann, *When God Talks Back,* 191–192.

44. Galton, *Inquiries into Human Faculty*, 155–177.

45. See Andreas Mavromatis, *Hypnagogia: The Unique State of Consciousness Between Wakefulness and Sleep* (London: Routledge & Kegan Paul, 1987).

46. Vladimir Nabokov, *Speak, Memory: An Autobiography Revisited* (New York: Penguin, 2012), 17.

47. On the relationship between hypnagogia and literature, see Peter Schwenger, *At the Borders of Sleep: On Liminal Literature* (Minneapolis: University of Minnesota Press, 2012).

48. Maurice M. Ohayon, Robert G. Priest, Malijaï Caulet, and Christian Guilleminault, "Hypnagogic and Hypnopompic Hallucinations: Pathological Phenomena?" *British Journal of Psychiatry* 169 (1996): 459–467, at 464.

49. R. C. Zaehner, *Mysticism, Sacred and Profane: An Inquiry into Some Varieties of Praeternatural Experience* (Oxford: Oxford University Press, 1961), 212.

50. André Breton, *What Is Surrealism? Selected Writings*, ed. Franklin Rosemont (New York: Pathfinder, 1978), 162.

51. Postscript to Samuel Taylor Coleridge, "Kubla Khan," the Crewe manuscript (c. 1797–1804), Add MS 50847, British Library: https://www.bl.uk/collection-items/manuscript-of-s-t-coleridges-kubla-khan

52. See the account of Coleridge's dreams in Alethea Hayter, *Opium and the Romantic Imagination* (London: Faber, 2015).

53. Samuel Taylor Coleridge to Thomas Wedgwood (September 16, 1803), in *Collected Letters of Samuel Taylor Coleridge*, 6 vols., ed. Earl Leslie Griggs (Oxford: Clarendon, 1966), 2:520.

54. Ernest Hartmann, "We Do Not Dream of the 3 R's: Implications for the Nature of Dreaming Mentation," *Dreaming* 10.2 (2000): 103–110.

55. Oliver Fox, *Astral Projection: A Record of Out-of-the-Body Experiences* (New Hyde Park, NY: University Books, 1962), 46.

56. Edmund Gosse, *Father and Son*, ed. Michael Newton (Oxford: Oxford University Press, 2004), 87.

57. Robert Louis Stevenson, *Across the Plains: With Other Memories and Essays* (London: Chatto and Windus, 1892), 234.

58. Fitz Hugh Ludlow, *The Hasheesh Eater: Being Passages from the Life of a Pythagorean* (New York: Harper and Brothers, 1857), 242.

59. Quoted in de Boismont, *Hallucinations*, 329.

60. Quoted in de Boismont, *Hallucinations*, 331.

61. Kevin Powers, "What Kept Me from Killing Myself," *New York Times* (June 16, 2018): https://www.nytimes.com/2018/06/16/opinion/sunday/books-saved-me-from-suicide.html

62. On reading's role in the recovery process, see Trysh Travis, *The Language of the Heart: A Cultural History of the Recovery Movement from Alcoholics Anonymous to Oprah Winfrey* (Chapel Hill: University of North Carolina Press, 2009).

63. Tim Page, *Parallel Play: Growing Up with Undiagnosed Asperger's* (New York: Doubleday, 2009), 103.

64. Mike Jay, *Mescaline: A Global History of the First Psychedelic* (New Haven: Yale University Press, 2019).

65. Havelock Ellis, "Mescal: A New Artificial Paradise," *Contemporary Review* 73 (1898): 130–141, at 132. See also S. Weir Mitchell, "The Effects of Anhelonium Lewinii (The Mescal Button)," *British Medical Journal* 2 (1896): 1625–1629.

66. Bo Roland Holmstedt and Göran Liljestrand, eds., *Readings in Pharmacology* (London: Pergamon, 1963), 208.

67. Aldous Huxley, *The Doors of Perception* and *Heaven and Hell* (New York: Perennial Classics, 2004), 19.

68. Philip B. Smith, "A Sunday with Mescaline," *Bulletin of the Menninger Clinic* 23.1 (1959): 20–27, at 22.

69. Quoted in Vladimir Lerner and Eliezer Witztum, "Victor Kandinsky, MD: Psychiatrist, Researcher and Patient," *History of Psychiatry* 14.1 (2003): 103–111, at 107.

70. T. M. Luhrmann and Jocelyn Marrow, eds., *Our Most Troubling Madness: Case Studies in Schizophrenia Across Cultures* (Oakland: University of California Press, 2016).

71. For more on the challenges faced by schizophrenic readers, see Robyn Lynette Hayes and Bethany Maree O'Grady, "Do People with Schizophrenia Comprehend What They Read?" *Schizophrenia Bulletin* 29.3 (2003): 499–507.

72. Quoted in Susannah Cahalan, *The Great Pretender: The Undercover Mission That Changed Our Understanding of Madness* (Edinburgh: Canongate, 2020), 277.

73. This sentence is taken from the chapter title "Paranoid Reading and Reparative Reading, or, You're So Paranoid, You Probably Think This Essay Is About You," in Eve Kosofsky Sedgwick, *Touching Feeling: Affect, Pedagogy, Performativity* (Durham: Duke University Press, 2003), 123–152.

74. On Kraepelin's role in the classification of mental illness, see Richard Noll, *American Madness: The Rise and Fall of Dementia Praecox* (Cambridge, MA: Harvard University Press, 2011), 49–73. The subsequent evolution of schizophrenia as a concept is traced by Kieran McNally, *A Critical History of Schizophrenia* (London: Palgrave Macmillan, 2016).

75. Quoted in Emil Kraepelin, *Dementia Praecox and Paraphrenia*, trans. R. Mary Barclay, ed. George M. Robertson (Chicago: Chicago Medical Book, [1919]), 105.

76. Emil Kraepelin, *Manic-Depressive Insanity and Paranoia*, trans. R. Mary Barclay, ed. George M. Robertson (Edinburgh: E. & S. Livingstone, 1921), 9.

77. "Anonymous," "An Autobiography of a Schizophrenic Experience," *Journal of Abnormal and Social Psychology* 51.3 (1955): 677–689, at 681.

78. Quoted in E. Fuller Torrey, *Surviving Schizophrenia: A Family Manual,* 7th ed. (New York: Harper Perennial, 2019), Adobe Digital Edition EPUB, 21.

79. Quoted in Torrey, *Surviving Schizophrenia,* 38.

80. Eugen Bleuler, *Dementia Praecox or the Group of Schizophrenias* (New York: International Universities Press, 1950), 106.

81. On the nature and prevalence of auditory hallucinations, see Charles Fernyhough, *The Voices Within: The History and Science of How We Talk to Ourselves* (London: Profile, 2016).

82. Quoted in Marjorie C. Meehan, "Echo of Reading: Impersonal Projection in Schizophrenia," *Psychiatric Quarterly* 16.1 (1942): 156–166, at 156. See also Ferdinand Morel, "L'Écho de la lecture: Contribution a l'étude des hallucinations auditives verbales," *L'Encéphale* 28.3 (1933): 169–183.

83. Quoted in Meehan, "Echo of Reading," 160.

84. William W. Ireland, *The Blot upon the Brain: Studies in History and Psychology* (Edinburgh: Bell and Bradfute, 1885), 28.

85. Jean-Étienne Dominique Esquirol, *Mental Maladies: A Treatise on Insanity,* trans. E. K. Hunt (Philadelphia: Lea and Blanchard, 1845), 323.

86. Quoted in Meehan, "Echo of Reading," 162.

87. Damien Droney, "Demonic Voices: One Man's Experience of God, Witches, and Psychosis in Accra, Ghana," in Luhrmann and Marrow, *Our Most Troubling Madness,* 122.

88. Carol S. North, *Welcome, Silence: My Triumph over Schizophrenia* (New York: Simon & Schuster, 1987), 78.

89. Quoted in Meehan, "Echo of Reading," 160.

90. Michael D. Kopelman, Elizabeth M. Guinan, and Philip D. R. Lewis, "Delusional Memory, Confabulation and Frontal Lobe Dysfunction," in *Broken Memories: Case Studies in Memory Impairment,* eds. Ruth Campbell and Martin A. Conway (Oxford: Blackwell, 1995), 145.

91. Daniel Paul Schreber, *Memoirs of My Nervous Illness,* trans. Ida MacAlpine and Richard A. Hunter (New York: New York Review of Books, 2000), 203.

92. Kristina Morgan, *Mind Without a Home: A Memoir of Schizophrenia* (Center City, MN: Hazeldon, 2013), 31.

93. Charles Dickens, *David Copperfield* (Oxford: Oxford University Press, 1994), 56.

94. Ken Steele and Claire Berman, *The Day the Voices Stopped: A Memoir of Madness and Hope* (New York: Basic Books, 2001), 7–8.

95. Steele and Berman, *Day the Voices Stopped,* 15.

96. Mark Vonnegut, *The Eden Express: A Memoir of Insanity* (New York: Seven Stories, 2002), 119.

97. Vonnegut, *Eden Express,* 119–120.

98. This portmanteau combines the diagnostic label "schizoaffective disorder" with the literary-critical term "the affective fallacy," outlined in William K. Wimsatt, with Monroe C. Beardsley, *The Verbal Icon: Studies in the Meaning of Poetry* (Lexington: University of Kentucky Press, 1954).

99. Stanley Fish, *Is There a Text in This Class?: The Authority of Interpretive Communities* (Cambridge, MA: Harvard University Press, 1980), 346.

100. See, for instance, A. Paula McKay, Peter J. McKenna, and Keith Laws, "Severe Schizophrenia: What Is It Like?," in *Method in Madness: Case Studies in Cognitive Neuropsychiatry,* eds. Peter W. Halligan and John C. Marshall (Hove, UK: Psychology Press, 1996), 100.

101. Clifford Whittingham Beers, *A Mind That Found Itself: An Autobiography,* 3rd ed. (London: Longmans, Green, 1913), 32.

102. Beers, *A Mind That Found Itself*, 53–54.

103. Benedict Anderson, *Imagined Communities: Reflections on the Origins and Spread of Nationalism*, rev. ed. (London: Verso, 1991), 6.

104. Richard McLean, *Recovered, Not Cured: A Journey Through Schizophrenia* (New South Wales: Allen & Unwin, 2003), 15; Amy June Sousa, "Diagnostic Neutrality in Psychiatric Treatment in North India," in Luhrmann and Marrow, *Our Most Troubling Madness*, 46.

105. May-May Meijer, "In the Garden of Eden: The Content of My Psychoses," *Schizophrenia Bulletin* 44.3 (2018): 469–471, at 469.

106. D. Walton and M. D. Mather, "The Application of Learning Principles to the Treatment of Obsessive-Compulsive States in the Acute and Chronic Phases of Illness," *Behaviour Research and Therapy* 1.2–4 (1963): 163–174.

107. See Eric Bennett, *Workshops of Empire: Stegner, Engle, and American Creative Writing During the Cold War* (Iowa City: University of Iowa Press, 2015).

108. Kurt Snyder, Raquel E. Gur, and Linda Wasmer Andrews, *Me, Myself, and Them: A Firsthand Account of One Young Person's Experience with Schizophrenia* (Oxford: Oxford University Press, 2007), 62.

109. Blake Morrison, "The Woman on the Doorstep," in *Mind Readings: Writers' Journeys Through Mental States*, eds. Sara Dunn, Blake Morrison, and Michèle Roberts (London: Minerva, 1996), 403–409.

110. Mira Bartók, *The Memory Palace* (New York: Free Press, 2011), 92.

111. Susan K. Weiner, "First Person Account: Living with the Delusions and Effects of Schizophrenia," *Schizophrenia Bulletin* 29.4 (2003): 877–879, at 877.

112. Quoted in Karen Nakamura, *A Disability of the Soul: An Ethnography of Schizophrenia and Mental Illness in Contemporary Japan* (Ithaca: Cornell University Press, 2013), 178.

113. Sylvia Plath, *The Bell Jar* (London: Faber, 2005), 120.

114. Plath, *The Bell Jar*, 149.

115. Elyn R. Saks, *The Center Cannot Hold: My Journey Through Madness* (New York: Hyperion, 2007), 29.

116. Lori Schiller and Amanda Bennett, *The Quiet Room: A Journey Out of the Torment of Madness* (New York: Grand Central, 2011), 17.

117. Saks, *The Center Cannot Hold*, 29.

118. Monroe Cole, "When the Left Brain Is Not Right the Right Brain May Be Left: Report of Personal Experience of Occipital Hemianopia," *Journal of Neurology, Neurosurgery and Psychiatry* 67.2 (1999): 169–173, at 170.

119. G. E. Berrios and P. Brook, "Visual Hallucinations and Sensory Delusions in the Elderly," *British Journal of Psychiatry* 144.6 (1984): 662–664.

120. Quoted in John C. M. Brust and Myles M. Behrens, "'Release Hallucinations' as the Major Symptom of Posterior Cerebral Artery Occlusion: A Report of 2 Cases," *Annals of Neurology* 2.5 (1977): 432–436, at 432.

121. Reinhard Schulz, Friedrich G. Woermann, and Alois Ebner, "When Written Words Become Moving Pictures: Complex Visual Hallucinations on Stimulation of the Lateral Occipital Lobe," *Epilepsy and Behavior* 11.1 (2007): 147–151.

122. Marc Rousseaux, Dominique Debrock, Maryline Cabaret, and Marc Stein-ling, "Visual Hallucinations with Written Words in a Case of Left Parietotemporal Lesion," *Journal of Neurology, Neurosurgery, and Psychiatry* 57.1 (1994): 1268–1271.

123. Gerda Saunders, *Memory's Last Breath: Field Notes on My Dementia* (New York: Hachette, 2017), 9.

124. Quoted in Bun Yamagata, Hitomi Kobayashi, Hideki Yamamoto, and Ma-saru Mimura, "Visual Text Hallucinations of Thoughts in an Alexic Woman," *Journal of the Neurological Sciences* 339.1–2 (2014): 226–228, at 226.

125. Quoted in Walter Freeman and Jonathan M. Williams, "Hallucinations in Braille: Effects of Amygdaloidectomy," *Archives of Neurology and Psychiatry* 70.5 (1953): 630–634, at 631.

126. D. H. ffytche, J. M. Lappin, and M. Philpot, "Visual Command Hallucina-tions in a Patient with Pure Alexia," *Journal of Neurology, Neurosurgery and Psychiatry* 75.1 (2004): 80–86, at 80.

127. Oliver Sacks, *Hallucinations* (London: Picador, 2012), 26.

128. Sacks, *Hallucinations*, 13, 140.

129. Sacks, *Hallucinations*, 13.

130. Sacks, *Hallucinations*, 81.

131. Sacks, *Hallucinations,* 222.

132. ffytche, Lappin, and Philpot, "Visual Command Hallucinations," 81.

133. Quoted in ffytche, Lappin, and Philpot, "Visual Command Hallucina-tions," 82.

134. Eric Nieman, "Charles Bonnet Syndrome," *Practical Neurology* 18.6 (2018): 434–435. My thanks to Dominic ffytche for sharing this account with me.

135. Quoted in Thomas M. Cox and Dominic H. ffytche, "Negative Outcome Charles Bonnet Syndrome," *British Journal of Ophthalmology* 98.9 (2014): 1236–1239, at 1236.

136. Saul Bellow, *Ravelstein* (New York: Penguin, 2001), 209.

137. On the scientific explanations of near-death experiences, see Susan Black-more, *Seeing Myself: The New Science of Out-of-Body Experiences* (London: Robin-son, 2017).

138. Apocalipsis 20:12.

139. These details are taken from Marvin J. Besteman, *My Journey to Heaven: What I Saw and How It Changed My Life* (Grand Rapids, MI: Revell, 2012); and Richard Sigmund, *My Time in Heaven: A True Story of Dying and Coming Back* (New Kensington, PA: Whitaker House, 2010).

140. Gary L. Wood, *A Place Called Heaven* (Kingwood, TX: RevMedia, 2008), 26.

CHAPTER 6

1. Terry Pratchett, *Shaking Hands with Death* (London: Corgi, 2015), 21. The ac-tor who finished the lecture was Tony Robinson, best known for playing Baldrick on the BBC television series *Blackadder* (1983–89).

2. Pratchett, *Shaking Hands with Death*, 21.

3. See Ian Lancashire, "Vocabulary and Dementia in Six Novelists," in *Language Development: The Lifespan Perspective*, eds. Annette Gerstenberg and Anja Voeste (Amsterdam: John Benjamins, 2015), 77–108.

4. Pratchett discusses how memory loss has affected his literacy in *Terry Pratchett: Living with Alzheimer's* (BBC, 2009). This documentary can be viewed at https://www.youtube.com/watch?v=KmejLjxFmCQ

5. William Shakespeare, *The Complete Works of Shakespeare*, ed. David Bevington, 4th ed. (New York: HarperCollins, 1992), 305. The chapter opening epigraph is from Virginia Woolf, "Charlotte Brontë," *Times Literary Supplement* 743 (April 13, 1916): 169.

6. On the various patterns of reading impairment, see Enrico Ripamonti, "Reading Impairment in Neurodegenerative Diseases: A Multiple Single-Case Study," *Aphasiology* 31.5 (2017): 519–541.

7. Jonathan Swift, *Gulliver's Travels*, ed. Robert DeMaria Jr. (New York: Penguin, 2001), 197.

8. For more information about the prevalence and impact of dementia, see the annual World Alzheimer Reports at: https://www.alz.co.uk/research/world-report

9. The name originated from Alois Alzheimer's treatment of a patient with a severe form of dementia, including rapidly increasing memory impairments. As Alzheimer noted of the patient, "While reading she would omit sentences, she would spell every word or read without intonation." Alois Alzheimer, "A Characteristic Disease of the Cerebral Cortex," in *The Early Story of Alzheimer's Disease: Translation of the Historical Papers by Alois Alzheimer, Oskar Fischer, Francesco Bonfiglio, Emil Kraepelin, Gaetano Perusini*, eds. Katherine Bick, Luigi Amaducci, and Giancarlo Pepeu (Padova, Italy: Liviana Press, 1987), 2.

10. Edward Fitzgerald to C. E. Norton (February 20, 1878), in Edward Fitzgerald, *Letters and Literary Remains of Edward Fitzgerald*, ed. William Aldis Wright, 3 vols. (London: Macmillan, 1889), 1:412.

11. Daniel L. Schacter, *How the Mind Forgets and Remembers: The Seven Sins of Memory* (London: Souvenir, 2001), 5.

12. Malcolm L. Meltzer, "Poor Memory: A Case Report," in *Injured Brains of Medical Minds: Views from Within*, ed. Narinder Kapur (Oxford: Oxford University Press, 1997), 9.

13. See, for example, Niall Tubridy, *Just One More Question: Stories from a Life in Neurology* (London: Penguin, 2019).

14. On the use of reading ability to diagnose dementia, see Hazel E. Nelson, *The National Adult Reading Test (NART): Test Manual* (Windsor, UK: NFER-Nelson, 1982).

15. Daniel L. Schacter and Elaine Scarry, "Introduction," in *Memory, Brain, and Belief*, eds. Daniel L. Schacter and Elaine Scarry (Cambridge, MA: Harvard University Press, 2000), 1. On memory loss as a condition of modernity, see Francis O'Gorman, *Forgetfulness: Making the Modern Culture of Amnesia* (London: Bloomsbury, 2017).

16. On the cognitive mechanisms behind memory formation, see Daniel L. Schacter, *Searching for Memory: The Brain, the Mind, and the Past* (New York: Basic

Books, 1996); and Charles Fernyhough, *Pieces of Light: The New Science of Memory* (London: Profile Books, 2012).

17. George Gissing, *The Private Papers of Henry Ryecroft* (Westminster, UK: Archibald Constable, 1903), 53.

18. Charles Darwin, *The Autobiography of Charles Darwin, 1809–1882*, ed. Nora Barlow (New York: W. W. Norton, 1969), 140; Michel de Montaigne, *The Complete Works: Essays, Travel Journal, Letters*, trans. Donald M. Frame (London: Everyman's Library, 2003), 359.

19. On the relevance of this term for literary criticism, see Andrew Elfenbein, *The Gist of Reading* (Stanford: Stanford University Press, 2018).

20. Milan Kundera, *The Curtain: An Essay in Seven Parts*, trans. Linda Asher (London: Faber, 2007), 150.

21. William James, *The Principles of Psychology*, 2 vols. (Cambridge, MA: Harvard University Press, 1981), 1:622.

22. Gabriel García Márquez, *One Hundred Years of Solitude*, trans. Gregory Rabassa (New York: Penguin, 2000), 48–49.

23. James Boswell, *Life of Johnson*, ed. R. W. Chapman (Oxford: Oxford University Press, 2008), 30.

24. Mary Hyde, "The Thrales of Streatham Park," *Harvard Library Bulletin* 24.2 (1976): 125–179, at 163.

25. Fred Barlow, *Mental Prodigies; An Enquiry into the Faculties of Arithmetical, Chess, and Musical Prodigies, Famous Memorizers, Precocious Children and the Like* (New York: Greenwood, 1969), 151.

26. Pliny, *Natural History*, trans. H[arris] Rackham, 5 vols. (London: Folio Society, 2012), 1:346.

27. *The Virgilian Tradition: The First Fifteen Hundred Years*, eds. Jan M. Ziolkowski and Michael C. J. Putnam (New Haven: Yale University Press, 2008), 76.

28. David Bevington, Martin Butler, and Ian Donaldson, eds., *The Cambridge Edition of the Works of Ben Jonson*, 7 vols. (Cambridge: Cambridge University Press, 2012), 7:517.

29. The USA Memory Championship still features poetry among its qualifying events. A sample poem (Patricia Anne Pinson's "Carpe Diem") is available on the organization's website: https://www.usamemorychampionship.com/events/

30. Mary Carruthers, *The Book of Memory: A Study of Memory in Medieval Culture*, 2nd ed. (Cambridge: Cambridge University Press, 2008), 143.

31. Joshua Foer, *Moonwalking with Einstein: The Art and Science of Remembering Everything* (New York: Penguin, 2011), 107–135.

32. William James learned by heart the first book of *Paradise Lost* as part of an experiment to test whether memorizing that poem would make it easier to memorize other poems. But spending twenty minutes per day (thirty-eight days total) learning the entire first book of *Paradise Lost* actually slowed the rate at which he absorbed other verses. William James, *The Principles of Psychology*, 2 vols. (Cambridge, MA: Harvard University Press, 1981), 1:627 fn 24.

33. Barlow, *Mental Prodigies*, 137; George Otto Trevelyan, *The Life and Letters of Lord Macaulay* (Oxford: Oxford University Press, 1978), 199; Harriet Martineau, *Autobiography* (Peterborough, Canada: Broadview, 2007), 62.

34. Robert E. Sullivan, *Macaulay: The Tragedy of Power* (Cambridge, MA: Harvard University Press, 2009), 28.

35. Alexander Aitken, *Gallipoli to the Somme: Recollections of a New Zealand Infantryman* (London: Oxford University Press, 1963), 107.

36. Ian M. L. Hunter, "An Exceptional Memory," *British Journal of Psychology* 68.2 (1977): 155–164, at 163.

37. F. C. Bartlett, *Remembering: A Study in Experimental and Social Psychology* (Cambridge: Cambridge University Press, 1932), 44.

38. John Abercrombie, *Inquiries Concerning the Intellectual Powers, and the Investigation of Truth* (Boston: Otis, Broaders, 1843), 80.

39. George M. Stratton, "The Mnemonic Feat of the 'Shass Pollak,'" *Psychological Review* 24.3 (1917): 244–247.

40. Elizabeth S. Parker, Larry Cahill, and James L. McGaugh, "A Case of Unusual Autobiographical Remembering," *Neurocase* 12.1 (2006): 35–49.

41. Jill Price, with Bart Davis, *The Woman Who Can't Forget: The Extraordinary Story of Living with the Most Remarkable Memory Known to Science: A Memoir* (New York: Free Press, 2008), 24. Subsequent cases of HSAM are documented in Linda Rodriquez McRobbie, "Total Recall: The People Who Never Forget," *Guardian* (February 8, 2017): https://www.theguardian.com/science/2017/feb/08/total-recall-the-people-who-never-forget

42. A. R. Luria, *The Mind of a Mnemonist: A Little Book About a Vast Memory*, trans. Lynn Solotaroff (Cambridge, MA: Harvard University Press, 1987), 30. For a profile of a modern-day mnemonist (who gave exhibitions in which he simultaneously played chess and bridge while reading a book), see Earl Hunt and Tom Love, "How Good Can Memory Be?," in *Coding Processes in Human Memory* (Washington, DC: V. H. Winston, 1972), 237–260.

43. Quoted in Luria, *The Mind of a Mnemonist*, 112.

44. Quoted in Luria, *The Mind of a Mnemonist*, 65.

45. Quoted in Luria, *The Mind of a Mnemonist*, 116.

46. Jorge Luis Borges, *Labyrinths: Selected Stories and Other Writings*, eds. Donald A. Yates and James E. Irby (New York: New Directions, 1964), 64.

47. John R. Hodges, "Transient Global Amnesia" in *Mental Lives: Case Studies in Cognition*, ed. Ruth Campbell (Oxford: Blackwell, 1992), 243.

48. Su Meck and Daniel de Visé, *I Forgot to Remember: A Memoir of Amnesia* (New York: Simon & Schuster, 2014), Adobe Digital Edition EPUB, 38.

49. Théodule-Armand Ribot, *Diseases of Memory: An Essay in the Positive Psychology* (London: Kegan Paul, Trench, 1882), 95.

50. On the selective impairments associated with amnesic syndrome, see Alan J. Parkin, *Memory and Amnesia: An Introduction*, 2nd ed. (Hove, UK: Psychology Press, 1997).

51. Narinder Kapur and David Moakes, "Living with Amnesia," in *Broken Memories: Case Studies in Memory Impairment*, eds. Ruth Campbell and Martin A. Conway (Oxford: Blackwell, 1995), 1–7.

52. Lisa Stefanacci, Elizabeth A. Buffalo, Heike Schmolck, and Larry R. Squire, "Profound Amnesia After Damage to the Media Temporal Lobe: A Neuroanatomical and Neuropsychological Profile of Patient E. P.," *Journal of Neuroscience* 20.18 (2000): 7024–7036, at 7024. Squire suggested that amnesia patients might continue reading the newspaper out of habit (email correspondence [May 20, 2020]).

53. Michael D. Lemonick, *The Perpetual Now: A Story of Amnesia, Memory, and Love* (New York: Doubleday, 2016), 135–136. On Johnson's ability to carry out skilled activities, see Emma Gregory, Michael McCloskey, Zoe Ovans, and Barbara Landau, "Declarative Memory and Skill-Related Knowledge: Evidence from a Case Study of Amnesia and Implications for Theories of Memory," *Cognitive Neuropsychology* 33.3–4 (2016): 220–240.

54. Christine Hyung-Oak Lee, *Tell Me Everything You Don't Remember: The Stroke That Changed My Life* (New York: Ecco, 2017), 14.

55. Lee, *Tell Me Everything*, 33.

56. Barbara A. Wilson, *Case Studies in Neuropsychological Rehabilitation* (Oxford: Oxford University Press, 1999), 30.

57. Wilson, *Case Studies*, 33, 32.

58. Quoted in Wilson, *Case Studies*, 42.

59. Deborah Wearing, *Forever Today: A Memoir of Love and Amnesia* (London: Corgi, 2005), 187.

60. Barbara A. Wilson and Deborah Wearing, "Prisoner of Consciousness: A State of Just Awakening Following Herpes Simplex Encephalitis," in *Broken Memories: Case Studies in Memory Impairment*, eds. Ruth Campbell and Martin A. Conway (Oxford: Blackwell, 1995), 18.

61. Suzanne Corkin, *Permanent Present Tense: The Unforgettable Life of the Amnesic Patient, H. M.* (New York: Basic Books, 2013), xii.

62. Philip J. Hilts, *Memory's Ghost: The Strange Tale of Mr. M. and the Nature of Memory* (New York: Simon & Schuster, 1995), 116.

63. Hilts, *Memory's Ghost*, 19.

64. Corkin, *Permanent Present Tense*, 216–217. Donald G. MacKay elaborates on the nature of Molaison's reading deficits in *Remembering: What 50 Years of Research with Famous Amnesia Patient H. M. Can Teach Us About Memory and How It Works* (Amherst, NY: Prometheus, 2019).

65. Luke Dittrich, *Patient H. M.: A Story of Memory, Madness, and Family Secrets* (New York: Random House, 2016), 258. My thanks to Dittrich for providing additional information about this case.

66. Peter Brooks, *Reading for the Plot: Design and Intention in Narrative* (New York: Vintage, 1985).

67. *Memento*, dir. Christopher Nolan, 2000 (Santa Monica: Lionsgate, 2012), DVD/Blu-ray.

68. For more on the genre of amnesia stories, see Jonathan Lethem, ed., *The Vintage Book of Amnesia: An Anthology* (New York: Vintage, 2000).

69. Jonathan Nolan, "Memento Mori," in James Mottram, *The Making of Memento* (London: Faber, 2002), appendix p. 193. The story originally appeared in *Esquire Magazine* (March 1, 2001): 186–191.

70. Nolan, "Memento Mori," 183.

71. Milt Freudenheim, "Many Alzheimer's Patients Find Comfort in Books," "The New Old Age" blog, *New York Times* (April 22, 2010): https://newoldage.blogs.nytimes.com/2010/04/22/many-alzheimers-patients-find-comfort-in-books/

72. Laura Bramly, Gilbert, AZ (April 26, 2010): https://newoldage.blogs.nytimes.com/2010/04/22/many-alzheimers-patients-find-comfort-in-books/. Bramly is the author of *ElderCareRead: Life Scenes 1: Scenes from Everyday Life for People with Moderate to Advanced Alzheimer's Disease and Other Forms of Dementia to See, Read, and Talk About* (self-pub., 2008).

73. On reading's potential benefits, see Julie M. Latchem and Janette Greenhalgh, "The Role of Reading on the Health and Well-Being of People with Neurological Conditions: A Systematic Review," *Aging and Mental Health* 18.6 (2014): 731–744; and Dawn DeVries et al., "The Impact of Reading Groups on Engagement and Social Interaction for Older Adults with Dementia: A Literature Review," *Therapeutic Recreation Journal* 53.1 (2019): 53–75.

74. Martin Orrell, Tom Dening, Nusrat Husain, Sally Rimkeit, Gillian Claridge, and Dalice Sim, "Reading for Dementia," in *Reading and Mental Health*, ed. Josie Billington (Cham: Palgrave Macmillan, 2019), 395–418.

75. Gary Mex Glazner, ed., *Sparking Memories: The Alzheimer's Poetry Project Anthology* (Santa Fe: Poem Factory, 2005).

76. Helle Arendrup Mortensen and Gyda Skat Nielsen, "Guidelines for Library Services to Persons with Dementia," *IFLA Professional Reports* 104 (2007): 1–16, at 9.

77. Jeffrey L. Cummings, John P. Houlihan, and Mary Ann Hill, "The Pattern of Reading Deterioration in Dementia of the Alzheimer Type: Observations and Implications," *Brain and Language* 29.2 (1986): 315–323.

78. Cynthia R. Green and Joan Beloff, *Through the Seasons: An Activity Book for Memory-Challenged Adults and Caregivers* (Baltimore: Johns Hopkins University Press, 2008), x.

79. Rosie May Walworth, "Adapting the Books on Prescription Model for People Living with Dementia and Their Carers," in *Bibliotherapy*, eds. Sarah McNicol and Liz Brewster (London: Facet, 2018), 149. The Pictures to Share catalogue is available at https://picturestoshare.co.uk/

80. Product information, "What the Wind Showed to Me: Volume 1 (Books for Dementia Patients)," Amazon (July 2, 2014): https://www.amazon.com/What-Showed-Books-Dementia-Patients/dp/1500664685/

81. Eliezer Sobel, *Blue Sky, White Clouds* (Faber, VA: Rainbow Ridge, 2013).

82. Lydia Burdick, *Wishing on a Star: A Read-Aloud Book for Memory-Challenged Adults* (Baltimore: Health Professions Press, 2009).

83. See, for example, Michael P. Jensen, "'You Speak All Your Part at Once, Cues and All': Reading Shakespeare with Alzheimer's Disease," *Borrowers and Lenders: The Journal of Shakespeare and Appropriation* 8.2 (2013/2014): https://openjournals.libs.uga.edu/borrowers/article/view/2256/2201

84. Melvyn Bragg, *Read to Care: An Investigation into Quality of Life Benefits of Shared Reading Groups for People Living with Dementia* (2014), 69: https://www.liverpool.ac.uk/media/livacuk/iphs/Read,to,Care,with,Melvyn,Bragg-1.pdf

85. Dovetale Press: http://www.dovetalepress.com/about-us

86. Sally B. Rimkeit and Gillian Claridge, "Literary Alzheimer's: A Qualitative Feasibility Study of Dementia-Friendly Book Groups," *New Zealand Library and Information Management Journal* 56.2 (2017): 14–22, at 18.

87. Arthur Conan Doyle, *Sherlock Holmes: The Adventure of the Blue Carbuncle*, adapted by Gillian Claridge and B. Sally Rimkeit (Wellington: Dovetale, 2016), 6.

88. Doyle, *Sherlock Holmes*, 63.

89. Charles Dickens, *A Christmas Carol*, adapted by Gillian Claridge and B. Sally Rimkeit (Wellington: Dovetale, 2016), 7.

90. For more on the visual cueing strategies appropriate to readers affected by memory deficits, see Michelle S. Bourgeois, *Memory and Communication Aids for People with Dementia* (Baltimore: Health Professions Press, 2014), 84–87.

91. Brooks, *Reading for the Plot*, 23.

92. Susan Ostrowski and Peter S. Dixon, "Reading and Dementia," *Perspectives of the ASHA Special Interest Groups* 1.15 (2016): 26–36, at 32. See also the organization's website: https://www.reading2connect.com/

93. G. Thomas Couser, "Memoir and (Lack of) Memory: Filial Narratives of Paternal Dementia," in *New Essays on Life Writing and the Body*, eds. Christopher Stuart and Stephanie Todd (Newcastle upon Tyne: Cambridge Scholars, 2009), 223–240.

94. Jesse F. Ballenger examines the negative perceptions of people with dementia in *Self, Senility, and Alzheimer's Disease in Modern America: A History* (Baltimore: Johns Hopkins University Press, 2006).

95. Lisa Snyder, *Speaking Our Minds: Personal Reflections from Individuals with Alzheimer's* (New York: W. H. Freeman, 1999), 1.

96. John Bayley, *Elegy for Iris* (New York: Picador, 1999), 259.

97. Bayley, *Elegy for Iris*, 62.

98. Rachel Hadas, *Strange Relation: A Memoir of Marriage, Dementia, and Poetry* (Philadelphia: Paul Dry, 2011), 73.

99. George Eliot, *Romola*, ed. Dorothea Barrett (New York: Penguin, 2005), 334.

100. Eliot, *Romola*, 447.

101. Eliot, *Romola*, 267.

102. Eliot, *Romola*, 310.

103. Jean Tyler and Harry Antifantakis, *The Diminished Mind: One Family's Extraordinary Battle with Alzheimer's* (Blue Ridge Summit, PA: TAB Books, 1991), 110.

104. Steph Booth, *Married to Alzheimer's: A Life Less Ordinary with Tony Booth* (London: Rider, 2019), 163.

105. Joseph Jebelli, *In Pursuit of Memory: The Fight Against Alzheimer's* (New York: Little, Brown, 2017), 183. On the difficulties following printed lines caused by Alzheimer's, see Keir X. X. Yong et al., "Facilitating Text Reading in Posterior Cortical Atrophy," *Neurology* 85.4 (2015): 339–348.

106. Marie Marley, *Come Back Early Today: A Memoir of Love, Alzheimer's and Joy* (Olathe, KS: Joseph Peterson, 2011), 32.

107. Quoted in Marley, *Come Back Early Today*, 192.

108. Jonathan Kozol, *The Theft of Memory: Losing My Father One Day at a Time* (New York: Crown, 2015), 208.

109. Robert B. Santulli and Kesstan Blandin, *The Emotional Journey of the Alzheimer's Family* (Hanover: Dartmouth College Press, 2015), 88.

110. Vicki Tapia, *Somebody Stole My Iron: A Family Memoir of Dementia* (Amarillo: Praeclarus, 2014), 167.

111. Candace Minor Comstock, *Remember Joan: An Alzheimer's Story* (self-pub., CreateSpace, 2011), Kindle edition, 135.

112. Richard Taylor, *Alzheimer's from the Inside Out* (Baltimore: Health Professions Press, 2007), 97.

113. Sarah Leavitt, *Tangles: A Story About Alzheimer's, My Mother, and Me* (New York: Skyhorse, 2012), 54.

114. Sally Magnusson, *Where Memories Go: Why Dementia Changes Everything* (London: Hodder and Stoughton, 2015), 149.

115. Marilyn Stevens, *Did I Ever Have Children?: An Alzheimer's Journey in Two Voices* (self-pub., CreateSpace, 2015), Kindle edition, 84.

116. Frank Kermode, *The Sense of an Ending: Studies in the Theory of Fiction* (Oxford: Oxford University Press, 2000), 23.

117. Jenni Ogden, *Trouble in Mind: Stories from a Neuropsychologist's Casebook* (Oxford: Oxford University Press, 2012), 368.

118. Sue Miller, *The Story of My Father: A Memoir* (New York: Alfred A. Knopf, 2003), 144.

119. Pamela Horner, *The Long Road Home* (self-pub., CreateSpace, 2017), Kindle edition, 247.

120. Pauline Boss, *Ambiguous Loss: Learning to Live with Unresolved Grief* (Cambridge, MA: Harvard University Press, 1999), 9.

121. Alex Witchel, *All Gone: A Memoir of My Mother's Dementia. With Refreshments* (New York: Riverhead, 2012), 138.

122. Faith Marshall, *I Miss You, Mom: A Daughter's Journey into Dementia Land* (self-pub., CreateSpace, 2018), Kindle edition, 25.

123. Andrea Gillies, *Keeper: One House, Three Generations, and a Journey into Alzheimer's* (New York: Broadway, 2009), 24.

124. Kate Swaffer, *What the Hell Happened to My Brain?: Living Beyond Dementia* (London: Jessica Kingsley, 2016), 19.

125. For an overview of narratives written by people with dementia, see Martina Zimmermann, *The Poetics and Politics of Alzheimer's Disease Life-Writing* (Cham: Palgrave Macmillan, 2017).

126. Anne Davis Basting, "Looking Back from Loss: Views of the Self in Alzheimer's Disease," *Journal of Aging Studies* 17 (2003): 87–99, at 88. For more on the ethics of dementia life writing, see Rebecca A. Bitenc, *Reconsidering Dementia Narratives: Empathy, Identity and Care* (London: Routledge, 2020).

127. See, for example, the various concepts of personhood outlined in Paul Higgs and Chris Gilleard, "Interrogating Personhood and Dementia," *Aging and Mental Health* 20.8 (2016): 773–780.

128. Charles Taylor, *Sources of the Self: The Making of the Modern Identity* (Cambridge, MA: Harvard University Press, 1989), 47. On the role played by narrative in identity formation, see the opposing stances represented by Jerome Bruner, *Making Stories: Law, Literature, Life* (New York: Farrar, Straus and Giroux, 2002); and Galen Strawson, "Against Narrativity," in *Real Materialism and Other Essays* (Oxford: Clarendon, 2008), 189–208. Marya Schechtman presents a third perspective on narration's role in *Staying Alive: Personal Identity, Practical Concerns, and the Unity of a Life* (Oxford: Oxford University Press, 2014), 103–109.

129. Stephen G. Post, *The Moral Challenge of Alzheimer Disease: Ethical Issues from Diagnosis to Dying*, 2nd ed. (Baltimore: Johns Hopkins University Press, 2000), 5.

130. See, for example, Patricia Meyer Spacks, *On Rereading* (Cambridge, MA: Harvard University Press, 2013).

131. Thomas DeBaggio, *Losing My Mind: An Intimate Look at Life with Alzheimer's* (New York: Free Press, 2003), 43.

132. Swaffer, *What the Hell Happened to My Brain?*, 31.

133. Lydia Davis, *Almost No Memory* (New York: Picador, 1997), 136.

134. Christine Bryden, *Dancing with Dementia: My Story of Living Positively with Dementia* (London: Jessica Kingsley, 2005), 119–120.

135. Cary Smith Henderson, *Partial View: An Alzheimer's Journal* (Dallas: Southern Methodist University Press, 1998), 23.

136. Henderson, *Partial View*, 23.

137. Quoted in Lisa Snyder, *Speaking Our Minds: Personal Reflections from Individuals with Alzheimer's* (New York: W. H. Freeman, 1999), 49.

138. Richard Taylor, *Alzheimer's from the Inside Out* (Baltimore: Health Professions Press, 2007), 97.

139. Taylor, *Alzheimer's from the Inside Out*, 97.

140. Wendy Mitchell and Anna Wharton, *Somebody I Used to Know* (London: Bloomsbury, 2018), 111.

141. Mitchell and Wharton, *Somebody I Used to Know*, 111.

142. Mitchell and Wharton, *Somebody I Used to Know*, 112.

143. For more on the fictional representation of memory loss, see Sarah Falcus and Katsura Sako, *Contemporary Narratives of Dementia: Ethics, Ageing, Politics* (London: Routledge, 2018).

144. Casting intellectuals is part of a venerable tradition among Alzheimer's stories. The Emmy Award–winning TV film *Do You Remember Love* (1985) features an English professor whose eccentric behavior is difficult to distinguish from the symptoms of her cognitive decline.

145. According to anecdotes, an aging Carl Linnaeus said while reading his own books, "How beautiful! What would I not give to have written that!" Quoted in Théodule-Armand Ribot, *Diseases of Memory: An Essay in the Positive Psychology* (New York: D. Appleton, 1882), 55.

146. Lisa Genova, *Still Alice* (New York: Simon & Schuster, 2007), 82, 165–166.

147. Walworth, "Adapting the Books on Prescription Model for People Living with Dementia and Their Carers," in McNicol and Brewster, *Bibliotherapy*, 141–151.

148. Greg O'Brien, *On Pluto: Inside the Mind of Alzheimer's* (Brewster, MA: Codfish, 2018), 56.

149. Mitchell and Wharton, *Somebody I Used to Know*, 140.

EPILOGUE

1. Gillian Rose, *Love's Work: A Reckoning with Life* (New York: New York Review of Books, 2011), 40.

2. Reports of reverse reading can be found in Arthur Sweeney, "Mirror-Writing, Inverted Vision, and Allied Ocular Defects," *The St. Paul Medical Journal* 2 (1900): 374–391, at 386; Byrom Bramwell, "Mirror Reading and Mirror Writing in a Left-Handed Epileptic Boy," *Clinical Studies: A Quarterly Journal of Clinical Medicine* 8 (Edinburgh: R. & R. Clark, 1910): 370–371; and J. E. Downey, "On the Reading and Writing of Mirror-Script," *Psychological Review* 21.6 (1914): 408–441, at 409.

3. John Hughlings Jackson, *Selected Writings of John Hughlings Jackson*, ed. James Taylor, 2 vols. (London: Hodder and Stoughton, 1932), 2:149. A modern-day example of reading backwards can be heard on "Meet the Backwards-Speaking Girl," *Weekend Edition Sunday*, National Public Radio (February 7, 2010): https://www.npr.org/templates/story/story.php?storyId=123463760&storyid=123463760&t=1565682068688?storyId=123463760&storyid=123463760&t=1565682068688

4. James Maxwell, "Towards a Definition of Reading," *Literacy* 8.2 (1974): 5–12, at 8.

5. Rudolf Flesch, *Why Johnny Can't Read—And What You Can Do About It* (New York: Harper and Brothers, 1955), 3; Alan G. Kamhi, "The Case for the Narrow View of Reading," *Language, Speech, and Hearing Services in Schools* 40.2 (2009): 174–177, at 175.

6. Maryanne Wolf, with Stephanie Gottwald, *Tales of Literacy for the 21*[st] *Century* (Oxford: Oxford University Press, 2016), 2–3.

7. Oliver Sacks, *Migraine: Understanding a Common Disorder* (Berkeley: University of California Press, 1985), 222. Emphasis in original.

8. G. Thomas Couser, "Disability, Life Narrative, and Representation," *PMLA* 120.2 (2005): 603–604.

9. A simulation of dyslexia can be found on Victor Widell's website Dsxyliea: http://geon.github.io/programming/2016/03/03/dsxyliea. Digital tools recreating the

experience of synesthesia include the Synesthesia Me Visualizer: https://synesthesia
.me/; Synesthesia VR: https://www.synesthesia.world/en/vr-experience; and Synes
thetize: https://chrome.google.com/webstore/detail/synesthetize/ldljgghnflfphlnp
neghciodeehilana?hl=en

10. Henri Bergson, *Matter and Memory*, trans. Nancy Margaret Paul and
W. Scott Palmer (London: Allen & Unwin, 1911), 126.

11. Leah Price, "Reading: The State of the Discipline," *Book History 7* (2004):
303-320, at 312.

Index

ABA (applied behavior analysis), 82
accessibility, 8
acedia. See depression
ADHD and ADD, 57–59
Adventures of Sherlock Holmes, The
(Conan Doyle), 189
aging, 169–70, 175–76
Aitken, Alexander, 179, 180
Alcoholics Anonymous, 45, 158
Alcott, Louisa May, 50–51
alexia: ability to write and, 109–10, 112,
117, 119; amnesia and, 182; aphasia
and, 105, 109, 110; causes of, 38,
104, 107, 114–16; denial and, 108–10,
118, 121; dyslexia and, 41, 110, 111;
historical examples of, 102–3, 104–5,
109–11; identity and, 105–6, 108, 115,
117–21; letter blindness and, 110, 113;
in literature, 105, 119–20; meaning
of, 3, 110; memoirs and, 116, 117–19,
121; mental health and, 103, 110, 115,
121; neurology and, 99–100, 104,
109, 110, 114, 117; pain and fatigue
and, 111, 115; prognosis and, 113–14,

118–19; pseudoreading and, 111–14;
reading aloud and, 110, 121; reading
speed and, 112–13, 119; recovery
from, 115–16, 118–19, 121; social
standing and stigma and, 106–7, 111,
115, 121; sudden onset of, 99–100;
word blindness and, 109–11, 113. *See
also* postliteracy
Alzheimer, Alois, 255n9
Alzheimer's disease. *See* dementia
Alzheimer's Poetry Project, 186
American Psychological
Association, 62
amnesia, 33, 60, 120, 181–86, *185*, 258n52.
See also dementia
Ancelin, Adèle, 107–8
Anderson, Benedict, 165
Andrews, Sally, 7
Antonetta, Susanne, 12
aphasia, 6, 23, 103, 105, 109–10. *See also*
speech and loss of speech
applied behavior analysis (ABA), 82
Asimov, Isaac, 36
Asperger, Hans, 75, 77, 89

hallucinations: appearance of text and,
158–59, 161; Belshazzar's feast and,
151–52, *152*, 169; blindness and, 170,
171; dementia and, 169–70; dreams
and hypnagogic visions and, 154–57;
drugs and, 154–55, 157–60; early research on, 142–43, 145–46, 147; hal-
lucinated text and, 168–71; hearing
voices and, 152–53, 161–63, 167–68,
171; neurology and, 3; interpretation and, 31, 172; memoirs and, 32,
162–63; mental illness and, 143–46,
149, 151–52, 154, 160–68; near-death
experiences and, 172–73; paranoia
and schizophrenia and, 32, 160–68,
171; reading as cause of, 144, 145–46,
149–50; reality versus unreality
and, 144, 146, 150–51, 160–61, 172;
supernatural and paranormal experiences and, 146, 149–54, *152*, 162,
172; universality of, 31–32, 143–46,
151, 154, 171–72
Hammond, Graeme, 48
Hampshire, Susan, 52–53, 55
Harry Potter series (Rowling), 24
Hartmann, Ernest, 155
Haweis, Mary Eliza, 142–43, *143*, 144
Hawthorne, Nathaniel, 154
Hayles, N. Katherine, 8
Head, Henry, 240n87
Heffter, Arthur, 158
Hellsing, Lennart, 93
hemianopia, 16
Hemingway, Ernest, 11
Henderson, Cary Smith, 197
Herodotus, 81
Hillinger, Michael, 5
Hinshelwood, James, 39–40, 110–11, 114,
219n22
Hirschman, Catherine, 59
historical record, neurodiversity in,
204–5
Homer, 178

Horace, 105
Hoskins, Argie, 60
Hoskins, Eugene, 75
Hughes, Ted, 178
Hulme, Kathryn, 69
Hunt, Nigel, 24
Hunter, Kathryn Montgomery, 23
Hustvedt, Siri, 142
Huxley, Aldous, 23, 159–60
Huysmans, Joris-Karl, 127
hyperlexia: autism and, 3, 27, 80, 82;
coining of term, 79; comprehension
and, 73–74, 77–82; deficits versus
abilities and, 79, 82–83, 88, 89, 92–93;
historical examples of, 76, 78, 81;
Kim Peek and, 67–69, *68*; meaning
of, 3; memoirs and other firsthand
accounts and, 83, 91; memory and,
67, 69, 71–75, 92; multiliteracy and,
71; *Rain Man* (film) and, 69; reading
in pictures and, 89–98; sound of language and, 74–75; speech and, 79–
80; what counts as reading and, 84,
88. *See also* autism and Asperger's
Syndrome; savant syndrome

illiteracy, 102, 114–16. *See also* alexia;
postliteracy
illness. *See specific types of illness*
International Dyslexia Association, 41
interpretation: autism and, 27–28;
complexity of reading and, 206;
dyslexia and, 27; hallucinations
and, 31, 172; paranoia and, 160,
163–66; perception and, 31; processing words before, 27, 38; schizoaffective fallacy and, 164; surface
reading and, 27–28, 84; synesthesia
and, 135, 141
Iowa State Psychopathic Hospital,
40–41
Irlen Institute, 62
Irlen, Helen, 62–64, 266n171

writer's block, 61, 109–10
Wuthering Heights (Brontë), 85

Xenophon, 81

Yeats, W. B., 48

Zaehner, Robert Charles, 154
Zalmon, Elijah ben Solomon, 178
Zasetsky, Lev, 114–15
Zunshine, Lisa, 215–16n86